EGYPT *at the* CROSSROADS

Domestic Stability and Regional Role

EGYPT
at the Crossroads:
Domestic Stability and Regional Role

edited by
PHEBE MARR

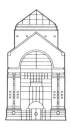

National Defense University Press
Washington, DC
1999

The Institute for National Strategic Studies

The Institute for National Strategic Studies (INSS) is a major component of the National Defense University (NDU), which operates under the supervision of the President of NDU. It conducts strategic studies for the Secretary of Defense, Chairman of the Joint Chiefs of Staff, and unified commanders in chief; supports national strategic components of NDU academic programs; and provides outreach to other governmental agencies and the broader national security community.

The Publication Directorate of INSS publishes books, monographs, reports, and occasional papers on national security strategy, defense policy, and national military strategy through NDU Press that reflect the output of NDU research and academic programs. In addition, it produces the INSS *Strategic Assessment* and other work approved by the President of NDU, as well as *Joint Force Quarterly*, a professional military journal published for the Chairman.

NDU Press publications are sold by the U.S. Government Printing Office. For ordering information, call (202) 512-1800 or write to the Superintendent of Documents, U.S. Government Printing Office, Washington, DC 20402.

Library of Congress Cataloging-in-Publication Data
Egypt at the crossroads : domestic stability and regional role / edited by Phebe Marr.
     p. cm.
     Includes bibiliographical references (p.   ).
     ISBN 1-5706-022-6
     1. Egypt—Politics and government—1981- 2. Egypt—Economic conditions—1981- 3. Egypt—Foreign relations—1981-   4. Regionalism—Egypt. I.   Marr, Phebe.
     DT107.87.E34   1999
     962.05'5—dc21   98-54860
                                                 CIP

First Printing, June 1999

Contents

II. EGYPT'S REGIONAL ROLE

III. U.S.-EGYPTIAN RELATIONS

Preface

This book is an outgrowth of a collaborative effort of two strategic studies centers, the Institute for National Strategic Studies at the National Defense University in Washington, and the National Center for Middle East Studies in Cairo, Egypt. Over a period of several years, a group of colleagues connected with these institutes has been engaged in conferences and discussions focusing on the future of Egypt and the U.S.-Egyptian relationship in the changing security environment of the post-Cold War Middle East.

This volume, the fruit of those labors, brings together the work of a distinguished group of Egyptians and Americans, combining the research efforts and long practical experience of authors of diverse backgrounds, including academics, military professionals, economists, and policy makers. Authors originally prepared their papers for two conferences, one on Egypt's domestic stability held in Washington, the other on Egypt's regional role, held in Cairo; their work has been updated to reflect changing events.

Egypt has a seminal role as a Middle East actor and is central in U.S. strategic planning on the Middle East. Because of Egypt's influence in the Arab and Islamic worlds, it is of paramount importance that Egypt remain a force for moderation. Any dramatic change in Egypt's position could alter the regional balance of power and the existing favorable security environment. Egypt's regional role as a moderating element depends on its domestic tranquility and its economic health. As authors in this volume emphasize, the domestic and regional aspects of Egypt's policy are inextricably linked. Without a reasonably sound economy and political stability, Egypt will be unable to undertake an active regional role. The reverse is also true—an active peace process and a growing regional economy are essential for Egypt's stability at home.

The combined essays tie together three essential components of the U.S.-Egyptian equation. The first part addresses domestic issues in Egypt and the prospects for Egypt's continued political stability. The second section concentrates on Egypt's regional role in the new post-Cold War environment. The third part looks at the future of the U.S.-Egyptian partnership. Authors have probed the underlying factors likely to persist well into the 21st century, rather than dwelling on episodic changes that may dominate tomorrow's headlines. It is hoped that exploration of these fundamental aspects of Egypt and the U.S.-Egyptian relationship will provide a sense of the forces at work in the region and of the issues with which U.S. strategists will have to grapple over the next decade.

Acknowledgments

I would like to thank the authors of this volume for their efforts and their patience in persisting through a number of revisions over the past year. In addition, a considerable debt of gratitude goes to the staff at the National Center for Middle East Studies, and in particular, to its director, Major General Ahmed Fakhr (Ret.). Without his intellectual acumen, efforts, and cooperation in this long joint venture, this book would not have been possible. Much appreciation is also due to two directors of the Institute of National Strategic Studies at the National Defense University, Drs. Hans Binnendijk (current director) and Alvin H. Bernstein (former director), whose sponsorship and encouragement of the project made it possible. I am also grateful to the generosity of Joseph Berger, former general manager of the National U.S.-Arab Chamber of Commerce, for providing financial support for a portion of this work. The book is also informed by contributions from a number of discussants and participants, both American and Egyptian, whose work is not directly acknowledged in specific chapters but whose insights are included in the introduction and conclusion. Last, but not least, I would like to thank members of the Publication Directorate at INSS for seeing this volume through to completion.

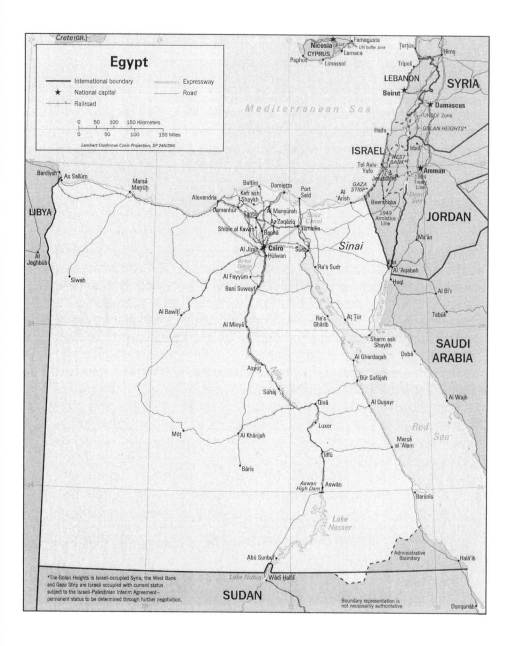

Egypt

PROLOGUE

PHEBE MARR

Why Focus on Egypt?

For much of its recorded history, Egypt has been a linchpin of regional trends and developments in the Middle East. As scholars have long recognized, there are some unique reasons why Egypt has been able to play such a central role. Today, in the post-Cold War era of flux and uncertainty, these reasons remain as valid as ever, although their context is changing. Chief among them has been demography.

From ancient times to the present, the Nile Valley has been able to sustain a larger, settled population than its desert neighbors. Today, with over 64 million inhabitants, Egypt is the most populous country in the Arab world; in the Middle East it is outstripped only slightly by the non-Arab countries of Iran (67 million) and Turkey (65 million). Its demographic size and the relative homogeneity of its population give it considerable political weight in the regional balance of power. Egypt also occupies a favorable geostrategic position, much to its advantage throughout its history. Situated at the intersection of three continents—Europe, Africa, and Asia—Egypt has been nourished by flows of population and ideas from all three and has, in turn, functioned as a vital connecting link among them. Even today, in an era of satellite downlinks and supersonic jets, Egypt remains an important focal point for communications and transport. The Suez Canal provides a vital shipping channel between the Mediterranean and the Indian Ocean through which passed 15,000 ships in 1996.[1] Overland routes via the Sinai tie Egypt to the Levant and the rest of southwest Asia. Egypt's lifeline, the Nile, inextricably links it to African nations further south.

Egypt's regional importance, however, hinges even more on its cultural influence than its geography. In ancient times, Egypt was a cultural crossroads, contributing to civilizations as diverse as those of the Phoenicians, the Nubians, the Greeks, and the Romans. Soon after the birth of the Islamic era, Egypt rapidly became a key center of Islamic learning and civilization, a position it still holds today. Al-Azhar, founded in Cairo in 970 A.D., is the oldest, continuously existing university in the world and still functions as the premier world center of Sunni law and theology.

In contemporary times, Egypt is an undisputed center of Arab and Islamic intellectual life. Its radio and TV programs, films, books, newspapers, and magazines spread Egyptian influence throughout the Arab world and beyond. No other Arab county has such overall media dominance. Egypt has also been at the forefront of the contemporary Islamic revival. The Muslim Brotherhood, founded by Hasan al-Banna in 1928, is still the largest and best organized of such movements, with offshoots in Syria, Iraq, Jordan, Saudi Arabia, and other Islamic countries.

From cultural influence has flowed political weight. Since World War II, the Arab world has often looked to Egypt for guidance. Egypt has led the Arab League from its inception in 1945 to 1979, and then again from 1989 to the present. While often ineffectual in practice, the league is the embodiment of collective Arab ideals and goals and the institutional framework for joint Arab action. Egypt's regional influence reached its apogee during the Nasser period (1952-70), when the Egyptian "Voice of the Arabs" was an instrument capable of shaking regimes (such as the pro-Western monarchy in Baghdad) and overturning Western plans (such as the Israeli, British, and French attempt to retake the Suez Canal in 1956). Notwithstanding repression at home and an ignominious defeat at the hands of Israel in 1967, Nasser and his "Arab vision" inspired a whole generation of Arabs and still has residual influence today. While Egypt's role has unquestionably declined since Nasser's day, in the less structured, more disordered post-Cold War world, there are signs that it may once again be reviving.

Finally, Egypt's regional importance lies in its role as a pacesetter for the region, in both domestic and foreign policy. In the

19th century, Egypt was at the forefront of the modernization process, borrowing from the West to build a modern army, a new bureaucracy, Western style educational and medical systems, and a modified Western civil code. Egypt was also the first—and most successful—Middle Eastern country to develop the attributes of a modern nation-state.

In recent decades, Egypt has been a pacesetter in foreign affairs. It was the first Arab state to make peace with Israel in 1979, a move so audacious that Egypt was ostracized by the rest of the Arab world for almost a decade. But by the mid-1990s, most Arab countries had followed suit and were engaged in a peace process designed to lead to normalization with Israel. Egypt was also a leader among former Soviet clients in making a clear break with its Communist patron and in reorienting its economy and society toward the West. This effort foreshadowed the collapse of the USSR and the near universal recognition of its failed system.

Egypt is currently in search of a new regional role in a Middle East that is increasingly without internal cohesion. While the nature and direction of that role are as yet unclear, Egypt's policy bears close watching as a forerunner for the region. Whatever role Egypt chooses to play, it is likely to be influenced both by domestic factors, such as a fragile but reviving economy and an Islamic resurgence, as well as a new and unpredictable regional environment still prone to conflicts and disruptions. Identifying these factors and the ways in which they may shape Egypt's foreign policy is the major focus of this volume.

The U.S.-Egyptian Relationship

For all these reasons, Egypt is of prime importance to the United States. Over several decades, Egypt and the United States have developed a close and mutually beneficial relationship in a number of areas. On the security front, the United States funds the modernization effort of the Egyptian military, conducts joint exercises with Egypt, and helps train its officers. In return, Egypt provides access to Egyptian facilities, including the Cairo West airport, when regional crises make it necessary. Egypt has cooperated with the United States and other NATO forces in war (in the Gulf) and in peace (in Somalia and Bosnia). In the economic arena, a high-level economic commission as well as economic aid from the United States assure continual cooperation on economic development and support for Egypt's structural reform program.

But these tangible benefits, while significant, are not the most important aspect of the relationship for the United States It is Egypt's political moderation and its willingness to cooperate with the United States and other Western allies on a broad array of regional issues that make the partnership so valuable. Chief among these has been Egypt's critical role in furthering the peace process as well as its support for the United States and its allies in the Gulf War and in subsequent efforts to contain Iran and Iraq. A substantial shift in this position would fundamentally alter the balance of power in the region and make the U.S. leadership role there far more difficult and certainly more expensive.

U.S.-Egyptian Relations in Historical Perspective

U.S.-Egyptian relations have not always been smooth. Up to the mid-1950s, when British troops withdrew from Cairo, Egypt was essentially a British preserve. U.S. interests in Egypt were primarily cultural, educational, and commercial. On political affairs, the United States generally deferred to Britain. This changed with the Egyptian revolution of 1952 that soon led to clashes between Britain and Egypt and, after the disastrous Suez crisis of 1956, to the removal of British influence from Egypt.

The Nasser era was a turbulent one for U.S.-Egyptian relations, which were often both ambivalent and conflicting.[2] Despite Nasser's anti-British position, the United States gave the new Egyptian Government some support at first, seeing it mainly as an anticolonial movement capable of providing a bulwark against the Soviet Union and desirous of progress and reform at home. But relations soon soured, as Nasser's anti-Western rhetoric emerged and Egypt turned to the Soviet Union for economic and military support. The United States also had difficulty in balancing its support for the newly created state of Israel with attempts to improve relations with newly independent Arab states, like Egypt, bitter over their loss of the 1948 war and the establishment of an Israeli state in Palestine.

Relations took a severe downturn in 1955 when Nasser turned to the former Soviet Union, first for arms and then for financing for the Aswan Dam, after the United States had abruptly withdrawn its own financing offer. Nasser then nationalized the Suez Canal Company, precipitating a crisis with Britain and the West that led, in 1956, to an ill-advised attack on Egypt by Israel, Britain, and France. Their effort to topple the regime and restore Western control of the canal failed. The United States, which did not condone this invasion, won some credibility in Egyptian eyes for pressuring its allies into withdrawing. Despite these strains with Egypt, the United States remained more fearful of Soviet penetration in the region than of Nasser's radical nationalism. Although cooperation with Egypt generated friction in American policy circles, the United States continued to deal with Nasser. Relations improved somewhat between 1958 and 1961, when Egypt and Syria formed the United Arab Republic (UAR) and Nasser used this opportunity to root out Syria's local Communists. In 1959, Egypt received $125 million in U.S. assistance and loans and credits from the International Bank for Reconstruction and Development (IBRD). By 1962, Egypt had signed on to a 3-year aid agreement that would transfer $430 million in food annually.[3]

But the honeymoon did not last. The breakup of the UAR in 1961 and Ba'th Party coups in Iraq and Syria in 1963 put anti-Communist (but not pro-Western) regimes in power in both countries. These events weakened Nasser and made Egypt less important to the United States. Equally significant in straining relations was Nasser's involvement in the Yemen civil war, which broke out in 1962. Egypt supported the republican forces with troops, while Saudi Arabia, an important U.S. ally, supported the monarchy. By the mid-1960s, Egyptian rhetoric against the United States and Israel had mounted, increasingly turning the U.S. administration against Nasser. Relations reached a nadir with the misadventure of the 1967 war and Nasser's decisive defeat. However, the seeds of a new Egyptian policy were also sown in that episode. Egyptian decisionmakers, disillusioned by the inability of their patron, the USSR, to come to their rescue or to thwart the policy of the United States and its allies, recognized the need for a turn to the West. Nasser's death in 1970 closed an era but also provided the opportunity for a new beginning.

It was not long in coming. U.S. relations with Egypt changed dramatically when Nasser's successor, Anwar Sadat, terminated Egypt's contractual relationship with its Soviet military advisors in July 1972, ending Egypt's status as a Soviet client. After numerous frustrating attempts to negotiate an end to Israeli occupation of the Sinai and the east bank of the Suez Canal (both legacies of the 1967 war), Egypt launched the 1973 attack against Israel, mainly as a means of attracting U.S. attention and breaking a political stalemate. In this, Sadat was successful. Although Egypt nearly lost the war to an Israeli counterattack, the effort drew the United States into the Middle East. Extensive shuttle diplomacy by Secretary of State Henry Kissinger saved Egypt's gains and helped it recover the Sinai. Negotiations over Sinai in 1974 and 1975 brought Egypt closer to the United States

Even more remarkable was Sadat's dramatic visit to Israel in October 1977, in an effort to break the Arab-Israeli impasse. This visit permanently changed the regional environment. More tough negotiations under President Carter finally led to a tripartite meeting among Sadat, Israeli Prime Minister Menachin Begin, and President Carter at Camp David in 1978, and eventually to a peace treaty between Israel and Egypt in 1979. The treaty secured considerable economic benefits for Egypt, including the opening of the Suez Canal; the return of the Red Sea and Sinai oil fields; and a flow of U.S. aid to Egypt totaling over $2 billion annually. It also cemented a firm bilateral relationship between the two countries, which has lasted to the present day.

Sadat took equally important domestic steps to orient Egypt westward.[4] Following the 1973 war, Sadat began to implement an "infitah" (opening) of the Egyptian economy to market forces, pursuing foreign investment and encouraging the development of Egypt's private sector. While progress in dismantling the Egyptian command economy established under Nasser has been slow, it has proceeded steadily in this direction ever since. On the political front, Sadat gradually dismantled Nasser's police state and opened up the political system. The army's role in the political process was reduced; a more open press was permitted; and the rule of law was strengthened. While still an authoritarian system, Egypt became a more relaxed society, more open to outside—especially Western— influence than it had been in the 1960s.

These moves cost Egypt much of its influence in the Arab world, where it was officially ostracized for signing the treaty with Israel. In 1979, the Arab League was moved from Cairo to Tunis, and Egypt was suspended as a member. Sadat's assassination in 1981 at the hands of a religious extremist can be blamed, in part, on his treaty with Israel and his tilt to the United States Husni Mubarak, as Sadat's successor, has continued the policy, with one noticeable change. From the first days of his presidency, Mubarak has engaged in a more pronounced Arab policy, aimed at bringing Egypt back into the Arab fold, while continuing to support peace with Israel; in this he has been successful.[5] Helped by the Iran-Iraq war (1980-88) that revealed the political weakness of the Arab world without Egypt, Mubarak managed to restore bilateral relations with most Arab states by 1988. In 1990, the Arab League was moved back to Cairo and an Egyptian was elected as its head, symbolizing Egypt's full return to the fold. Egypt was an early and important participant in the allied coalition to liberate Kuwait in 1991 and has been an indispensable partner in furthering the Madrid peace process that followed.

In the meantime, the relationship with the United States has been strengthened by a substantial economic aid program. By 1996, despite severe cuts in the U.S. foreign aid budget, Egypt absorbed 40 percent of U.S. Foreign Military Financing and 34 percent of Economic Support Funds, receiving $1.2 billion in military aid and $815 million in civilian aid. Since its inception in 1978 through 1997, Egypt has received a total of $49 billion.[6] Military transfers go mainly into equipment (purchased from U.S. suppliers), while civilian aid has played a major role in such economic and social projects as sanitation, irrigation, pest control, family planning, and communications.[7]

New Challenges for the Future

Since 1970, the U.S.-Egyptian relationship has matured, but there is still a certain element of fragility, and in the post-Cold War era it faces new challenges. Many of them have been clearly identified in this volume. In the wake of the Soviet collapse, the United States has been left the sole super power, with increasing dominance—some would say hegemony—over Middle Eastern policy. At the same time, the 1991 Gulf War revealed a fragmented Middle East unable to manage its own security affairs and deeply divided over a number of issues, including relations with the United States.

The spread of weapons of mass destruction (WMD) and their delivery systems has raised tensions in the region and made management of the security environment more difficult. Egypt has foregone the nuclear option but is clearly concerned about Israel's undeclared nuclear arsenal and the seemingly permanent military imbalance this poses within the region. The United States and Egypt have divergent views on future reductions and how to achieve them, especially where Israel is concerned.

Prior to the 1995 election of the Likud government in Israel, pursuit of the peace process drew Egypt and the United States together. The direction and the pace of the process have now changed and, in a worst case scenario, could be stalled or reversed. Either of these two prospects would put strains on U.S. relations with Egypt and could contribute to a change of direction within Egypt itself.

The post-Cold War era has also seen the emergence of destabilizing domestic forces in the Middle East, including pressures for "democratization" and greater popular participation in political systems as well as continued challenges from Islamic revivalist forces seeking major political changes in secular, often pro-Western, states. Egypt is on the cutting edge of the solution to this problem.

Last, and perhaps most important of all, as this volume makes clear, domestic economic development issues have come to the fore throughout the region. A decade of decline in regional economic growth and per capita income, a pressing need in almost all countries for major structural reform, and the relentless competition imposed by economic globalization are forcing economic policy to the top of the regional agenda. Egypt is no exception; indeed, it is a primary example of a Middle Eastern state that needs to focus on economic issues, even as talk of cuts in foreign aid surface in Washington.

All these changes in the regional security environment pose new challenges and new opportunities for the United States and Egypt as they seek to extend their close working relationship into the 21st century. This book illuminates the character of the challenges and suggests ways in which both countries can address them.

This book is divided into three parts. The first, *Egypt's Domestic Stability,* explores the prospects for Egypt's domestic stability, its potential for economic, political, and social growth, and its ability to deal with opposition challenges from Islamic movements. Two authors look at Egypt's domestic political dynamics. Tahseen

Basheer addresses the question of systemic change in Egypt and the prospects for political reform, examining several basic issues: whether Egypt can accommodate new forces in society and move away from an authoritarian, overly centralized government; whether its leadership is too cautious in opening the system to the forces of change; and whether such an opening might envelop the system and put an end to an era of stability. In short, when does stability become rigidity?

Egypt's future will repose in a new generation of leaders. In a searching analysis, John Waterbury examines past patterns of leadership recruitment in Egypt and points to the different directions it could take in the future. He questions whether leaders with political skills, capable of mobilizing the population in new directions, will emerge, or whether the system will continue to produce competent but relatively passive technocrats, capable of keeping the system in operation but unable to break new barriers.

The most serious challenge to Egypt's domestic stability over the last decade has come from Islamic opposition movements, which feed on underlying economic and political discontent. Two authors explore this phenomenon and what it might hold for the future. Saad Eddin Ibrahim documents the cycles of violence initiated by extremist Islamic movements and, in a succinct but penetrating analysis, pinpoints their causes. While the violence has declined, he questions whether the causes have been adequately addressed or the movements have simply gone underground to await more fortuitous circumstances. John Esposito, in turn, analyzes the ideology of Islamic movements and their appeal to various segments of the population, and the ability of Islamic movements to accommodate modern concepts of economic development and political participation. Above all, he outlines regime strategies for dealing with mainstream movements and what can be learned from examples of repression and accommodation.

Few subjects are more critical to Egypt's future than its progress on the economic front. While Egypt has made measurable progress in a number of areas, it still has a critical distance to traverse before it is out of an economic danger zone. Two economists versed in social as well as economic analysis tackle economic issues. Alan Richards looks at the need for rapid structural adjustment in Egypt, addressing such problems as privatization, job creation, and the costs, long and short term, of postponing difficult decisions. He wonders whether Egypt will make a "break for the market" or compound its difficulties by "dilatory reform." Hanaa Kheir el-Din examines the economic decisions that go into encouraging investment and the growth of the private sector in Egypt. Egypt's economic progress and its ability to attract foreign investment depend on its domestic stability. She raises questions about the costs, political and social, of rapid structural adjustment and whether painful adjustments could derail Egypt's stability and, in consequence, its ability to attract investment.

Essential to any discussion of Egypt's stability is the role of its military in domestic society. While greatly reduced in political importance from Nasser's days, the Egyptian military is still a bulwark of support for the regime and a significant player in Egypt's economy. Stephen Gotowicki surveys the domestic role of Egypt's military establishment, addressing its impact on Egypt's future economic growth and its future role in the constitutional structure.

The second part, *Egypt's Regional Role,* explores Egypt's regional role and the direction it may take in the future. As authors recognize, this role will be directly related to Egypt's domestic stability and its economic capacity for growth. Two authors chart the potential trajectory of Egypt's regional policy in the coming era. In a carefully nuanced chapter, Rosemary Hollis examines the ways in which Egypt may strike out in new directions and the factors likely to affect its policy. She wonders whether Egypt will show more "distance" from the United States and the ways in which a new strategic environment might place constraints on an ambitious regional role. In a wide-ranging and comprehensive essay, Abdul Monem Sa'id Ali explores the evolution of Egypt's regional role over the past few decades and provides a political road map for the future. He probes Egypt's priorities in a new security environment and the ways in which Egypt's economic difficulties may affect its regional role in an era in which global economic competition is likely to be of ever increasing importance.

Egypt's ability to assume its chosen role will be affected by the changing security environment beyond its borders, bringing a multitude of new challenges as well as a continuation of some that are as old as Egypt's history. George Joffe and Ali Hillal Dessouki map out the new regional environment. Joffe points to an increased lack of regional cohesion as well as the addition to the region of non-Arab countries in the Caucasus and Central Asia and asks whether these will not compete with and possibly reduce Egypt's regional role. In the same vein, he questions how Egypt will deal with economic challenges from an increasingly competitive European Union (EU) and, given Egypt's domestic economic and social problems, how much of a regional role Egypt will be able or willing to afford. Dessouki, like Joffe, sees a fluid regional environment subject to accelerating change. He explores the challenges for Egypt as a status quo power in such an environment, as well as the strains it may raise within the U.S.-Egyptian partnership.

Egypt's military posture will be an essential component of its regional role. Two authors address key questions regarding Egypt's military. In a changing (and presumably more benign regional environment), what should be the size, role, and mission of Egypt's military? What threats to its security does Egypt perceive and how have these changed since the Gulf War and the start of the peace process? And what kind of a military can and should Egypt sustain? The answers to these questions could impact on the U.S. relationship and U.S. willingness to fund continuing military improvements.

In this arena some significant differences emerge between the authors addressing the subject. Ahmed Abdul Halim looks at Egypt's "geostrategic" and "geoeconomic" goals in restructuring its military. He addresses the issue of Egypt's military posture and how Egypt should deal with the military imbalance in the region posed both by Israel's conventional and nonconventional military force and the large military forces of potential regional adversaries. In contrast, Chas. Freeman poses questions about Egypt's ability to sustain a substantial military force economically. He suggests some innovative ways in which Egypt might modernize its forces, meet economic challenges, and carve out a new role involving more integral military cooperation with the West.

The book concludes with *U.S.-Egyptian Relations*, a section that discusses the future of the U.S.-Egyptian partnership. In a searching assessment of the U.S.-Egyptian strategic partnership thus far, Ahmed Fakhr questions how strong and enduring the partnership really is and the extent to which U.S. and Egyptian views converge or diverge, and then asks what changes need to be made to meet the new political, economic, and security challenges. He points to a number of differing assumptions that underlie the relationship, many of them not readily apparent, and suggests the need for a new strategic vision.

Phebe Marr integrates the various threads in Egypt's domestic and foreign policies outlined in the book, and the ways in which these are likely to affect the joint partnership. She points to the remarkable value the United States has received from Egyptian cooperation over the past two decades—on the Arab-Israeli front, in the Gulf, in maintaining a balance of moderation in the region, and in peacekeeping functions. But a new environment, she argues, requires a new, joint vision that answers to the needs of both countries as they face an era dominated not by the Cold War, but by domestic pressures for economic growth, political reform, and reduced involvement in expensive foreign ventures.

Notes

1. Douglas Jehl, "Trying to Revive a Canal That is Out of the Loop," *New York Times*, April 30, 1997, A4.

2. For this era see, Peter Hahn, "National Security concerns in U.S. Policy toward Egypt, 1949-1956" and Malik Mufti, "The United States and Nasserist Pan-Arabism," in *The Middle East and the U.S.,* ed. David Lesch, (Boulder, CO: Westview Press, 1996).

3. Mufti, 176-179.

4. John Waterbury, *Egypt, Burdens of the Past/Options for the Future* (Bloomington: Indiana University Press, 1978), 207-209; John Waterbury, *The Egypt of Nasser and Sadat: The Political Economy of Two Regimes* (Princeton, NJ: Princeton University Press, 1983), ch. 15.

5. Louis J. Cantori, "Egypt Reenters the Arab System," in *The Middle East from the Iran Contra Affair to the Intifada*, ed. Robert O. Freedman, (Syracuse, NY: Syracuse University Press, 1991), 341-344.

6. Duncan Clarke, "U.S. security assistance to Egypt and Israel: Politically untouchable?" *Middle East Journal* 51, no. 2 (Spring 1997): 201.

7. Eric Hooglund, "Chapter Two," in *Egypt: A Country Study*, ed. Helen Metz (Washington: Government Printing Office, 1991), 109-110.

Select Egyptian Statistics

Social	1985	1997
Population	48,305,000[1]	64,824,466[2]
Population growth rate	2.6%	1.90%[2]
Total fertility rate	NA	3.5[2]
Infant mortality rate	94/1,000[3]	71/1,000[2]
Age structure		
0-14	NA	36%[2]
15-64	NA	60%[2]
65 and over	NA	4%[2]
Literacy:		
Population	40%	51.4%[4]
Male	NA	63.6%[4]
Female	NA	38.8%[4]

Economic	1985	1995
GDP(gross domestic product)	$21.2 billion (current $)[3]	$183.9 billion[5] (purchasing power parity)[6,7]
GDP real growth rate	3.5%[3]	5%[8]
Labor force:	13 million [3]	17.4 million[5]
Public sector	36% (1984 est.)[3]	NA
Agriculture	34% (1984 est.)[3]	NA
Mfg. and service	20% (1984 est.)[3]	NA
Unemployment	7%[1]	20%[6]

Defense	1985	1997
Total fit for military service	8,209,000 (1986)[9]	10,987,037[2]
Defense expenditures:		
Total (in current $)	$3.4 billion[9]	$3.28 billion[2]
Percent of total government budget	13%[9]	8.2%[2]

1. *World Fact Book 1985*, Central Intelligence Agency (Washington: Government Printing Office).
2. *World Fact Book 1997*.
3. *World Fact Book 1987*.
4. 1995 estimated.
5. 1996 estimated.
6. *World Fact Book 1996*.
7. The CIA changed the method of calculating the GDP for this reference. The purchasing power parity is a weighted figure using international dollar amounts for goods produced in country. Therefore, the 1985 and 1995 estimates of the GDP are not comparable measures.
8. Fiscal year 1998.
9. *World Fact Book 1986*.

I. Egypt's Domestic Stability

THE EGYPTIAN STATE
IN TRANSITION

Tahseen Basheer

Since 1954, presidents in Egypt live and die; they are never changed by popular choice. Understandably, this historical record discourages leaders from introducing major changes in a system that has provided a proven security net. The forces of change have to overcome the entrenched embattlements of inertia.

The Egyptian state system, with its focus on a highly centralized government, represents the oldest known model of a centralized state system. From its inception under the Pharaohs, this political model has withstood the vicissitudes of history with little basic change in domestic power relationships. It has survived changes of regime, ideology, patterns of leadership, and, in modern times, transformations in modes of production and social structure. It is not an exaggeration to say that in the beginning came the state and within that state the Egyptian nation developed.

Ambassador Tahseen Basheer is a member of the Consultative Board of the National Center for Middle East Studies in Cairo. He is also a former Ambassador to Canada. Currently he concentrates his efforts on conflict resolution in the Middle East and Africa and writes and lectures on this subject.

Historically, most changes in Egyptian life have been generated from the top down; revolts initiated from a popular base have succeeded only in a few cases, primarily under circumstances when the populace felt that their leadership was abandoning their belief system or in cases when Egypt was ruled by foreign occupiers. In most situations, Egyptians have favored stability and demonstrated patience under adversity, especially if its leadership possessed the mantle of legitimacy and legality.

Nevertheless, Egypt today is hardly a mere carbon copy of its past. Egypt's image as a "grainery," inherited from Roman times, is no longer valid. Nor is Egypt any longer a simple "gift of the Nile." No more than 40 percent of Egypt's population is engaged in agriculture, and its agricultural production is now insufficient to feed half of its population.

Egypt has ceased to be a living museum of the past. The country is in transition and its people are in a process of change. The Egyptian people are the key to this transformation, and the renewal of Egypt will depend to a large extent on what they do. Their knowledge, education, productivity, and social organization, together with the quality of their leadership, will play a decisive role in shaping their future. It is the interplay between the new forces of change and the solid rock of inertia that will determine the new Egypt to emerge.

Political Stability: The Past as an Indicator (1952-81)

The army coup d'etat of 1952, which ushered in the Nasser regime, was preceded by considerable intellectual ferment and a period of political turmoil, which culminated in the "burning of Cairo" on January 26, 1952.[1] These activities predisposed the public to accept and support the new political regime. Popular alienation from the monarchy, the rise of resistance to the British occupation of the Suez area, and the impotence of existing political parties all facilitated the demise of Egyptian "liberalism" that had developed since the 1919 revolution.[2]

The coup officers, under the unique leadership of Gamal Abdul Nasser, developed not another military junta but a new political system that remains as the source of legitimacy for the Egyptian

Government today, despite erosions and embellishments. Under Nasser, a tacit political compact emerged wherein the presidential leader was fully supported by an overwhelming public acquiescence in exchange for government-provided jobs, free education and medical care, low-cost housing, and a symbolic sense of dignity.

The army was provided a comfortable status and income so long as it reciprocated with loyalty and noninterference in political life. The military tacitly underwrote the system by delegating to the president management of the political realm. Intellectuals, labor unions, and the media all played a part in developing the charismatic role of the president. Egypt was neither a military dictatorship nor a military junta nor a democracy. Rather, it was a workable accommodation between the military and political constituents, where the president emerged from the armed forces and continued to be the Supreme Commander, but the Army itself was kept outside the sphere of direct political action. The system produced a simple political party run by political administrators posing as politicians who were selected by the president and continued in office at his discretion. Changes or modifications of the system emanated from the top. Any conflicting or competitive political factions were coopted into the single party organization, leaving the basic structure intact. Thus, irrespective of government successes or failures, no one was able to topple or destabilize the system. The leadership on the top was able to maintain momentum, even when it suffered reversals, and was always able to attain enough popular support for its policies.

When President Anwar Sadat succeeded to the presidency in 1970, he moved toward a degree of pluralism, opening the door to a multiparty system. In this, he encountered passive resistance from the bureaucracy. The system Sadat developed allowed other political parties a minor sphere of action but established a licensing process that kept the dominant party (the National Democratic Party) as the gatekeeper of political activities. This produced the appearance of political pluralism on the surface while preserving the real political levers in the hands of the president. This metamorphosis from a simple political monopoly to a quasi-monopoly helped absorb some of the shock of change without changing the basic system of control.

Under President Husni Mubarak, who came to office in the wake of Sadat's assassination in 1981, further political advances were achieved, particularly in freedom for the opposition press. Mubarak also has a consistent record of respect for court decisions. However, these positive contributions have been marred by the re-emergence of emergency laws and martial courts, in an attempt to curb the Islamic opposition.

Through these changes, the unwritten political compact has proved enduring. It stood the test of the crisis of 1954, in which President Naguib lost most of his power, and Nasser publicly became the leader of the coup d'etat; the secession of Syria from the United Arab Republic (UAR) in 1961, which was a major setback for the cause of Arab nationalism espoused by Nasser and showed the failure of the revolutionary leader to unify with Syria; the debacle of Arab defeat in 1967;[3] and the assassination of President Sadat. The system has proved almost coup-proof, a function it has developed to near perfection. As a result of this success, the Egyptian public has become ever more passive, while stability at the top has reached a level of stagnation.

Alternation of political office by legal action is unknown in contemporary Egypt. Presidential replacement has been left to the will of God. Since 1954, presidents in Egypt live and die; they are never changed by popular choice. Understandably, this historical record discourages leaders from introducing major changes in a system that has provided a proven security net. The forces of change have to overcome the entrenched embattlements of inertia.

The Role of the Armed Forces

Since the creation of the modern Egyptian state in the early decades of the 19th century, the development of the Egyptian Armed Forces has been the first priority of governments. As a result, the Egyptian Army is the most modernized element of Egyptian society in both technological and managerial skills.

In addition, the military fulfills a number of political and social roles in Egyptian society. It has been the guardian of Egypt's

6

regional role, a function it accomplishes both in peace and war. The army is also a provider of mass education, training the poorest illiterates of Egyptian society. At the same time, institutions of higher education, medical facilities, and factories run by the military are among the best in the country. In 1954, after an initial period of unrest in the armed forces, the Egyptian Army was restructured in a manner that kept it out of politics. The Army respected the well-established tradition of operating within the legal system and abstained from meddling in political affairs. It has established a tradition—which has a long record of being maintained—of moderation and stability.

Egyptian Armed Forces are now recognized as the ballast of the ship of state. There is every reason to believe that the Army will continue to be the cornerstone of the Egyptian political order for some time to come, and the refuge of last resort should the country be threatened from within or without.

However, the multitransitional processes of modernization and change enveloping Egypt today necessitate a fresh look at military roles and missions. The Egyptian Armed Forces must be able to modernize and to maintain stability to keep up with developments in the region. Modernization should be achieved at a cost consistent with Egyptian capabilities. One role for the military is to continue down a path it has already taken—organizing and training peace-keeping forces for service in Africa, the Middle East, and wherever Egypt can contribute to U.N. Security Council peace efforts. Domestically, the military should also continue its role as a modernizing force in training and industrialization, a function that benefits Egyptian economic development. Some of the Army-run enterprises, particularly in the construction of public works, have proven equally and sometimes more efficient than either the public or private sector civilian enterprises.

Unlike the Turkish Army since Ataturk, which performs the function of periodic direct intervention in political processes to correct any deviation from the Ataturk tradition, the Egyptian Army basically limits its role to the defense of the country and is reluctant to intervene in domestic political affairs. It sees its function as both the defender of the country against foreign enemies and the ballast for the stability of the political system.

The Egyptian Army will continue to play a stabilizing role, providing the political regime and society as a whole with a sense of order. On the regional scene, the Egyptian Army has played an active and sustained role in supporting the Arab-Israeli peace process. As a spearhead of the twin Egyptian goals of modernization and moderation, the military will continue to live up to its expected responsibility.

The Intellectual Spectrum

The debacle of the Arab defeat in the 1967 war was a watershed in the political and intellectual life of Egypt. This episode had two ideological consequences. On the one hand, the period that followed this crisis became one of political retrenchment. The Egyptian mainstream, which represented the majority opinion among civilians and military, concentrated its efforts on the consolidation of the Egyptian defense posture. Egyptians wanted to correct the weaknesses in their defense establishment so as to eventually concentrate on the retrieval of their lost territories and help the other Arabs do the same. On the other hand, the crisis quietly unleashed the re-Islamization of intellectual life. Theleologies and political explanations derived from both traditional and radical Islamic writings provided answers to questions raised by those in the younger generation who felt betrayed by the failure of the Nasser revolution to deliver on its promises.

The two political trends that dominated the political scene were the pro-Nasser nationalist mainstream and the new Islamic revivalist movements. While these trends were in opposition to one another, they both sought to find solutions from the past. Both produced past-oriented prescriptions instead of examining global challenges in terms of the present and future. In both, changes were viewed through the lens of the past. This backward looking approach to the present and the future colors almost all intellectual schools of thought in Egypt today. The intellectual climate produced by this orientation results in giving Egyptians a sense of living "outside of history," of providing an optic increasingly out of focus with current developments.

The "oil epoch" of the mid-1970s had a negative effect on Egyptian intellectual life. The avalanche of petro-dollars that resulted from the oil price increases of that decade was used to "buy" the Arab media and publishing world. Gulf leaders created a "cultural desertification" in the Arab world, using intellectuals as tools in a campaign to weed out critical thinking and the introduction of new ideas. This campaign had as its aim the return of the Arab mind to acceptance of a simplistic, literalist interpretation of the past. The sheikhs of the Gulf, as well as their policies, became immune to examination. Saddam Hussein and Muammar Qadhafi, on the other hand, were able to mobilize writers of nationalist and leftist persuasion, who portrayed these mavericks as liberators. These developments gradually fragmented the intellectual mainstream in Egypt and its cohesion was lost. Meanwhile, new talent lost its integrity through the lure of oil money. These trends were intensified by the second Gulf War, which further polarized Arab thinkers. Subsequent attempts to heal the wounds of that war have proved superificial as well as counterproductive.

The professional classes have increased in number, but respect for professional norms is threatened. Recently, Egypt has witnessed a power struggle among elites that pits the old guard against aspiring newcomers. Sons and daughters of professors miraculously rise to the top of their class at an alarming rate. Meanwhile, the Egyptian attorney general cannot tolerate press criticism of the selection of attorney generals as unfair and corrupt. Monopolistic trends are rampant in professional life. Those who remain outside the system and its benefits have been isolated and are deprived of public attention, their voices being heard only faintly. The system has conveniently encouraged mediocrity and is now paralyzed by it.

Bureaucracy and the Issue of Corruption

Lethargic though it may be, Egyptian bureaucracy has performed some useful functions. It has kept a steady statecraft functioning and allowed Egypt to adjust to sudden gusts of change that could upset the ship of state. However, the expansion of the bureaucracy and the pay bureaucrats receive relative to the private sector have encouraged a new attitude on the part of civil servants. They are now using their positions as a source of private enterprise. Those sectors of the bureaucracy engaged in production for profit have been "privatized." This privatization benefitted small cliques of businessmen that represented the rise of a new moneyed class composed of former public sector managers who had turned to the private sector and who knew private sector managers with close ties to the government. This semimonopolistic group benefits enormously from the patronage they receive from the government. This process accounts for the perception of widespread corruption that used to be limited in scope and under continuous government scrutiny. It has now developed into a phenomenon of what the Egyptians call "fat cats," a group that dominates the privatization process in all of its economic aspects. The widespread perception of corruption, though difficult to prove, is mainly the result of the expansion of government patronage. The government's bidding procedures and its allocation of the public domain are heavily loaded to benefit this new class. Economic reform, which should be open and transparent, unfortunately is now conducted in a climate of secrecy and a fog of double talk.

Structural adjustment of the economy without concurrent political and social reform tends to increase the power of patronage at the disposal of the state. Forced privatization in a small capital market like Egypt has increased the gap between economic classes and provided the central government with a means of patronage that it has used to buy political support. This kind of "privatization" has increased the irrational and selfish use of government patronage, causing the poor to suffer from declining incomes.

Impact of External Factors

International and regional relations have also affected Egypt's domestic politics and perceptions in ways not clearly understood in the West. The painfully slow (although real) progress on the Arab-Israeli peace process; the change in the regional balance of power in favor of one, dominating super power; the intrusion of the

International Monetary Fund (IMF) and the World Bank into Middle Eastern economies with policies that cause the most pain, at least in the short run; and above all, the perception that the West applies a "double standard" when dealing with the Arabs and Israelis have all left the average Egyptian feeling enfeebled and disempowered. Globalization has worked in the same direction and is viewed as a new form of imperial order. The developing world has to cooperate or be marginalized. The rich and powerful develop the rules of the game; countries like Egypt have to play by them.

These perceptions are gathering momentum in Egypt, and a search for new options and substitutes for the "new world order" is underway. As long as these perceptions persist, the state will be driven to resist change, especially when it appears to come from external factors. This will weaken the resolve of the central government to stay the course on structural reforms, despite the fact that a social, political and organization adjustment, with explicit norms of performance, is long overdue. Without such a structural adjustment, Egypt will resemble a one-legged stool, which cannot stand on its own.

The Economic and Demographic Challenge

The population growth rate has decreased substantially during the past 4 years as a result of many factors, including massive governmental and nongovernment family planning efforts; the rate of growth has decreased from 2.9 percent in the 1970s to an estimated 1.9 percent in 1996.[4] Despite this relative success, the population is still growing by 1.8 million a year. This increase has, for a number of years, exceeded the job-creating capacity of the economy, resulting in an increase in open unemployment and in underemployment. The World Bank estimated per capita GNP in 1994 at $710; by 1996, it was a little over $1,000. It also estimates that the number of poor increased from 2.96 million (5.6 percent of the population) in 1990 to 3.44 million (6.5 percent of the population) in 1994.[5] The Egyptian deputy prime minister for planning has estimated that Egypt's private sector must create sufficient employment opportunities to absorb a labor force that is increasing by some 400,000 to 500,000 new entrants each year.

In Egypt, as in most other countries that undertake economic reform, real gross domestic product (GDP) growth slowed after the Economic Reform and Structural Adjustment Program was initiated by the Egyptian Government with the IMF, from an average of 2.5 percent per annum from FY89-91 to 0.41 per annum in fiscal year from FY 92-93. Yet Egypt has managed to absorb a population increase of about 14 to 15 million between 1981 and 1993, equal to the population of Jordan, Israel, and Palestine combined. This remarkable fact indicates the elasticity of the Egyptian economy and its capacity for growth. However, it is estimated that Egypt will require a consistent growth rate of no less than 5 percent per annum to absorb the expected increase in population at the present level of per capita income. Although Egypt achieved a 5 percent growth rate by 1997, it is not yet clear that this level can be sustained.

Without a substantial decline in population growth or an increase in employment, Egypt faces the specter of a gradual erosion of the significant gains in the standard of living Egypt has made over the previous decade. A supply-side approach to increase the productivity of the economy is needed, in addition to the economic reform program. Mobilization of new resources and skills on the national, regional, and international levels is urgently required to ensure growth, employment, and stability.

These economic, social, and demographic factors represent the main short- and long-term challenge to political leadership in Egypt. What are the chances that Egypt will be able to rise to this challenge?

Some Political Conclusions

Based on these political trends, one can draw several conclusions about Egypt's future political direction over the next decade.

Violence by Islamic extremists may undergo periods of expansion and contraction, but such activities are not likely to threaten regime continuity. Their main impact will lie in the social and economic costs they exact. One of these costs may be to solidify the government's defensive posture and to polarize domestic politics further. This will make it more difficult for Egypt to pursue economic reform. Egypt will, nevertheless, be able to fulfill its obligations in the field of domestic and regional security.

The political scene will remain deadlocked. All parties are currently mired in an outlook that reflects a backward, rather than a forward, view. Current leadership is, for the most part, uncreative, yet it blocks the rise of youthful talent and new, imaginative ideas. The process by which new leadership is selected is still quasi-monopolistic and authoritarian. Islamic groups are no exception; they produce new and younger leaders, but most of the "amirs" are authoritarian.

Economic growth and social change hold the key to the Egyptian future. Egypt needs to launch an immediate program of social and political adjustment to augment and enhance the program of economic adjustment. Programs to increase productivity in agriculture, industry, and services are urgently needed to ensure sustained economic growth. Egypt must mobilize nationally to retrain and educate its population and to create a public awareness of new technologies and better management techniques. Such a campaign would help to create a more positive intellectual climate. The quality of higher education and standards of professionalism need reinforcement. An approach that stresses quality over quantity would improve the effectiveness of elites.

To assure continuity and confidence, all changes should be institutionalized within a clear, legal framework. The system requires the institution of serious measures of accountability from top to bottom. To be effective, such programs should concentrate on the future. Past inequalities can best be corrected through improved tax measures.

The President's Dilemma

Egypt's current circumstance confronts the president with a dilemma. Since 1981, Mubarak has been committed to a policy of stability and respect for the constitutional process. He has kept faith with this course, limiting his role to that of a "corrector" of abuses in the system. Domestic stability and regional support for the peace process have been the hallmarks of his presidency. Constitutional changes have been resisted and, until now, no vice president has been appointed. Up until 1990-91, this modus operandi proved successful.

In 1991, when economic conditions became difficult, Mubarak accepted the structural adjustment program but opted for a gradualist approach. As a result, Egypt's record of performance has been merely satisfactory, not decisively successful. Egyptian economic policies have remained mired in bureaucracy, imposed from the top down. The private sector has been encouraged, but failure to simplify legal and administrative structures has slowed it down. The president has intervened to correct mistakes, but reforms have not yet been institutionalized.

Faced with the costs of the extremist violence that bleeds the economy, threatens domestic stability, and embarrasses the government, the president has opted for a "law and order" policy; after a period of patience, he has resorted to emergency measures. The use of martial law courts instead of civil courts to bring extremists to justice has increased the numbers of victims and opened Egypt to international criticism for its human rights record. The excellent Egyptian record of following the current constitutional processes has been tarnished.

The president's dilemma is that of most politicians: can he change a successful modus operandi that has served him well for over a decade? He has been a successful military commander and president by "staying the course." Can he now change course dramatically and if so, how?

Based on the political assessments above, the prognosis is not good, and recent events do not provide much optimism. In July 1993, 441 of the 454 members of the People's Assembly signed a petition to nominate the incumbent President Mubarak, for a third 6-year term. In December 1993, amid huge fanfare, he received a 94 percent vote approving his third term in a public referendum. Widespread expectations of pending reforms, floated during the reelection campaign, came to a sudden halt when the president, in his inaugural speech, opted for "consolidation" rather than rejuvenation and renewal. After 12 years at the helm, the president has failed to name a vice president, leaving uncertainty about his succession. The cabinet changes introduced after his election were limited and unspectacular. New programs turned out to be boring repetitions of the old programs; new slogans were stale versions of the old justifications for political inertia. "Staying the course" remains the supreme compass of political direction. Mummification of the state structure and the elected legislature has become a hallmark of the regime.

Public perceptions of government incompetence, widespread rumors of corruption in high places, and a general erosion of public confidence in government have fallen on deaf ears. The leadership, fearful of uncontrolled change, has opted for strict consolidation. The one exception, and it is a marginal one, has been the initiation of a "national dialogue." However, the participants did not include any serious opponents or critics of the government, such as the Muslim Brotherhood. The rosy hopes that were entertained of the government opening the political space for more participation were dashed when the dialogue was aborted by the government.

The 1995 elections for the *majlis al-Sha'ab*—the Parliament—and for the local council were marred with violence and election rigging. In dealing with the problem of terrorism, which still flares up intermittently, the government heavily relies on "emergency laws" and "emergency courts." This "law and order approach" failed to uproot this phenomenon, because the government was not able to combine its policing efforts with serious measures to reduce the disparity of income and to permit a greater role for political participation. Government wavering between a tough crackdown on these terrorist groups on the one hand and a vague and hesitant policy toward the official Islamic establishment—which exercises more influence on the direction of traditionalist and fundamentalist orientations—on the other, led to the squeezing of the government between two Islamic pressures—the illegal Muslim gama'at (groups), and the traditional Islamic institutions. This zigzagging paints government policy as incoherent, bureaucratic, heavy handed, and uncreative.

The official version of Islam, which represented the consensus of Islamic interpretation from the 1919 revolution until today, is eroding from above as well as from below. Government leadership has failed to create an atmosphere that can help the Egyptian public respond creatively to the ideological challenge that comes with rapid development. If the past 10 years give us any guide, the future does not look very prepossessing. At best, Egypt may simply be in for more of the same. The Egyptian state will not collapse; the centrality of its power will be maintained by a higher degree of coercion, and the vitality of the country will be increasingly wasted by the inertia of leadership and the weight of a decaying bureaucracy. The rejuvenation of Egypt will have to await a period of more creative policies, a more equitable distribution of wealth, a more productive economy that will trickle down to the poor, and above all, a more open political system that will encourage political participation.

Notes

1. Armed British troops attacked an Egyptian police station in the Suez area. The Egyptian police defended their posts with small shotguns, and a number of them were killed in the encounter. Riots against the British spread in Cairo, and in the midst of the riots many parts of downtown Cairo were set on fire by unknown perpetrators. King Farouk dismissed the constitutionally established Egyptian Government of the Wafd Party and declared martial law. The army was deployed to control the city, and a period of political instability ensued that ended with the military coup of July 23, 1952.

2. The 1919 Revolution was a popular civilian uprising against the British presence in Egypt, calling for British evacuation and a constitutional parliamentary system in Egypt that would limit the powers of the monarch. This revolution ushered in a constitutional period in Egyptian history, and is historically referred to as "the liberal age."

3. The grave debacle of 1967 was explained by the government as a temporary reversal—*naksa* in Arabic—and most of the Egyptian public still supported Nasser.

4. *Claiming the Future: Choosing Prosperity in the Middle East and North Africa* (Washington: The World Bank, 1995), 92, and "Sovereign Report: Egypt," Fitch International Bank Credit Analysis, August 1997.

5. Ibid., 29.

WHENCE WILL COME EGYPT'S FUTURE LEADERSHIP?

John Waterbury

An overriding question is whether or not any regime will tolerate, no less encourage, the development of political institutions beyond the control of the government itself; or the development of what others have called civil society. . . . Since the Nasserist period, all such groups in Egypt have been extensions of the political regime itself, with little effective independence.

For over 40 years, Egypt's presidents have been military men, and although there has been creeping civilianization of the cabinet, the country's leaders have never strayed far from their military base of support. When the incumbency of Husni Mubarak comes to an end some time early in the next century, it may fall to civilian leadership to take up the reins of power. That is by no means a foregone conclusion, however. It is as likely that some form of lightly veiled military rule will continue. Before the collapse of his government, General Suharto of Indonesia showed that military, authoritarian rule could be made compatible with rapid growth, provided the

---

Dr. John Waterbury is President of the American University in Beirut. Previously he was a professor of politics and international affairs at Princeton University. He has written several books on the Middle East.

government made use of the best civilian experts in economics and finance, stimulated the indigenous private sector, and attracted foreign investment. With the collapse of the Asian tigers, however, some of these concepts have been questioned. Egypt will need to do all that and more if it is to make a successful transition to a market economy while meeting the challenges of a rapidly growing workforce and the opposition of an entrenched Islamist movement. The past and present sources of leadership will heavily influence what is likely, as opposed to what is possible, in the emergence of Egypt's future leadership.

Political Patterns, Past and Present

At least three political generations are currently represented in the Egyptian elite. There are a few "dinosaurs" from the pre-1952 era, such as Fuad Serag al-Din, the second-most powerful man in the Wafd Party prior to the revolution in 1952, and its undisputed leader since the death of Nahhas Pasha, and Ibrahim Shukry, former MP and leading member of Young Egypt after World War II and today the leader of the Egyptian Labor Party. As leaders of marginalized "opposition" parties, Serag al-Din and Shukry do not carry much weight in the system. There are remnants of the Nasserist era who are today, despite the relaunching of a Nasserist party, mainly in retirement or in honorific positions. Only Khalid Muhyi al-Din, former officer and core member of the 1952 Revolutionary Command Council, as leader of the Tagammu' Party, and Hassanein Heikal, former editor-in-chief of Egypt's most prestigious daily, *al-Ahram*, who continues to be the country's most influential pundit, can be said to have any current prominence. Most of the salient figures of the Sadat era , no longer occupy center stage, including the likes of Ahmad Osman, former chief executive officer of the giant construction firm, Osman Contractors; Sayyid Marei, long-time minister of agrarian Reform; Kemal Hasan Ali, senior officer and former vice president; and Abdul Aziz Higazi, university professor and former prime minister. In some ways Dr. Yussuf Wali, secretary-general of the National Democratic Party and minister of agriculture, is the most important holdover from the Sadat era.

The main actors today in the governmental elite are those who occupied positions in the politico-administrative hierarchy directly beneath the key players of the Sadat years—deans or rectors of universities, deputy ministers, provincial governors, and senior military figures. There has thus been a succession of generations, and a rather orderly one at that, with no leapfrogging into younger age cohorts.[1] Only militant Islamic groups, which obviously play only an adversarial and largely illegal role in the political system, have produced leaders in their twenties and thirties.

The smooth generational transition of Egyptian leadership is mirrored in its meritocratic characteristics. To understand better what is at stake, we may draw on the abundant literature on Latin American political elites, which often highlights the balance between technicos and politicos.[2] The former are politically powerful by virtue of their technical competence and training. They tend to be powerful in the financial, production, and military sectors of the state and political system. They live with and often depend on the politicos, who are politicians of diverse backgrounds to be found in both democratic and authoritarian settings. They are the deal makers, the brokers, and the strategists, and they need the technicos in order to make deals and strategies that work; the technicos need the politicos in order to protect and promote their careers in highly politicized and often dangerous environments.

When one looks at Egypt since 1952, what is most striking is the dominance of technicos. Men, and one or two women, have arrived at positions of power on the strength of their training, education, and technical expertise.[3] This does not mean that they ignore conventional politics, but it was not political skills that brought them to prominence. In looking back over the last four decades, the only *politico* of long standing and real power discerned in Egypt's elite is Sayyid Marei.

By contrast, Egypt's elite has been overwhelmingly drawn from what Manfred Halpern called years ago, "the new middle class."[4] Unlike conventional, property-owning middle classes, this new class, Halpern argued, owned intellectual capital, acquired through technical training and higher education. As a result it was and is a class that places a premium on performance, competence, and know-how. It is an empirical question whether or not this class in fact existed in Egypt or anywhere else and further whether or not it was able to maintain the ideals Halpern attributed to it. But the simple fact is that the type of one's education in Egypt is as powerful a predictor of one's path to power as one can find.[5] I am not arguing that expertise guarantees elite status, but it is a requisite, and the type of expertise will indicate in what realm status will be achieved.

The Dominance of Technocrats

As the years passed after 1952, and especially after Egypt moved into "state socialism" between 1956 and 1963, patterns of elite recruitment became fairly clear and well known. The realm of public finance, banking, and trade was initially dominated by civilians with business experience of one kind or another, but they gradually gave way to experts in economics, accounting, and banking recruited from universities and institutes of higher education. In all instances, this sphere of the elite has been dominated by civilians. Subsequently economic planning was added to this sphere, and the Ministry of Planning and the Institute of National Planning (a kind of governmental think tank) were staffed increasingly by holders of advanced degrees from Soviet and Eastern European institutions. Egypt's two most recent prime ministers, Atif Sidqi, a professor of accounting, and Kamal Ganzouri, a Ph.D. in economics from the United States and for many years an expert in the Ministry of Planning, typify the kind of technocrats with which President Mubarak feels most comfortable.

The productive sectors tended to be dominated by engineers. Industry, agriculture, energy, construction, transportation, and the like were captained by engineers with appropriate training and experience. Some, but always a minority, were drawn from the military. Specific subsectors, such as public sector textiles, chemicals, or automobiles, came to supply top-level leadership, including the minister of industry.

The defense sector, including military production, ports, and airfields, has been the strict preserve of the military itself. Moreover, the military, in conjunction with the intelligence and internal security apparatuses, has claimed the Ministry of Interior and provincial governorships (Ahmad Guweily notwithstanding: see note 1). The Ministry of Foreign Affairs appears to be the most hybrid public agency in Egypt, drawing its experts from the faculties of political science, intelligence, the military, and other parts of the administration.

Few, if any, positions of power exist outside the public sector sphere. Even rectors of universities and editors of major newspapers have often been quasi-official figures, as have the heads of professional syndicates, until recently. The dominant political organizations of the last 40 years—the National Union, the Arab Socialist Union, and the National Democratic Party—have not provided alternate career paths to power. Rather, the government has seconded public officials to serve in the ranks of the political formations. Thus, the political class of Egypt is small and atrophied. Because technicos rather than politicos dominate, individuals with the capacity to mediate among diverse groups or to mobilize multiple constituencies, are in short supply.

Future Political Scenarios

Having examined the patterns of leadership recruitment of the past, what are the prospects for change in the future? In the 21st century, the sources of leadership will depend, in part, on at least four possible political scenarios.

The first is a continuation of the status-quo—an authoritarian, centralized political structure, dominated by technocrats and the military/intelligence apparatuses. The appointment of Kemal Ganzouri as prime minister after the national elections of November-December 1995 represents a change in style but not the introduction of new blood. Ganzouri had served as minister of planning and deputy prime minister for 9 years.

New types of leaders will be rare and in marginal positions. The brief passage of Fuad Sultan as minister of tourism would be an example. He is both a civilian and a businessman who previously occupied no high office in the government or in any political formation. He was expected to bring his private sector experience to bear on re-shaping policy toward public enterprise, but beyond limited reforms within the tourism sector, he was effectively stymied. In early January 1996, Nawwal al-Tatawi, a Ph.D. in economics from Wisconsin and similar in background to Sultan, was appointed to the important position of minister of economy and international cooperation. She was an expert in the World Bank, then a senior officer in the Arab Investment Bank in Cairo after 1978.

The second scenario would witness the engineering of some sort of democratic opening. In that event, real politicians, advocating programs or promoting specific interests, would emerge, replacing in part nominally apolitical technocrats. Such politicians would have to compete for votes, and their success or failure would depend at least as much on their ability to address the needs of parts of the electorate as it would on their access to the top-most power wielders in the regime.

In the third scenario, a seizure of power by Islamic groups, whether by violent or peaceful means, takes place. The type of leadership that would emerge would depend on the groups that seize power and with whom they ally. One possibility is a regime little different from that which we see today, except for the fact that its ideology will be explicitly Islamic. It would be based on a technocracy, a dominant single party, and an alliance with the military. Pakistan under General Zia al-Haqq provides an example.

A fourth scenario would be seizure of power by extremist groups with a social revolutionary agenda and relying on peoples' militias, and local committees. Unlike the first Islamic variant, there would be plenty of politics, grassroots leaders, a certain contempt for the technocracy, and probably a fairly short life span for the regime itself. Islamic romantics cannot change the realities of managing a complex economy thoroughly enmeshed in international commodity and financial markets. Islamists of whatever stripe will share with the current regime a deep suspicion of anything we might label pluralist, an obsession with political control, and a preference for loyal, apolitical technocrats.

In the first two scenarios (the status quo and a democratic opening), the medium- and large-sized private sectors are likely to be increasingly important sources of leadership. First, business organizations and lobbies will enjoy greater prominence in the political sphere as the private sector is called upon to lead the economic development effort. Second, in the democratizing scenario, business persons are likely to play direct or indirect roles in formal politics, as candidates in elections or as financiers of parties and of the media. In the third scenario, Islamic business figures may gain prominence if conservative Islamic forces gain power. If, however, the fourth scenario comes to pass, and radical, populist Islamic groups win power, only the petty entrepreneurs of the small-scale manufacturing and trading sectors are likely to enjoy any political legitimacy.

The four scenarios are each composed of pieces and elements that can be combined in a variety of ways. An overriding question is whether or not any regime will tolerate, much less encourage, the development of political institutions beyond the control of the government itself, or the development of what others have called civil society. We would look to the press, radio, and television, to the universities, to the professional associations, and to voluntary and charitable groups to be the building blocks of civil society. Since the Nasserist period, all such groups in Egypt have been extensions of the political regime itself, with little effective independence. They have been instruments through which the regime has exerted control over specific parts of society. If they achieve financial and organizational autonomy, they become political arenas in their own right, in which new leaders can gain skills and experience.[6] In addition they can begin to supply leadership to the national—and presumably somewhat decentralized—political system. The flourishing of such groups provides alternatives to political life and death within the formal system. There may be a flow back and forth between the quasi-autonomous units of civil society and the structures of governance and economic management.

Such a development would also encourage a new breed of politicians whose claims to power or representation are not based solely on technical competence and training but rather on the interests in whose name they speak or on the programs they advocate. Two consequences would seem to flow from this. First, political pluralism, with its attendant risks, would have to be officially tolerated. Second, it would be possible to be powerful without being part of the government. Only the extremist Islamic groups offer that possibility today. It is ironic that the hallmarks of Egypt's political stability—smooth generational transfers and meritocratic recruitment—have become liabilities in the sense that to young, politically ambitious Egyptians those two characteristics are the manifestations of an impenetrable and unyielding system.

The Missing Technicos

There is one group of leaders so far missing in Egypt and that will be crucial under any scenario. It is the economic and financial technocracy, vital to economic reform and to a dynamic, competitive private sector. Relative to other large, developing countries (Mexico, India, Brazil, Turkey, Indonesia, etc.), Egypt has but a handful of highly trained economists or those with advanced business training.[7] The public sector needs high-caliber experts in the Central Bank, the Ministry of Finance, the Ministry of Economy, the Capital Market Board, the Business Sector Office, and so forth. The private sector needs them in banking, marketing, and management. For the moment, the needs of the public sector are the more crucial in that the experience of other countries tends to demonstrate that a strategically placed, officially blessed, and highly trained team of economic experts is required to carry any reform program forward.[8] Egypt does not yet have such a team, although the government of Kemal al-Ganzouri appears to be moving in that direction.[9] Any regime from among those described above will need one, except the militant Islamic variant, which will not seek such expertise and which will consequently slide toward economic paralysis.

The Diaspora as a Source of Leadership

Egypt has a large diaspora. Parts of it hold substantial wealth; other parts have achieved the highest levels of professional competency in their respective spheres. The diaspora could be a major source of new leadership, particularly in private sector development. It is unlikely that the Egyptian public sector, as currently constituted, will draw expertise from the diaspora. It is unlikely, though not inconceivable, that returning sons and daughters would seek overtly political roles; resentment from those who stayed behind, as it were, would be too strong.

However, in the business realm itself, the talent of the diaspora could come to play a major leadership role. Something of the same process could take place in the university and higher education systems. Something along those lines happened after the death of Nasser, when a number of those who had their businesses nationalized or their property sequestered returned from abroad, principally from Saudi Arabia and the Gulf, to take advantage of Sadat's *infitah.* In addition, some technocrats from the international financial institutions, politically at odds with Egypt's socialist experiment, also returned at that time. Two of the most prominent were Abderrazak Abdul Maguid, former World Bank expert and minister of economy in 1980, and Fuad Sultan, who left the IMF to return to Egypt in the early 1970s. Yusuf Boutros Ghali and Nawwal al-Tatawi represent contemporary examples. While fraught with friction and resentment, the kind of leavening such a return flow produces is generally creative. In the last decade, India and Turkey have been quite successful in utilizing the skills that have accumulated in their respective diasporas, and their model is worth emulating.

The Private Sector Role in the Political Process

Under virtually any political scenario, it appears inevitable that the private sector in general, and individual entrepreneurs in particular, will come to occupy a much more prominent place in the political system. This is so for the simple reason that growth in the economy will depend to a significant degree on increased private investment. It is inherent in the fiscal crises Egypt has weathered since the collapse of oil prices in the early 1980s that the state itself cannot generate resources sufficient to meet more than the recurrent budget and investment necessary for basic infrastructure and social services. The investment required for increased production and structural change must come primarily from private sources, whether Egyptian or foreign.

The real question is, how will the prominence of the private sector in the economic domain translate itself into the political domain? There are a number of possibilities, already alluded to above. There could be a kind of authoritarian alliance of private capital with military and/or Islamic rulers that might look like the arrangements that characterized Brazil, Argentina, and Mexico in the 1970s. On the other hand, we might witness something closer to the Turkish experience, in which TÜSIAD, the Turkish Businessmen's Association, and other private professional associations have taken on an independent, quasi-political role as frequent critic of governmental economic policy. The Turkish industrial bourgeoisie, while no longer subordinated to the state through the corporatist arrangements pioneered by Atatürk, has not yet gained enough legitimacy to play an independent role as financier of political parties or as a source of candidates for political office. But Turgut Özal himself is an example of a technocrat-cum-businessman who rose to be the founder of a political party, prime minister, and president of the Republic.[10]

It is safe to say that any alliance of capital and political authoritarians will tend to degenerate into oligopolized markets, corruption, and rent seeking, as we see today in Iran and in Algeria. Only democratic institutions provide incentives to control such behavior (which is not to say that the incentives always work). Failing the emergence of such institutions, we should expect to see the replacement of corruption and rent seeking within dominant state sectors with corruption and rent seeking in alliances of fiscally constrained states with private interests. The most likely short-term outcome in Egypt is an authoritarian alliance of the state with private capital, but such an alliance will bear the seeds of its own failure. It will be a narrow alliance, with limited private sector partners, and will thus be unable to meet Egypt's investment needs.

The alliance will remain narrowly based because there is no indication that Egypt's current leadership is contemplating any major changes in the political status quo. This means that leadership and power will continue to be monopolized by the government (although illegally contested by Islamic groups), and leaders will continue to be recruited out of technocratic/military/intelligence backgrounds.

That status quo is viable only if strong economic growth is restored, but such growth under present arrangements appears highly problematic. Maintenance of the status quo may send very negative signals to private actors who may feel that a centralized, authoritarian, bureaucratized government cannot be trusted to make irreversible commitments to stimulate private activity. And without substantial private investment, real growth is probably unachievable. So we come full circle, to the paradox that the political status quo is viable only if accompanied by strong growth, which in turn may come about only by abandoning the political status quo.

Notes

1. It is for that reason that when a relatively young individual makes it into elite circles that he or she is so carefully scrutinized. That is the case of Dr. Ahmad Guweily, former Professor of Agricultural Economics at Zagazig University, who became governor of Damietta Province in the late 1980s and then was brought into the cabinet as minister of supply. Guweily is probably in his early fifties.

2. See Janet K. Escobar, "Comparing State Enterprises across International Boundaries," in *Public Enterprises in Less-Developed Countries*, ed. Leroy Jones (Cambridge, United Kingdom: Cambridge University Press, 1980), and Miguel Centeno, "The New Leviathan: the Dynamics and Limits of Technocracy," *Theory and Society* 22 (1993): 307-335.

3. I present evidence on this point in *Exposed to Innumerable Delusions: Public Enterprise and State Power in Egypt, India, Mexico, and Turkey*, ed. John Waterbury (New York and Cambridge, United Kingdom: Cambridge University Press, 1993), ch. 7.

4. Manfred Halpern, *The Politics of Social Change in the Middle East and North Africa* (Princeton, NJ: Princeton University Press, 1963).

5. I have explored these issues in greater detail with respect to Egypt in two books, *The Egypt of Nasser and Sadat: The Political Economy of Two Regimes* (Princeton, NJ: Princeton University Press, 1983), and *Exposed to Innumerable Delusions*. See also Nazih Ayubi, *Bureaucracy and Politics in Contemporary Egypt* (London: Ithaca Press, 1980), and *The Centralized State in Egypt* (Beirut: Center for Arab Unity Studies, 1989); Sarah Farid, *Top Management in Egypt: its Structure, Quality and Problems* (Santa Monica, CA: Rand Corporation, 1970); and Ali Leila,

El-Sayyid Yassin, and Monte Palmer, "Apathy, Values, Incentives and Development: the Case of the Egyptian Bureaucracy," *Middle East Journal* 39, no. 3 (1985): 341-361.

6. The research of Carrie Rosefsky-Wickham on the politics of professional associations amply illustrates this point.

7. John Waterbury, *Exposed to Innumerable Delusions.*

8. Ibid., ch.1, and Anders Aslund, *How Russia Became a Market Economy* (Washington: Brookings Institution, 1995).

9. As evidence of this trend, in 1997 Yusuf Boutros Ghali, the MIT-trained point man for the IMF under the previous government, was appointed minister of economy.

10. See Metin Heper, ed., *Strong State and Economic Interest Groups; The Post-1980 Turkish Experience* (Berlin: Walter De Gruyter, 1991), and Ay Bue Ra, *The Centralized State in Egypt* (Beirut: Center for Arab Studies, 1994).

THE CHANGING FACE OF EGYPT'S ISLAMIC ACTIVISM

Saad Eddin Ibrahim

The persistent vibrancy of Egypt's Islamic activism is a cause for concern but not for panic. Despite its marked problems, the Egyptian state remains strong and will no doubt prevail in its armed confrontation with radical Islamic militants.

Concepts and phrases such as "Islamic revival," "Islamic resurgence," "Islamic fundamentalism," "Islamic militancy," and "political Islam" have received wide circulation in academic circles and the mass media during the last two decades. Dramatic events in the Middle East, such as the Iranian Revolution (1978-79), the assassination of Egypt's President Sadat (1981), and escalating violence in Algeria and Egypt have added to growing interest and anxiety in Egypt and abroad over the potential implications of this Islamic activism. Moreover, such events have compounded the confusion over the meaning to be associated with such phenomena.

Dr. Saad Eddin Ibrahim is Professor of Political Sociology at the American University in Cairo. He has also taught at several American universities. Dr. Ibrahim is the author of several books and over 100 scholarly articles on the Middle East.

In this chapter, "Islamic activism," a less value-loaded term, will be used to tackle the subject. Its use will designate "collective sociopolitical action aimed at changing the status quo in the direction of what is believed to be the proper Islamic order." Such action may be peaceful, semiviolent, or violent. Islamic activism, as used here, should be distinguished from the official or semiofficial Islamic "establishment," that is, Islam as represented by al-Azhar, the Ministry of Awqaf, and the Supreme Council of Islamic Affairs. In reality, these are extensions of the state that regulate the spiritual lives of Egyptians in accordance with state objectives. Islamic activism should also be distinguished from *sufi* Islam. Represented by many *tariqas* (orders), *sufism* is apolitical, emphasizing religious mysticism. However different, neither establishment nor *sufi* Islam poses any political or security threat to the regime or the state. On the contrary, if they were well tuned and functioning properly, establishment and *sufi* Islam would reduce Islamic activism to political and sociological irrelevance.

Activists raising Islamic banners in a quest for power have existed since the first century after Muhammad (7th century A.D.). In modern Egyptian history, Islamic activism has appeared forcefully in three major waves; first at the turn of the 20th century, then at midcentury, and now toward its end. Each wave climaxed in violence and resulted in assassinations of top political figures: Prime Minister Boutros Ghali in the first wave, Ahmed Maher and Mahjoud F. al-Noukrashy in the second, and President Anwar Sadat in the third. Like their tidal counterparts, as each wave of Islamic activism subsided, the genesis of a new wave was laid.

Research suggests that these waves of Islamic activism are not random in their contextual appearance, the social strata to which they appeal, their religious textual discourse, their strategy and tactics, or the actions to which they resort. The concern here is with the third wave that started in the mid-1970s and escalated in an unprecedented manner since the early 1990s. Longer in duration, larger in following, more pervasive in its penetration of society, and more brutal in its violence, this third wave of Islamic activism poses an unprecedented domestic threat to society, the regime, and the contemporary Egyptian state.

Since the inception of this third wave, the Egyptian state has managed to prevail in a succession of armed confrontations with Islamic militants. There is no compelling reason to suppose that the Egyptian state will not continue to do so in the foreseeable future. However, the cost of the confrontation in human and material terms is becoming progressively higher.

Origins of the Third Wave

The symbolic date of the start of Egypt's third wave of Islamic activism is April 18, 1974. On that day, a group of young cadets, aided by some civilian comrades, took over the Technical Military Academy (TMA) in the Abbusiya district of Cairo. They seized its arsenal and prepared to march on the headquarters of the Arab Socialist Union, where President Sadat and his top aides were meeting. Their plan was simple: arrest (or kill) Egypt's political elite, occupy the nearby radio and television building, and declare the birth of "the Islamic Republic of Egypt."

Their attempt was foiled before they could march out of the TMA grounds, but not before a shootout with the state security forces that lasted several hours, in which several people were killed and wounded. The militants were arrested, tried, and sentenced either to death or to long prison terms. In retrospect, these youngsters, invariably called the TMA group, turned out to be the precursors of the violent wing of Egypt's Islamic movement known as the Jihad (Holy Struggle). Jihad is the group that carried out the assassination of President Sadat on October 6, 1981.

During the last two and a half decades (1974-98), other militant Islamic groups have emerged to engage the Egyptian state in similar violent confrontations. The best known of these has been the Takfir wal Hijra (Repentance and Flight) and the Gamaa Islamiyya (Islamic Group). These militant organizations have all been splinters of the Muslin Brotherhood (MB) founded by Hasan al-Banna in 1928.

The MB itself went through a violent phase (1945-65) before deciding to disavow violence and pursue the quest for an Islamic order peacefully. This decision was only made after heated debates during a period in the late 1960s, when MB elders were in Nasser's prisons. At the time, the majority opinion was shaped by Hasan al-Hudhaibi, Supreme Guide of the MB, whose stand was formulated in a book, *Advocates Not Judges*. However, a steadfast minority of younger Muslim Brothers rallied behind the views of another elder, Sayyid Qutb. In his book, *Landmarks on the Road*, Qutb asserted that the contemporary Egyptian regime, state, and society were sinfully repugnant and irredeemable. All had to be destroyed to pave the way for a truly Islamic order.

Following Nasser's death in 1970, President Sadat assumed the reins of power. He faced the task of consolidating his power in the face of detractors—Nasserists, leftists, and pan-Arabists. In this quest, he contemplated an accommodation with the MB and was successful in negotiating a deal with their elders, inside and outside prison. Sadat released the MB members from prison. In return, they agreed to support Sadat against his opponents and to refrain from using violence against the regime—and the MB has honored its side of the bargain.

When he concluded this agreement, Sadat did not know of the split in the MB. Sayyid Qutb had been executed by Nasser in 1965, and his followers were too young and inexperienced to be known to Sadat or his aides. These young dissidents were, nevertheless, released along with their elders. A few years later—too late to remedy—the regime discovered the true implications of the MB split.

Streams in Egypt's Islamic Activism

By the late 1970s, Egypt's Islamic activism had separated into two broad groupings; nonviolent and violent. Both had the same ultimate objective—capturing state and society and transforming them into an ideal Islamic order—but the two groups have gone about the task in different ways.

The nonviolent mainstream of Islamic activism consists of the Muslim Brotherhood, their sympathizers, thousands of Islamic private voluntary organizations (IPVOs), and tens of Islamic investment companies (IICs). Legal and quasi-legal components of this mainstream have managed to duplicate the state, to take advantage of its defective performance, and slowly and steadily to infiltrate Egypt's public space. During the last two decades, this kind of Islamic activism has become entrenched in the mass media, educational institutions, and community social services. It then marched systematically into elected councils at both national and local levels. With a definite agenda in mind, the MB has manipulated activities in professional associations and even managed to obtain a decent representation in the People's Assembly (Egypt's parliament) in 1984 (12 seats out of 455) and 1987 (38 seats).

But the most stunning performance of the MB has been its growing ability to capture a majority of seats in Egypt's major professional syndicates, including those representing doctors, engineers, dentists, lawyers, pharmacists, businessmen, and university professors (see figure 1). The same is true of university student unions.

While not organically linked to the MB, IPVOs registered with the Ministry of Social Affairs now outnumber the secular organizations (8,000 out of a total of 14,000). IPVOs generally are better financed and managed. In times of crisis, such as the Egyptian earthquake of October 1992, IPVOs and the MB-controlled professional syndicates outperform not only their secular counterparts but the state itself. At least, that is how it appeared to the public at large and to the foreign media.

Though much smaller in numbers, the more militant Islamic groups are the ones that have captured the headlines and embarrassed the Egyptian Government. Since 1974, three main Islamic groups have engaged in violent confrontation with the Egyptian state: the Jihad, the Takfir wal Hijra, and the Gamaa Islamiyya.

To be sure, Islamic militants have not had a monopoly of politically motivated violence. In modern Egyptian history, such actions have also been undertaken by secular political groups, but militant Islamic activists unquestionably have appropriated the lion's share of this violence.

Table 1 shows selective indicators of sociopolitical unrest in Egypt between 1952 and 1993. Some of this unrest was

Figure 1. Islamist and Secularist Representation on the Boards of Major Professional Syndicates, 1993

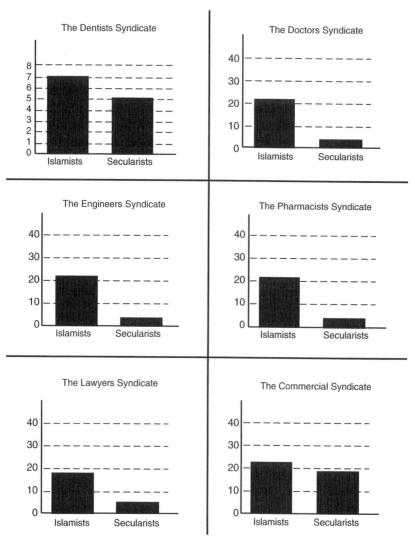

Source: Division of Minorities Affairs, Ihn Khaldoun Center for Development Studies, Cairo.

Table 1. Selective Indicators of Sociopolitical Unrest, 1952-93

Indicators	Nasser Years, 1952-70	%*	Sadat Years, 1971-81	%*	Mubarak Years, 1982-93	%*	Total
Demon-strations	10	16	16	26	35	58	62
Strikes	2	7	13	42	15	52	31
Riots	3	5	6	9	55	86	64
Attempted coups	2	50	2	50	0	0	4
Attempted Assassi-nations	2	12	2	13	12	75	16
Assassi-nations	0	0	2	11	16	89	18
Arrests detention orders	14,000	24	19,000	33	25,000	43	58,000
Hard labor sentences	42	24	69	40	53	36	174
Death sentences	27	37	20	27	27	37	74
Total	14,088	43	19,110	33	25,215	43	58,413
Annual average	782		1,910		2,292		1,181

*Percent over total period, 1952-93.
Source: Ibn Khaldoun Center for Development Studies, Islamic Activism Research Project.

spontaneous (riots), while some was instigated by interest groups (workers and students). However, much of the sociopolitical unrest correlates with Islamic activism during the three successive regimes of Nasser, Sadat, and Mubarak. Table 1 indicates a quantum leap in the incidence of unrest under each regime. The annual average of such incidents doubled between the Nasser and the Sadat eras and then tripled between Sadat and Mubarak. It may legitimately be argued that the rise of unrest is commensurate with the increase in Egypt's population (from 22 million in 1952 to 60 million in 1994). However, like all averages, these figures conceal important specificities within each regime. In the Nasser period, much of the unrest was in the early years (1950s); under Sadat it occurred in the later years (1974-81); under Mubarak it has been quite recent (since 1986). These factors diminish the significance of a simple demographic explanation.

Table 2 shows casualties between 1952 and 1995. In these 43 years, there were some 3,090 casualties from politically motivated violence; 92 percent of them occurred in the last 13 years. More dramatic still is the fact that during the first 4 years (1982-85) of Mubarak's tenure, there was hardly any violence—an average of eight casualties annually. Table 3, which shows political violence between 1992 and 1995, indicates that these years were by far the bloodiest, not only for the Mubarak presidency but for the entire century. In these 4 years there were 2,707 casualties, an average of 677 casualties annually.

Table 2. Total Casualties, 1952-95

Nasser Years, 1952-70	(%)	Sadat Years, 1971-81	(%)	Mubarak Years, 1982-95	(%)	Total
49	(2)	205	(7)	2,836	(92)	3,090

Source: Compiled from Ibn Khaldoun Center for Development Studies, Islamic Activism Research Project

Some ominous observations are worth noting from these and other statistics. First, the number of total casualties has been increasing since 1990, although there has been a slight decline since 1994. Second, table 3 indicates a growing parity between casualties suffered by Islamic activists and those suffered by security forces. In 1993, more police were killed than Islamic activists. Third, the number of civilian bystanders caught in the crossfire now exceeds both police and activists. It is also noteworthy that several assassination attempts have been made by Islamic activists on the lives of high ranking public figures. Two of them succeeded: Dr. R. al-Mahgoub, former Speaker of Parliament died in October 1970 and Dr. Farag Fouda, Egypt's most outspoken secular intellectual, in June 1992. The activists also managed to assassinate four police generals, including the top-ranking antiterrorist officer, General R. Khairat, killed on April 9, 1994. There were close attempts on the lives of the minister of information in April 1993, the minister of interior in August 1993, and on the prime minister in November 1993. Most spectacular of all was the attempt on President Mubarak during his visit to Adis Ababa in 1995.

Table 3. Scoreboard of Political Violence, Egypt 1992-95

Population Group		1992	1993	1994	1995	Totals	Annual Average
Police	Kill	23	120	93	108	**334**	86
	Wound	38	181	112	95	**426**	107
	Total	61	301	205	203	**771**	193
Extremists	Kill	39	111	159	217	**526**	132
	Wound	83	252	30	15	**380**	95
	Total	122	363	189	232	**906**	227
Civilians	Kill	32	101	52	90	**275**	69
	Wound	107	341	213	95	**766**	192
	Total	139	442	265	185	**1,031**	258
Total	Kill	94	332	304	415	**1,145**	286
	Wound	228	774	355	205	**1,562**	391
	Total	322	1,106	659	620	**2,707**	677
Arrested	Civil	128	594	291	489	**1,502**	376
	Extremists	3,645	17,191	6,523	3,630	**30,989**	7,747

Source: Ibn Khaldoun Center for Development Studies, Islamic Activism Research Project.

The Changing Face of Islamic Militants

Several trends in militant activities changed by the mid-1990s. In armed confrontations, militants are more daring and they are willing to take the initiative in operations and often outmaneuvered government forces. Their choice of targets has widened to include Christian Copts, secular Muslim thinkers, foreign tourists, and/or objects they consider repugnant, such as cinemas, cafes, video shops, and Nile cruisers.

The methods of Islamic militants also show greater sophistication. Not only do they demonstrate skillful use of arms, explosives, and remote control devices, but they also manufacture some material themselves. They display remarkable acumen in intelligence gathering. Some of these upgraded skills are no doubt the result of experience accumulated over the previous two decades. Equally important is the combat experience many acquired as volunteers with the *Mujahideen* in Afghanistan during the 1980s. As a result, their operations are longer and more protracted. In the 1970s, their operations took hours or days; in the 1990s, they take weeks and months.

Unlike their counterparts in the 1970s and early 1980s, today's Islamic militants have modern communication skills. They are skillfully maximizing media exposure to conduct psychological warfare against the Egyptian state. For example, among the hundreds of casualties during Mubarak's tenure, until 1997 fewer than a dozen had been foreign tourists—but that tiny figure succeeded in destroying two tourist seasons (1992 and 1993) and depriving Egypt of badly needed currency ($30 billion). Again, in November 1997, a massacre of 58 foreign tourists in Luxor resulted in a significant downturn in tourist numbers and revenues for the 1997-98 season. (This may be compared with the much milder reaction to the deaths of several foreign tourists in Florida.)

However, the greatest change of all lies in the socioeconomic profile of the 1990s. Islamic militants, compared to their counterparts of the two previous decades, are younger and less well educated. Many of them come from deprived regions such as rural areas, small towns, and urban shanty towns. (Table 4 indicates some significant comparisons over decades, compiled from available data on those killed, wounded or arrested.)

The average age of Islamic militants arrested and charged with acts of violence has dropped from 27 years in the 1970s to 21 in the 1990s. Of the 30 militants arrested, tried, and convicted for attacks on tourists, three were below the age of 20 (19, 18, and 16). Likewise, there has been a sharp decline in the formal education of Islamic activists, based on this sampling—in the 1970s, as many as 80 percent were college students or graduates. In the 1990s, that percentage had dropped to 20 percent. Among these, those majoring in elite subjects, such as medicine and engineering, dropped from 51 to 11 percent.

These data suggest that alienation and discontent sufficient to create extremism have now spread to younger and less well-educated Egyptians. This may, in part, explain their disposition to lethal violence. Table 4 also shows that this sense of despair is spreading from large cities to rural areas and shanty towns filled with rural immigrants. In the 1970s, 55 percent of these militants came from large cities; today only 15 percent do. Two decades ago, 8 percent came from rural areas or shanty towns; today the figure has risen to 54 percent. In the 1970s, no rural residents were among arrested activists; today the Egyptian public hears about villages in the governorate of Asyut as scenes of sustained armed confrontations between Islamic militants and the state security forces. Another new scene of confrontation has been the so-called ashwai'iat, or shanty towns, on the fringes of major cities that divide urban from rural areas. A case in point is Western Munira, a shanty town on the edge of the old district of Imbaba across the Nile from Cairo's elite suburb, Zamalik. About the same geographic size as Zamalik (21 square kilometers), Western Munira has more than 10 times its population. By the late 1980s, this slum, with no schools, hospitals, clubs, sewage systems, public transportation or
even a police station, had become a Hobbesian world of violence and vices. A small group of Islamic militants, led by 27-year-old Shaikh Jabir, was able to take over and rule Western Munira for 3 years, collecting taxes and imposing Islamic codes of morality. By

Table 4. Socioeconomic Profile of Egypt's Islamic Militants, 1970s-1990s

Factor	1970s	1980s	1990s
Age			
Fewer than 20 years	5	11	23
25-30 years	38	31	48
20-25 years	61	53	24
Above 30 years	0	5	5
Formal Education			
Below secondary	2	5	9
Secondary	8	12	29
Junior College	11	24	42
College and post-graduate	79	59	20
Elite majors (e.g., medicine)	51	27	11
Community of Residence			
Villages	0	7	18
Shanty-towns	8	16	36
Towns	37	43	31
Large cities	55	34	15
Total	100	100	100

Source: Ibn Khaldoun Center for Development Studies, Islamic Activism Research Project.

December 1992, when the Egyptian state finally took note of what was happening, it took some 14,000 security forces with armored vehicles to restore government control over the area. The process took 3 weeks, cost some 100 casualties from both sides, and resulted in the arrest of some 600 suspected militants.[1]

Toward an Explanation

The data in this chapter contain only part of the story behind the present wave of Egypt's Islamic activism. When more data are available and better analyses possible, the story of the third wave may not be very different in its sociological background and inner logic from that of the first and second waves. It may well be similar to the story currently unfolding in Algeria or to other religious-political movements throughout Arab-Islamic history. That story is one of "politicized Islam" as an idiom for expressing profound worldly grievances.[2]

Concentrating on the Egyptian case at hand, it seems clear that the swift rise and spread of Islamic activism, whether violent or nonviolent, is associated with a number of real or perceived simultaneous crises—social, economic, political, cultural, regional, and international. The social crisis arises from worsening social inequity, rising unemployment, misery in the lower classes, and a spreading sense of relative deprivation. The economic crisis is associated with Egypt's narrow resource base, a rapidly growing population, external debt, and inadequate investment—factors that slowed Egypt's economic growth for a decade, until it began to pick up in the mid-1990s. The political crisis flows from the slow and sluggish process of democratization and government's failure to make the transition from the highly mobilized society of the 1950s and 1960s to a genuinely participatory polity in the 1980s and 1990s. The cultural crisis emerged from the persistence of the century-old, but now flaring, debate over values and norms. On the one side are advocates of "authenticity," who look inward and to the past; on the other are partisans of "modernity," who look outward and to the future. The regional crisis relates to the perception of Egypt's declining role in leading or shaping events in the Arab Middle East and the feeling that Egypt has lost ground compared to

Israel, Iran, and the oil-rich Arab countries. The international crisis springs from a growing collective sense that, during the last half century, Egypt has become more dependent than ever on the West and is unable to chart a meaningful course in a fast changing world.

Whether real or perceived, these multiple crises are affecting Egypt's various socioeconomic strata differently, in degree if not in kind. The new middle class (professionals, technocrats, and bureaucrats) is becoming impoverished and feels itself losing its role as the leading socioeconomic-political force in society. The "lumpen proletariat" is the fastest growing of Egypt's socioeconomic formations. No longer confined to small corners of large urban centers, this group now constitutes one-fourth to one-third of Egypt's total population, and has spread to rural areas and the rural-urban fringes of middle-sized towns. It is the most flammable and manipulable socioeconomic group. From its ranks, lower middle class Islamic activists can easily recruit, indoctrinate, and deploy followers. The third significant socioeconomic stratum is the upper class, which, in the last two decades thanks to Sadat's open-door policy, has grown much richer and less socially and civically responsible. Internationally oriented by virtue of its connections and multiple foreign residences and bank accounts, this class has grown more detached from the rest of society and less culturally sensitive to its behavior. It flaunts its wealth conspicuously. While concerned, like most Egyptians, about the rise of militant Islamic activism, members of this detached upper class would probably leave the country in a few days, or even a few hours, should anything too serious occur. In this respect, they would not be very different from their Iranian or Kuwaiti counterparts in 1979 and 1990, respectively.

The crises have been intensified by a quantum deterioration of societal problems, with the state or the ruling elite unable or unwilling to contain, manage, or resolve them in a timely manner. In the course of the Sadat-Mubarak regimes, a period of 27 years, the state has retreated from Nasser's populist "social contract." Among other things, that contract had traded the provision of immediate goods and services and a loftier vision of the future for the temporary suspension of basic freedoms and democratic participation. For better or worse, the majority of Egyptians appeared to have consented to this contract, at least until the 1967 Arab-Israeli war. Egypt's crushing defeat in that war stirred Egyptian doubts about their populist social contract. When Sadat capitalized on these doubts by de-Nasserizing Egypt, few Egyptians objected in any serious manner, at least not initially.

However, the state's retreat from the Nasserite contract appeared disorganized. Dazzling under Sadat and lack luster under Mubarak, the alternative contract—sociopolitical-economic liberalization—bogged down. It left sizable sections of Egyptian society with inadequate socioeconomic safety nets or unsatisfying political participation. The most adversely affected have been the young, ambitious members of the lower middle class, a substratum that has always been the "sensitive nerve" of Egyptian society. From its ranks have risen all of Egypt's potent sociopolitical movements and articulate leadership in the last century—Urabi, Zaghlul, Nasser, Sadat, and Mubarak. At present, this substratum is the most alienated and discontented in Egypt, and from its ranks now come the leaders and most cadres of the third wave of Islamic activism. As this substratum and the lumpen proletariat have grown in size and become more disenfranchised, Islamic activism has increased in outrage, propensity for violence, and participants.

What has made this situation even worse in recent years is the short supply of political imagination in the ruling elite and the virtual absence of elite circulation. The average age of cabinet members was 63 (in the mid-1990s); the average age of an Islamic militant, as we saw, was 21. This is a gap of 42 years, nearly two generations.

The hardening of Egypt's political arteries has been multiplied by a heavy and inefficient bureaucracy. Demoralized and increasingly impoverished, its upper ranks have become disposed to corruption on a grand scale, and its lower ranks, on a petty scale. Petty corruption has long been taken for granted, and even sympathetically tolerated; in the last few years, exaggerated tales of grand corruption have been rampant.

Gallant but clumsy, Egypt's security forces have been compelled to confront growing Islamic militants almost alone for much of the last decade, without a supportive and politically mobilized public opinion. Two successive ministers of interior have complained in the People's Assembly of the absence of eyewitnesses ready to come forth and testify, even when acts of violence are committed in broad day light in public markets. A good example is the assassination of a police general and his drivers in 1993.

However, by 1998, the situation was improving, because of strategic and tactical mistakes committed by the Islamic militants, the steady improvement in the capabilities of security forces, and, most importantly, a reaction from Egypt's civil society, especially the artistic community.[3] Violent actions, such as the November 1997 execution of tourists in Luxor, appeared more sporadic and more confined to upper Egypt. It is hoped that this improvement will not lull the Mubarak regime into a premature sense of victory against Islamic militants or make it oblivious to badly needed sociopolitical reform.

Conclusion

The persistent vibrancy of Egypt's Islamic activism is cause for concern but not panic. Despite its marked problems, the Egyptian state remains strong and will no doubt prevail in its armed confrontation with radical Islamic militants. The state possesses tremendous resources for this task, most of which have scarcely been tapped: a political culture that values moderation, continuity, and stability; a potent civil society; a powerful media; a cohesive, loyal professional army, and security forces; its own religious establishment; and its good regional and international relations.

However, there is legitimate concern over the regime's inability to mobilize and manage these considerable resources. So far, the government has relied in its confrontation with the Islamic extremists only on its security forces. Even with limited use of its resources, the Egyptian state is already turning the corner in containing them. But the problem is not merely one of achieving a "physical" victory over Islamic extremism, but in dealing forcefully with the root causes that give rise to militancy. Here it is imperative for the regime to develop a clear and comprehensive strategy of reform.

So far, the Mubarak regime has been narrowly obsessed with economic reform. While economic growth is necessary and vital, such one-sidedness has had serious negative repercussions in social and political arenas; these now threaten the positive effects of the economic reform itself. It may not be a coincidence that the present round of violence began in the summer of 1991, just 3 months after Egypt signed the structural adjustment agreement with the IMF (April 1991). Belatedly the government earmarked several billions of Egyptian pounds to upgrade depressed areas in upper Egypt and to create about one half million new jobs. The regime also announced plans for "national dialogue" with the long neglected and marginalized opposition parties and professional associations. Had these two measures been taken a few years earlier, much of the violence might have been averted. Late as they may be, these and similar measures in education and in the media illustrate the imperative to comprehensive social and political reform, needed to complement economic adjustment.

Evolving a comprehensive reform package is the domestic responsibility of Egyptians, but there is a significant role to be played by external actors. This is particularly true of the United States, which has a stake in regional stability in the Middle East and the Arab world. Egypt is the cornerstone of such stability, not only because of its demographic and military weight, but more importantly because of its moral and cultural influence. A stable, prosperous Egypt is a necessary condition for Arab and Middle Eastern stability. Hence, whatever comprehensive reform package Egypt develops, must be fully supported, morally and materially, by those keen on enhancing the processes of peace and regional cooperation in the area.

Notes

1. "Tourists are the Latest Victims of Egypt's Civil Strife," *Africa Report* 38, no. 1 (January 1993): 10.

2. For elaboration of this thesis, see S. E. Ibrahim, "Islamic Activism as a Means of Conflict and Change," *Security Dialogue* 25, no. 2 (1994): 377-381.

3. Reference is to a series of well-received antiterrorism TV dramas and films that appeared early in 1994.

THE ISLAMIC FACTOR

John L. Esposito

Islamic activism in Egypt . . . has not receded; rather it has rooted itself more deeply and pervasively in Egyptian society. . . . The reality of Egyptian society today contributes to a climate in which the influence of Islam and activist organizations on sociopolitical development will increase rather than diminish.

For sometime headlines from Egypt have been dominated by the force of religion in politics. For more than two decades, Egyptian rulers have been grappling with a resurgence of Islam that has significantly challenged the state and its ruling elites.[1]

Egypt has often been regarded as the Arab and Muslim vanguard of development in political, social, intellectual, and religious fields. So, too, contemporary Islamic revivalism ("Islamic fundamentalism") in its origins and manifestations has strong, indeed formative, roots in the Egyptian experience. This experience has had a regional and international impact on transnational Islam and on the West. The Muslim Brotherhood has provided ideological and organizational models for the growth and development of Islamic movements across the Muslim world from North Africa to

Dr. John L. Esposito is Director of the Center for Muslim-Christian Understanding and Professor of Religion and International Affairs at Georgetown University, Washington. The author of many books, he is also editor-in-chief of the Oxford University Press *Encyclopedia of the Modern Islamic World.*

Southeast Asia. In particular, Hasan al-Banna (1906-49) and Sayyid Qutb (1906-66) provide formative influence as their pamphlets, books, and tapes are disseminated globally.

In the 1990s, Egypt continues to provide an example of the many faces of contemporary Islamic activism: the institutionalization of Islam socially and politically; the struggle of government and ruling elites to maintain their world and its lifestyle, power and privileges; the growing polarization in many Muslim societies between Islamists and secularists; and finally the confrontation of state security forces and militant Islamists.

Islam and Modern Egyptian Politics

Much of the character and politics of contemporary Egypt have been influenced by the revolution of 1952 and the subsequent rule of Gamal Abdul Nasser (1952-71). Nasser redefined Egyptian nationalism and promoted Arab nationalism and socialism both at home and abroad. He both centralized and refined the apparatus of an authoritarian, "security" state and projected himself as a regional and world leader.

Although Nasser and the revolution had initially enjoyed the support of the Muslim Brotherhood, that support turned to opposition as it became clear that Nasser did not intend to establish an Islamic state. Before long, the government and the Brotherhood became entangled in a sporadic battle that on several occasions erupted in violence. Both Nasser and his ministers were subjects of assassination attempts that the government attributed to the Brotherhood; these attempts resulted in mass arrests and suppression of the Brotherhood. Finally, in 1966, Nasser moved decisively to eradicate the Brotherhood, executing (among others) Sayyid Qutb, its chief ideologue, arresting and imprisoning thousands, and driving many others underground or into exile. By the late Nasser period, the state had coopted the religious establishment and silenced its Islamic opposition.

Anwar Sadat inherited a defeated and demoralized Egypt in 1971. He took power in the wake of the Arab defeat of 1967 and the subsequent death of Gamal Abdul Nasser, the charismatic leader who was mourned by millions in Egypt and the broader Arab and Muslim worlds. Sadat sought to forge his own political identity and legitimacy, using Islam to blunt the power of the Nasserites and leftists as well as to enhance his legitimacy and mobilize popular support. He utilized both the state-sponsored religious establishment and fostered the reemergence of the Islamic movement, a step that led to the reassertion of a repoliticized Islam, the resurrection of a rehabilitated Muslim Brotherhood, and the emergence and proliferation of more militant Islamic organizations.

Sadat, who referred to himself as the "believer-president," was photographed regularly at Friday prayer, promoted the building of mosques on an unprecedented scale, released Muslim Brothers from prison and allowed them to function in public life, and supported the creation of Islamic student organizations on campuses to counter the influence of Nasserites and leftists.

As a result of these policies, the Muslim Brotherhood, which had emerged from prison and exile a seemingly broken remnant of the past, reconstituted itself and reestablished its publications and activities. However, chastened by repression, imprisonment, and torture, the Brotherhood took an unequivocal position against violence and adopted a clear policy of working for change within the system.

At the same time, younger radical Islamic groups emerged. Many were led by former Muslim Brothers whose prison or underground experience had reinforced their belief that the government was anti-Islamic and that the only option was the violent revolutionary overthrow of the government. By the mid-1970s radical groups were active. Among these, the most significant were the Islamic Liberation Organization (also known as Muhammad's Youth, Shabab Muhammad); Gamaat al-Muslimin (the Society of Muslims) or, as it was more popularly known, Takfir wal-Hijra (Repentance and Flight); Gamaat al-Jihad (Society of Holy War); and Salvation from Hell. The Islamic Liberation Organization successfully seized Cairo's Technical Military Academy in April 1974, while in July 1977, Takfir wal Hijrah kidnapped and subsequently killed Husayn al-Dhahabi, an Azhar shaikh and former minister of religious endowments who had been a strong critic of extremists. Although leaders of both Muhammad's Youth and the

Takfir were executed and others imprisoned, many militants went underground and became active in other radical groups such as the Jund Allah (Soldiers of God) and Jihad, which subsequently assassinated Anwar Sadat.

Sadat's Islamic initiatives proved counterproductive, as he discovered what many have realized in other contexts: Islam is a two-edged sword capable of legitimating and delegitimating, of mobilizing support but also mobilizing opposition. Increasingly, the regime found itself taken to task by the Brotherhood and the militant Gamaa Islamiya (Islamic Group), then an umbrella organization for student groups. They criticized his visit to Israel and signing of the Camp David Accords, his support of the Shah of Iran, and enactment of family law reforms, dismissed as Western inspired. Sadat's "open door" (infitah) economic policy was seen as increasing Egypt's economic dependence on the West and as promoting Western cultural penetration and benefitting an economically privileged, westernized elite.

Having let the genie out of the bottle, Sadat then attempted to put the lid back on. He declared official separation of religion and politics, tightened the reins on the Brotherhood, banned Islamic student groups, and attempted to nationalize Egypt's mosques. During the 1970s, the number of private mosques had doubled from approximately 20,000 to 40,000; out of 46,000 mosques in Egypt, only 6,000 were controlled by the Ministry of Religious Endowments.[2]

Sadat's growing authoritarianism and suppression reached its apogee in 1981, when he imprisoned more than 1,500 people, from a cross section of Egyptian society (Islamic activists, professionals, political opponents, ex-government ministers). These activities left in their wake a more radicalized Islamic terrain, which ultimately culminated in the assassination of Anwar Sadat on October 3, 1981, by members of the Organization for Holy War (Jihad) as he reviewed a parade commemorating the 1973 war.

Mubarak and Political Islam

Vice President Husni Mubarak assumed the presidency with a vivid and personal sense of the power of militant Islam, having witnessed the assassination of Anwar Sadat. The style of Islamic revivalism changed in the 1980s after the death of Sadat, from a movement of confrontation and violence to the entrance of Islamists into the mainstream and the institutionalization of Islamic activism.

Initially, Mubarak's style also changed. He pursued a path of political liberalization and tolerance while at the same time responding quickly and firmly to those who resorted to violence to challenge the authority of the government. He distinguished more carefully between religious and political dissent and direct threats to the state. Religious critics were allowed public outlets for their opposition: to compete in parliamentary elections, to publish newspapers, to voice their objections in the media.

However, in the late 1980s, Mubarak's flexible policy, which failed to coopt or silence effectively his Islamic opposition, gave way to a more aggressive response to the challenge of both religious extremists (those who advocate the violent overthrow of the government) and moderates (those who participate within the established political and legal framework). The Mubarak Government became less discriminating and broadened its battle beyond the militant groups, using harassment and imprisonment to curb the growing strength and challenge of more moderate Islamist movements such as the Muslim Brotherhood.

Institutionalization of the Islamic Movement

The breathing space of the early Mubarak years had enabled Islamic political and social activism to grow more rapidly, to expand its institutions, and to become part of mainstream society. The revivalist spirit, as well as increased religious consciousness and observance, was evident throughout much of society and had become institutionalized in personal religious observances, the growth of Sufi mysticism, the proliferation of Islamic institutions, and social welfare services.

During the 1980s a number of prominent intellectuals and professionals, formerly secularist and even Marxist, "returned" to Islam. These included leftist intellectuals Muhammad Amara, Tariq al-Bishri, and Anwar Abdul Malak, as well as the respected Islamic scholar Khalid Muhammad Khalid, who had decades earlier gained attention when he argued for a secular state. Islamists could also be found among prominent journalists such as Fahmy Howeidy and Adil Hussein, editor of *Al-Shaab*.

Perhaps the most significant development was the extent to which the Muslim Brotherhood and other Islamically oriented organizations became effective agents of social and political change, developing alternative socioeconomic institutions and participating in the political process. They attracted members from the middle and lower middle classes (businessmen, bureaucrats, doctors, engineers, lawyers, journalists) and revenue from members working in the oil rich countries of the Gulf. They engaged in a broad range of activities, from the creation of Islamic charitable associations and banks to electoral successes in parliamentary and professional association elections. Their hospitals, clinics, day care centers, youth clubs, legal aid societies, publishing houses, and drug rehabilitation programs multiplied. A stinging indictment of the government and public testimony to the effectiveness of Islamists in responding to social crises occurred in October 1992, when they, rather than the government, were the first to respond to a devastating earthquake.

Professional associations also felt the influence of Muslim Brothers and other Islamic activists, who captured the leadership in professional organizations of lawyers, doctors, engineers, and journalists. Operating within the political system, moderate activists such as the Muslim Brotherhood couched their criticisms and demands within the context of a call for greater democratization, political representation, social justice, and respect for human rights.

Democratization

The clearest testimony to the main streaming and institutionalization of Islamic revivalism or activism was the emergence of the Muslim Brotherhood as a political force in electoral politics. During the 1980s moderate Islamic activists in Egypt, North Africa, and Jordan demonstrated a gradualist, bottom-up approach to political change by participating within the political system.[3] Relative to the expectations of some, they scored stunning successes. While banned as a political party in Egypt, the Muslim Brotherhood formed coalitions with political parties and emerged as the strongest political opposition group. In the 1984 elections, the Brotherhood joined with the Wafd Party and the coalition won 65 of 450 seats to become the largest opposition group in the Parliament. Subsequently, in the 1987 elections, the Brotherhood formed a new coalition, the Islamic Alliance, with the Socialist Labor Party and the Liberal Party. Campaigning on the slogan "Islam is the solution" and calling for the implementation of Islamic law, they won nearly 20 percent of the vote, emerging as the chief political opposition of the Mubarak government. Islamic candidates (mainly Muslim Brotherhood) held 36 of the Alliance's 60 seats.[4]

The moderate approach of the Brotherhood was reflected in a platform that, while critical of the status quo, did not reject society as un-Islamic. It did not call for revolution but rather for a process of Islamic reform in which Islamic values would gradually inform the political, economic, social, and educational spheres as well as the media. The Islamic Alliance was inclusive rather than exclusive, including Copts on its list of candidates and in its 1989 program affirming that "brother Copts in particular and the 'people of the book' in general have the same rights and obligations as Muslims."[5]

Mubarak's War Against Extremism

By the late 1980s and 1990s, radical violent alternatives, more silent in the early Mubarak period, were boldly and directly challenging and attacking the regime. Islamic student organizations once again dominated university student unions. In Asyut, Minya, Cairo, and Alexandria, they pressed for an Islamic revolution, the implementation of Islamic law, curriculum reform, and separation of the sexes in classes. Their growth was fed by the Government's inability to address continued chronic socioeconomic realities that were having a particularly disastrous effect upon the more than half of Egypt's 60 million citizens below the age of 20. Hundreds of thousands of university graduates found jobs and housing impossible to obtain. Young couples often lived with their families or delayed marriage for years until they could find adequate housing.

Islamic groups, often organized into cells called families (usrah), offered a sense of community and a new feeling of hope. More importantly, their community was based upon an Islamic ideology that provided a sense of identity and religiocultural continuity. It offered a critique of modern Egyptian society and an agenda for radical corrective change, rooted in a religious world view. Radical groups, like their more mainstream counterparts, extended their influence through a network of educational and social welfare societies. They formed Quran study groups for the faithful and social centers that offered food, clothing, and assistance in obtaining housing. Student organizations at universities assisted with free books, clothes (including "Islamic dress" for women), tutoring, and housing.

The chief militant Islamic challenge to the Mubarak government has come from the Gamaa Islamiyya (Islamic Group) and the Jihad, both of which have been locked in a deadly battle with security forces and police during the 1990s. The Gamaa Islamiyya evolved (or perhaps more accurately "devolved") from student groups active on university campuses and in politics in the early Sadat days to become an umbrella organization that includes a host of underground extremist groups active in Cairo, Alexandria, Asyut, Minya, and Fayyum. The Gamaa regards Shaikh Omar Abdul Rahman—the blind cleric arrested, tried, but released in the trial of the assassins of Anwar Sadat and convicted in 1995 in New York for attempted bombings in the United States—as its spiritual leader. Bent upon destabilizing the Egyptian economy and overthrowing the government, they have attacked and murdered foreign tourists, Coptic Christians, and government officials, as well as bombed banks and government buildings.[6] Militants believe that the liberation of Egyptian society requires that all true Muslims undertake an armed struggle or holy war against a regime which they regard as oppressive, anti-Islamic, and a puppet of the West.

The Egyptian military, though generally loyal to the government, has not been impervious to Islamist penetration. Despite attempts to weed them out, the military has proved vulnerable to infiltration by Islamists. In December 1986, 33 activists, including four military officers who were allegedly connected to al-Jihad, Sadat's assassins, were arrested and charged with plotting to wage a holy war in order to overthrow the government. The government has continued quietly to purge those suspected of being "fundamentalists," thwarted several apparent attempts on Mubarak's life by officers, and used its military courts to try and execute secretly those who have challenged the regime. However, despite government vigilance, some argue that a surprising degree of Islamist presence and sympathizers remains in the military among junior officers and soldiers. While the bulk of the army remains loyal, signs of fundamentalist infiltration and presence continue in the military, including the officer corps. Tight press control regarding both the military courts and dissent has not prevented stories of attempted coups, including a report that at a military trial, "a white robed defendant, brandishing the Koran and screaming for President Mubarak's death . . . turned out to be an army lieutenant."[7] In March 1994, three officers were found guilty of an attempt to blow up the president on an airstrip near the Libyan border.[8]

Islamic movements and associations (moderate and extremist) in Egypt have received support from a broad spectrum of governments (Libya, Saudi Arabia, the Gulf States, Iran, and Sudan). In the aftermath of the Gulf War, in which Islamists generally sided against Saudi Arabia and Kuwait, government funding has dried up. The Egyptian Government had accused Iran and Sudan of funding "religious extremists," but now attention has shifted to the role of Usama bin Ladin. Bin Ladin, the son of a wealthy Saudi family, had fought in the Afghan war against Soviet occupation. Returning to Saudi Arabia, his criticism of the presence of American forces in Saudi Arabia, both during and after the Gulf War, eventually led to his loss of Saudi citizenship and exile, first to Sudan (1994-96) and now to Afghanistan. Increasingly, he was identified as a supporter of a network of militant Islamic groups, including the Egyptian Gamaa Islamiyyah and the Islamic jihad. However, although outside assistance can serve as a catalyst, the strength and credibility of Islamic organizations are rooted in domestic conditions and actors rather than outside agitation.

The Mubarak government has aggressively responded to what it clearly perceives as a major threat of Islamic radicalism to the stability of the government and to regional security. In the process, the lines between radical and moderate Islamists have often been blurred. In its war against "terrorism," a broad government crackdown and massive arrests of suspected extremists and sympathizers have included not only extremists but also moderate Islamists and family members of suspects in an attempt to silence and intimidate any and all Islamic opposition. In 1989, as many as 10,000 Islamic militants were arrested. Thousands were held without charge; the Arab Human Rights Organization accused the government of routine torture.[9] An Amnesty International report noted that security forces "appear to have been given a license to kill with impunity."[10] Special military courts, which do not permit defendants a right of appeal, have been created. They quickly and often quietly mete out swift, harsh sentences; the number of those executed has vastly exceeded those for past politically motivated crimes, such as the attempt to kill Nasser or the assassination of Sadat. Lawyers for suspected militants have themselves been arrested. The death of "prominent Muslim militant lawyer" Abdul Harith Madani, one day after his arrest, prompted the Egyptian Bar Association and international human rights groups to call for an investigation, suspecting "that security guards had tortured him to death."[11] The February 1994 State Department human rights report on Egypt on noted that the government "perpetrated many abuses, including the arbitrary arrest and torture of hundreds of detainees, the use of military courts to try accused terrorists, the failure to punish officials responsible for torture."[12]

The Mubarak government's attempt to control the institutionalization of Islamic revivalism or activism extended to professional associations. In 1993, the government changed the election laws that govern associations in order to counter the Muslim Brotherhood's control and influence. More ominously, in June 1994, in a move reminiscent of the actions in Tunisia and Algeria, the Mubarak government extended its war not against just the terrorism of the Gamaa Islamiya but also Egypt's strongest opposition group, the Muslim Brotherhood. It moved "to curtail not only those movements that have carried out violent attacks, but also one that has come to dominate many municipalities, professional and labor associations and university faculties."[13] Increasingly, the Mubarak government has blurred its earlier distinction between violent extremists like the Gamaa Islamiyaa and the more moderate Muslim Brotherhood, accusing it of indirectly supporting Islamic militants. As the presidential election of November 1995 approached, it initiated a pre-election crackdown against the Brotherhood, harassing and arresting many of its leadership and trying them before military courts. In mid-November, 54 Brothers, including parliamentary candidates, were given jail terms, and the Brotherhood's Cairo headquarters was closed. Husni Mubarak was reelected with 94 percent of the vote with no opposition, and the state remained totally dominated by the ruling National Democratic Party. While many believe that the Mubarak government had broken the back of extremist groups, grim reminders of their presence are to be found: an attempted assassination of Mubarak in Addis Ababa in 1995, the killing of 17 Greek tourists in 1996, and, in 1997, a string of attacks against Coptic Christians and the massacre of 68 tourists and three Egyptians at Luxor.

Power and Potential of Political Islam

The most important characteristic of Islamic activism in Egypt today, and its potential source as a challenge to the government and ruling elites, is the extent to which revivalism has become part and parcel of moderate, mainstream life and society, rather than merely a marginal phenomenon limited to small extremist groups or organizations.

Contemporary Islamic activism provides an alternative system or infrastructure and an implicit critique of the failure and inability of the state to adequately respond to the needs of its citizens. This, combined with the remarkable growth of Sufism and other nonpolitical religious organizations, creates a potential pool of politically and nonpolitically oriented Muslims. Given the right conditions (failure of the system, lack of viable political or Islamic alternatives), they can be politically mobilized to vote for those who proclaim, "Islam is the solution."

That Islamists are specific in their indictment of the government but general in terms of their own programs tends to work in their favor. They are able to criticize the failings of the government, from employment and housing to corruption and maldistribution of wealth, without having to offer their own specific solutions to seemingly intractable problems. They employ Islamic rhetoric and symbols and call for an Islamic solution and the implementation of the sharia, but they do not delineate precisely what these would mean in terms of specific policies.

The major accomplishment of the Islamic movement, and the Muslim Brotherhood in particular, and the source of its strength is the extent to which it has created an alternative, normative order. Its alternative order provides an ideological worldview based on and legitimated by religion and an alternative social system of services that demonstrates the relevance and effectiveness of religion to social realities and problems. As a result, the Islamic factor is regarded as both an effective change agent and challenge or threat. While many Muslims find meaning, direction, assistance, and a sense of empowerment, others (in particular the government and many elites) see Islamic movements as an indirect critique of the government's failures, a challenge to its legitimacy, and a direct threat to the stability of the Egyptian Government and society.

Policy Issues

While the threat of radicalism and terrorism must be countered, failure to distinguish between extremists who are avowedly committed to the violent overthrow of the prevailing system and those organizations that have demonstrated a willingness to participate within the system has led to indiscriminate state repression of both kinds of Islamic organizations. This approach runs the risk of setting in motion a spiral of state violence and a movement of counterviolence that can lead to the creation of self-fulfilling prophecies: radicalization, terrorism, and the polarization of society. The attempt to indiscriminately suppress or "decapitate" Islamic movements can lead to the radicalization of moderates, as has occurred in Algeria and is increasingly a risk in Egypt. It would be more productive to discriminate between moderates and violent extremists and thus drive a wedge between them rather than create conditions that will cause them to close ranks.

The history of two different policies, one toward the Muslim Brotherhood in Egypt and the other toward Jama'at-e-Islami in Pakistan, is instructive. Gamal Abdul Nasser's repression of the Muslim Brotherhood, and the spiral of violence and counterviolence that accompanied it, spawned the more militant ideological interpretation of Sayyid Qutb and the ascendance of a radical wing within the Muslim Brotherhood. More than a decade later, prison experience and state repression led to the formation of violent extremist splinter groups like Takfir wal Hijra and the Jihad, and their offshoots today, many of whom are clustered under the umbrella of the Gamaa Islamiyya.

In contrast, Islamic movements such as the Jamaat-i-Islami in Pakistan (or Jordan's Muslim Brotherhood) have been able to function within the system. The Jamaat has been politically influential but never an electoral or violent revolutionary threat. Indeed, while Pakistan has been a theater for significant Islamic political activity, Islamic activists and organizations have generally participated within the system. Islamic groups play a role in government and in opposition. As a result, Pakistan has avoided much of the extremism that has plagued the Middle East. Indeed, in a more open atmosphere without a common enemy and repression to unite them, many Islamic organizations would fall victim to the personality and ideological factors that divide them. This phenomenon can be seen in Sudan, where Sadiq al-Mahdi's Ummah (Islamic Community) party and Hasan al-Turabi's National Islamic Front have often been in contention.

President Mubarak's blurring of the distinction between extremist and participatory organizations in recent years may indeed contribute to Egypt's future instability. Measures that further restrict political parties and professional associations contribute to the growing polarization in society in which citizens are, for all practical purposes, forced to choose sides between the government and a "radical fundamentalist threat" as the middle ground erodes.

Many in the Muslim world and the West believed that Islamic organizations were simply radical, fringe groups that were not representative of their societies and would simply be repudiated by the electorate. The relative successes of the Muslim Brotherhood and its emergence as the leading political opposition in Egypt proved disconcerting, if not a threat to ruling elites. Those who once dismissed Islamist claims as unrepresentative and who denounced Islamic radicalism as a threat to the system now accuse Islamist organizations that wished to participate within the system of an attempt to "hijack democracy."

Concerns in Egypt as elsewhere that Islamic movements might use the ballot box to come to power and then make their "win" permanent ("hijack democracy") are rooted in a realistic possibility. Certainly the examples of the Islamic republics of Iran, Pakistan (under Zia al-Haqq), and Sudan (under Numairi and currently under Omar al-Bashir) offer little reassurance. At the same time, this issue must be balanced by an equal awareness that, however liberal Egypt may have appeared relative to many other countries in the region, it is an authoritarian state. Its rulers are more dependent on the military and security apparatus for legitimacy and stability than the popular support of an electorate.

Too often the lessons of the past have been forgotten. Authoritarian Middle Eastern governments, such as Egypt, regard effective opposition by populist movements, whether in the name of nationalism, socialism, or Islam, as a threat. Such movements challenge the privilege and the way of life of rulers and entrenched elites. This reality can be seen in recent years quite graphically in Tunisia and Algeria, where the relatively successful electoral showing of Islamic movements has resulted in government repression and torture documented and criticized in reports by major international human rights organizations and the U.S. Department of State. At the same time, Islamic organizations such as Egypt's Gamaa Islamiyya and Jihad and Algeria's Armed Islamic Group, as well as the Islamic republics of Iran and Sudan, have engaged in their own brand of authoritarianism, repression, and terrorism in the name of Islam.

The Muslim Brotherhood, like Islamic movements in other parts of the Muslim world, should be challenged to prove by their actions, as well as their promises, that if elected, they will honor the very rights of opposition groups and minorities that they now demand for themselves. They should be challenged to be as vociferous in their denunciation of extremism and terrorism done in the name of Islam as they are of government repression and western imperialism. Like governments, they must demonstrate an awareness that authoritarianism, whether religious or secular, in the name of God or the state, is counterproductive and dangerous.

The United States and other Western governments that advocate the promotion of self-determination and democracy should demonstrate by their policies that they respect the right of any and all, religious as well as secular movements and parties, to participate within the political process. Some Western officials have taken a realistic stance. Edward Djerijian, formerly Assistant Secretary of State for Near East Affairs, has pointed out on several occasions that the United States does not regard Islam or Islamic movements as the enemy, that the United States recognizes the right of movements to participate within the electoral process provided that they did not come to power motivated by a belief in "one man, one vote, one time."[14] However, the test came in Algeria, when the Islamic Salvation Front (FIS) electoral victories raised the specter of an Islamic movement actually coming to power through the ballot box. The intervention of the Algerian military tested the democratic commitment of Muslim and Western governments alike. The policy failures evident in American and European responses toward the subversion of the electoral process and indiscriminate repression of the FIS in Algeria discredit, in the eyes of Islamists, the democratic commitment of the West. They reinforce the perception that the United States and many European governments are guilty of employing a "double standard," a democratic one for the West and selected allies and another for the Middle East and Islamic movements.

Islamic-oriented political actors and groups should be evaluated by the same criteria as any other potential leaders or opposition parties. While some are rejectionists, most Islamic-oriented leaders or governments can be expected to be critical and selective in their relations with the United States. However, like their secular counterparts, on most issues many would operate on the basis of national interests and demonstrate a flexibility that reflects acceptance of the realities of a globally interdependent world. American policy should be carried on in the context in which ideological differences are recognized and accepted or at least tolerated where U.S. interests are not directly threatened.

The electoral strength of the Egyptian Muslim Brotherhood has come not only from a hard core of dedicated followers but also from the fact that they are the most credible and effective alternative to the current government. Their support includes a spectrum ranging from MB members, sympathizers or supporters, and other Muslims who simply wish to vote for an Islamic agenda, to those who wish to cast a vote against an ineffective or discredited government. It must be emphasized that the membership of the Muslim Brotherhood constitutes a numerical minority *not* a majority of the population. Egypt should be challenged to become more inclusive and willing to create conditions that will allow strong alternative parties and opposition groups to develop and have access to power. Finally, the realities of a more competitive political system where Islamic parties are compelled to come to power and rule amidst diverse interests will force them to adapt or broaden their ideologies and programs. The history of Egypt's Muslim Brotherhood and examples in Jordan, Tunisia, Kuwait, Pakistan, and Malaysia bear out this process of development and transformation.

Conclusion

Islamic activism in Egypt as in much of the Muslim world has not receded; rather, it has rooted itself more deeply and pervasively in Egyptian society. Its variety and diversity and its many faces and postures have long been overshadowed by its equation in the West with a monolithic, radical, fundamentalist threat. The broader significance and impact of Islamists are reflected in the extent to which they have gained cultural legitimacy and become part of mainstream Muslim life and society. They are not solely members of marginalized and alienated groups. Secular institutions are now complemented or challenged by Islamic-oriented counterparts, which provide much needed services and underscore the limitations and continued failures of government. Similarly, the emergence of modern educated but more Islamically oriented professionals in society offers an alternative political and social elite that challenges the Western, secular presuppositions and lifestyles of many in the establishment.

The reality of Egyptian society today contributes to a climate in which the influence of Islam and activist organizations on sociopolitical development will increase rather than diminish. Egypt continues to exist in a climate of socioeconomic crisis and cultural alienation in which many experience the failures of the state and of secular ideologies. The ruling elites or classes possess tenuous legitimacy in the face of mounting disillusionment and opposition: in these circles, Islamic activists remain the most vocal, best organized, and effective. The extent to which the government fails to meet socioeconomic needs restricts political participation, is unable to incorporate Islam and moderate Islamists into the body politic more effectively, and appears increasingly Western is the extent to which political Islam will appeal as an alternative. Resorting to repression, whatever its apparent short-term gains, will only contribute to further radicalization and long-term instability in Egypt.

Notes

1. See, for example, Nazih Ayubi, *Political Islam: Religion and Politics in the Arab World* (London and New York: Routledge, 1991), ch. 4; Raymond William Baker, *Sadat and After: Struggles for Egypt's Political Soul* (Cambridge: Harvard University Press, 1990), ch. 8; John L. Esposito, *The Islamic Threat: Myth or Reality?* (New York: Oxford University Press, 1992), ch. 4-5; John Esposito, *Islam and Politics*, 3rd rev. ed. (Syracuse, NY: Syracuse University Press, 1991), ch. 4-5; Amira El-Azhary Sonbol, "Egypt," in *The Politics of Islamic Revivalism*, ed. Shireen T. Hunter (Bloomington, IN: The University of Indiana Press, 1988), ch. 2.

2. See for example, Ayubi, 197.

3. For an analysis of this issue, see John L. Esposito and John O. Voll, *Islam and Democracy* (New York: Oxford University Press, 1996); John L. Esposito and James P. Piscatori, "Democratization and Islam," *The Middle East Journal* 45 (Summer 1991); John L. Esposito, "Islam, Democracy, and U.S. Foreign Policy," in *Riding the Tiger: The Middle East*

Challenge After the Gulf War, eds. Phebe Marr and William Lewis (Boulder, CO: Westview Press, 1993); *Islam and Democracy: Religion, Politics, and Power in the Middle East* (Washington: U.S. Institute of Peace, 1993).

4. Mona Makram-Ebeid, "Political Opposition in Egypt: Democratic Myth or Reality?" *The Middle East Journal* 43, no. 3 (Summer 1989): 423-436, and Ayubi, 85.

5. John O. Voll, *Islam: Continuity and Change in the Muslim World*, 3rd rev. ed. (Syracuse: NY : Syracuse University Press, 1994), 116.

6. Sonbol, 25.

7. *Irish Times*, February 23, 1994.

8. *South China Morning Post*, March 27, 1994.

9. Jane Freedman, "Democratic Winds Blow in Cairo," *The Christian Science Monitor*, January 17, 1990.

10. Christopher Hedges, "Seven Executed in Egypt In Move to Suppress Islamic Rebel Group," *The New York Times*, July 9, 1993.

11. "U.S. Said to Ask Egypt About Lawyer's Death," *The New York Times*, May 27, 1994.

12. Ibid.

13. Chris Hedges, "Egypt Begins Crackdown on Strongest Opposition Group," *The New York Times*, June 12, 1994.

14. The policy was reiterated by Robert Pelletreau, Djerijian's successor.

DILATORY REFORM *vs.*
MAKING A BREAK FOR THE MARKET

Alan Richards

The short-, medium-, and long-run challenges to the Egyptian economy all point toward the same conclusion: a process of export-led growth must be launched. The role of the private sector must greatly expand; the effectiveness of the government in providing public goods . . . must markedly improve.

The Past as Prologue

On the eve of the Gulf War, the Egyptian economy was in shambles. After the heady boom of the late 1970s, economic growth slowed during the early 1980s, then turned negative in the late 1980s. Per capita GNP declined from $680 in 1986 to $610 in 1991. By 1990 the country had amassed international debts of nearly $50 billion, roughly 150 percent of the GDP. Most economists agree that the level of open unemployment roughly doubled during the decade. The quality of government, health, transportation, and educational

---

Dr. Alan Richards is Professor of Economics at the University of California, Santa Cruz, and a former senior analyst with Chemonics International, where he worked on sociopolitical change in Egypt. He has also been a consultant to U.S. AID missions and the RAND Corporation.

services declined precipitously from levels that were already quite poor. This situation could be, and was, exploited by Islamist extremists to create an internal security problem.

The origin of this economic mess is no secret: it is the fruit of three decades of state-led industrialization strategies, featuring import substitution. This strategy manifestly could not increase exports and heighten efficiency while maintaining a minimal social safety net and increasing investment in human capital. It is a tall order, but given Egypt's paucity of natural resources and its abundant labor, the only strategy that will work is export-led growth in manufacturing, with an expanded role for the private sector.

Economists increasingly agree not merely on the broad outlines of change, but even on many of the details. A coherent Egyptian reform requires cuts in the budget deficit by targeting food subsidies, eliminating energy and all other producer subsidies, and reducing the number of public-sector employees. Competition needs to be stimulated by unifying and lowering tariff rates and by reducing government restrictions. Price distortions should be eliminated as quickly as possible, and the regulatory environment radically reformed to promote the growth of private manufacturing. Finally, many believe that even with the best policy package, success will be impossible without a substantial reduction in Egyptian debt.

Dilatory Reform

Despite consensus on the remedies and gravity of the disease, the policy doctors did little before the Gulf War. The Egyptian Government paid lip service to change, even signing a letter of intent with the IMF in May 1987, from which it quickly backed away; the agreement was dead within 6 months. The president claimed that the "limits of popular patience with change" had been reached, even though hardly anything had changed. The government pursued a strategy of "dilatory reform."

It is hardly unusual for a government to delay adopting essential economic reforms. Stabilization and structural adjustment are painful: of necessity, losers outnumber winners in the short run. Further, the losers often include many, perhaps most, members of the ruling coalition; this is especially likely in strongly statist political economies, like Egypt's.

This phenomenon is a necessary but not sufficient condition for explaining dilatory reform in Egypt. There are always losers from economic reform, and they usually have some political influence. Yet economic reforms have occurred all over the world. Many reforming countries face far less severe imbalances than Egypt. Egypt's ability to delay reforms is remarkable, perhaps unique and demands an explanation.

One answer has been the escape afforded by economic rent, a key underpinning of the dilatory reform strategy. The bulk of Egyptian export revenues in the 1980s came directly or indirectly (via workers' remittances) from petroleum revenues, which are largely economic rent. These had risen from essentially nothing in the early 1970s to nearly 20 percent of government revenue in 1982.[1] Oil revenues permitted the Sadat regime to pursue "economic business as usual" while reorienting the country's foreign policy. Despite the vaunted Open Door policy, the Sadat government deepened many of the baleful economic legacies of Nasserism: the number of civil servants doubled, while enrollments in the universities (the ticket to government employment) rose over 250 percent.[2] There was much talk of reform but very little action during the Sadat era.

The collapse of oil rents in the early 1980s greatly increased the pressure for reform. Although there were some reforms (particularly of the government budget), a consistent reform program was not even formulated until mid-1986, not implemented until May 1987, and abandoned in November 1987. Throughout the 1980s, the government procrastinated as problems mounted.

Strategic Rent

The reason was simple. Egypt could, and did, collect another form of rent: strategic rent. Egyptian leaders were able to exploit their unique position as the largest Arab nation, and the only one to have signed a peace treaty with Israel, to extract concessions from the United States, the European Community, and through these powers, international agencies such as the International Monetary

Fund (IMF) and the World Bank. The Mubarak government skillfully utilized "strategic rent" to delay reforms for half a decade after the oil price collapse of mid-1986.

But even strategic rent had its limits. By the eve of the Gulf War, pressure for change was mounting. The IMF took a harder line, while the U.S. connection was endangered when Egypt failed to meet the targets of the May 1987 standby agreement with the IMF. The patience of all parties was running out, as Egyptian policy makers appeared to take an ever shorter perspective on the problem.

Enter the *deus ex machina*, in the unsavory person of Saddam Hussein. The Gulf crisis created an entirely new situation, which allowed the government to obtain a very favorable deal from its creditors. The essence was simple. Egypt would adopt a reasonably conventional stabilization and structural adjustment package in exchange for massive debt relief. Such a bargain was attractive both economically—the reduction of up to $20 billion of debt would cut yearly interest payments by $2 billion for the next 10 years—and politically—the deal could be sold domestically by the government plausibly arguing that its creditors were shouldering part of the burden of past mistakes. Creditors hoped to avoid a rerun of 1987 by making debt relief heavily conditional, with reforms "front-loaded," that is, required early in the process.

Stalled Reform

Many of the basic elements of the reform have been achieved, but there are danger signals. Although financial stabilization has worked well, the deeper problems that the structural adjustment is designed to address continue to grow. Progress toward relaxing the hold of the state in industry has been minimal, and international developments (continued decline of oil prices, recession in Egypt's main export markets in the Former Soviet Union) have not helped matters. The government has made impressive progress in reforming the macro and financial economy but has continued to dither on privatization, trade liberalization, and deregulation. Consequently, a massive inflow of capital to the country remains cautiously parked in highly liquid instruments, rather than invested in employment-creating activities. Investors have returned to Egypt, but they remain very wary, thanks to the government's pathological caution. Consequently, the reforms have yet to produce many jobs.

One cannot help wondering whether it all may have been too little, too late. By delaying deep reform until 1991 (in the case of macroeconomic reform) or even until today (privatization), the regime may have allowed socioeconomic problems to mount so high that any reform package risks being swamped by a backlash of political violence, which, in turn, distracts both public and private actors from the tasks of economic reform and development. The government may now be caught on the horns of a dilemma, one which procrastination has done much to create.

Serious questions remain on the relationship of security concerns to economic problems. What will be the impact of continued political violence on the economy? Will the reform process be deepened and extended? Will it create enough jobs and sufficiently mitigate poverty to undercut the extremists' appeal? In sum, can the Government both reform the economy (necessary to meet the underlying socioeconomic challenges of the 1990s) and also contain the mounting Islamist threat? The Government sometimes resembles a "deer caught in the headlights." It is so paralyzed by fear of Islamists that it delays reform. The Islamist challenge creates a powerful temptation to revert to the "dilatory reform" strategy, to argue that "reforms now will only play into the hands of the extremists." While understandable, this position is mistaken.

Making a Break for the Market

The best strategy for containing militants is to *accelerate* the process of reform, to "make a break for the market," for several reasons:

- Most of the most painful aspects of economic reform have *already* occurred.
- Fears of additional unemployment from privatization are probably grossly exaggerated.

- A dramatic gesture of additional reform might well induce the (very considerable) volume of Egyptian savings into employment generating activities.
- The government badly needs to redirect public servants toward serving the public and providing a social safety net, a task which has been virtually abandoned to the Islamists.

In short, the government's best economic strategy for promoting internal security is a two-pronged reorientation of the role of government: get it *out* of the direct production of goods and services (privatization), and get it back *in* to providing basic social services (recapturing the social safety net from the extremists). Such a policy mix is simultaneously a useful component of a short-to-medium-term counterinsurgency strategy, and also a sound medium-to-long-term economic development strategy.

Economic Mismanagement and Security Problems

The Economic Policy Inheritance

At the core of Egypt's macroeconomic crisis are three microimbalances: the gap between domestic savings and investment, between imports and exports, and between government revenues and spending. The first gap is illustrated in table 1. The collapse of savings may be attributed to the decline of public sector savings as oil revenues have dwindled and as public sector companies have accumulated losses. Private savings available to the economy have been held down by negative real interest rates on Egyptian pound deposits and by great uncertainty manifested by private wealth holders as to the future direction and credibility of economic policy. The problem is not Egyptian savings propensity; the World Bank estimates that in 1991 over $80 billion in assets were held by Egyptians abroad.[3] Rather, until reform, there were few incentives for wealthy Egyptians to place their savings in the domestic banking system.

The pattern of investment has also been unhelpful. Most funds have gone into infrastructure, which received some 45 percent of investment from 1982 to 1987, rather than into traded goods production.[4] Although some infrastructure investment may have been necessary to launch export-led growth (it is difficult to do business without telephones), the relative neglect of manufacturing did little to foster exports and create jobs. Further, investment had a capital intensity bias: the incremental capital-output ratio (ICOR) rose from about 2.5 in fiscal years 1976-81 to 8.78 in 1988-91.[5] The average capital-output ratio rose from 2.7 in 1972-82 to just under 7.0 in 1982-87.[6] Still worse, the capital-labor ratio rose at just under 15 percent *per year* from 1975 to 1985.[7]

Table 1. The Gap Between Domestic Savings and Investment

	'65	'80	'85	'86	'87	'90	'91	'92
GDI*	18	27.5	26.7	21	20	20.4	20.4	18.1
GDS*	14	20.6	12.5	12.0	8.0	1.6	11.8	19.6
Resource Gap	-4	-6.9	-4.2	-9.0	-12.0	-18.8	-8.6	1.5

*As percent of theGDP
Source: *World Development Report,* The World Bank, 1992.

The weaknesses in the volume and pattern of investment have contributed to the second gap, that of the current account. The gap between exports and imports of commodities and nonfactory services is shown in table 2. The gap has shown little tendency to decline since the early 1980s; if anything, the resource gap has widened. In 1989 the current account deficit was 7.2 percent of the GDP; by 1991, it was 10.2 percent.[8] Since roughly two-thirds of Egyptian imports are intermediate and capital goods, there is relatively little room for remedying the resource gap through reduced imports. Modest import growth resumed in 1990 and 1991. Since the Gulf War, the balance of trade has remained heavily in deficit, slightly above $5 billion, thanks to the lackluster performance of exports. On the other hand, the current account has fared much better, moving into surplus in 1992, thanks to the large influx of capital and remittances following the macroeconomic and financial reforms which followed the war.

Export developments during the 1980s were dominated by the decline in the value of petroleum sales, which fell from $2.9 billion in 1983 to $1.36 billion in 1987. Other traded goods failed to take up the slack. Agricultural exports continue to deteriorate, with cotton export volume in 1990 only one-third that of the early 1980s, when it had already declined by 50 percent in comparison with 1974. In 1987 the deficit for agricultural trade was some $2.8 billion, or about one-third of the total trade deficit. Industrial exports performed only slightly better. Textiles and related products account for some 60 percent of such exports; these and other expanding industrial exports (aluminum) enjoy substantial subsidies. Successful private sector performers such as horticultural products and rugs were simply too small to plug the trade gap.

Table 2. Balance of Payments, 1980-1992

	1980	1985	1990	1991	1992
Exports*	6.3	6.9	7.9	9.3	9.7
Imports*	9.2	12.7	13.7	13.9	13.6
Balance of Trade	-2.9	-5.8	-5.8	-4.6	-3.9
Net Current Transfers	2.8	3.5	3.8	3.8	5.5
Current Account Balance	-4.4	-3.2	-3.7	-2.4	1.4
Reserves	2.5	1.6	3.6	6.2	11.6

*Goods and nonfactory services, $billion.
Source: The World Bank.

Invisible earnings fared better. Tourism grossed over $2 billion per year on the eve of the Gulf crisis and provided the only really bright spot in the economy. Although the 1991 season was badly hit by the Gulf War, tourism quickly rebounded and enjoyed a substantial boom, until the October 1992 Islamist attacks on tourists. Workers' remittances outperformed most predictions until the Gulf crisis. Estimates of the number of Egyptians violently repatriated during the Gulf crisis range from 490,000 to 700,000.

From a macroeconomic perspective, the rebound after the Gulf War was strong: private transfers rose from $4 billion in 1991 to $6 billion in 1992.

Economic Gaps

Until the Gulf War, remittances were insufficient to cover the difference between imports and exports, and savings and investment. Egypt, like so many middle-income countries, plugged the twin gaps by borrowing from abroad. Direct private investment was severely inhibited by the mire of Egyptian bureaucratic regulations and the macro-problems enumerated above. Such deficiencies, combined with the political volatility of the region, inhibited private bank lending as well. Accordingly, Egypt relied overwhelmingly on borrowing from foreign governments. Although there are conflicting estimates of Egypt's debt, a rough estimate indicates that Egypt's foreign debt climbed from about $2 billion in 1970 to just under $50 billion in early 1990. This latter figure was roughly 150 percent of GNP; in 1990 debt service payments consumed over 25 percent of exports. The situation in mid-1990 may fairly be characterized as one of crisis. Egypt narrowly averted disaster by the last-minute largesse of Gulf States.

The twin gaps were exacerbated by the government deficit. Although its size fell somewhat by the end of the 1980s, the average deficit for fiscal years 1982-90 was 21.2 percent of the GDP; the deficit in 1991 was some 21.9 percent of the GDP. By this time, some 80 percent of government spending consisted of subsidies, public sector salaries, interest on the public debt, and the military. The last two were sacrosanct, forcing all adjustment on the spending side onto the first two.

As new foreign lending dried up in the latter half of the 1980s, the deficit was increasingly financed by the banking system. Accordingly, inflation rose to roughly 25 percent, with the usual baleful results: further distortion of price signals, sharply negative real interest rates that exacerbated the savings-investment gap, and (thanks to fixed nominal rates) a steadily increasing overvaluation of the exchange rate. Such underpricing of increasingly scarce foreign exchange discouraged the production of traded goods and favored imports over exports; in short, it greatly exacerbated the trade gap.

The decision of the Egyptian Government to reduce the government wage bill by freezing nominal wages and new hires rather than by layoffs crippled governmental effectiveness. Real wages in the public sector in 1989 were only 55 percent of their 1973 level; official incomes of lower level public servants fell below the poverty line.[9] As the old joke in Communist lands went, "We pretend to work and they pretend to pay us." It is unsurprising that the quality of governance was impaired as public servants necessarily devoted as little time as possible to their public duties while scrambling to eke out a living on the margins of the private sector by moonlighting.

Microeconomic distortions reinforced these macroimbalances. Egyptian price distortions of the 1970s and 1980s were internationally notorious. The divergences between private and social rates of return in industry were little short of astonishing. In the second half of the 1980s, price reforms began to be implemented in agriculture, but cotton remains underpriced even today. Prices in Egypt have borne little relation to social scarcities. At the same time laws that made it almost impossible to fire workers converted labor, every textbook's example of variable costs, into overhead. This is but one example of the regulatory environment of which it has been aptly said, "That which is not explicitly allowed, is forbidden."[10]

Economic Reform and Security

The parlous state of Egypt's economy has nourished political extremism by providing a mass of willing recruits, whether active or passive, to the Gama'a Islamiyya (Islamic Group) and their allies. Of course, the origins of current security problems are varied and complex. They range from deficiencies in the educational system to constriction of the "safety valve" of emigration abroad, to the Afghan experience. But many of those who sympathize with the extremists do so because they have lost hope that the current system can provide them and their children with a decent standard of living. The legions of young men who cannot find a job or a

74

home provide particularly lush soil for the growth of fanaticism. *Any successful long-term strategy of containing the security threat must address the social problems that have spawned it in the first place.*

The Employment Problem

The most pressing immediate economic dimension to security is the employment problem. Egypt needs to create a minimum of six million jobs during the 1990s, simply to keep up with additions to the labor force. If current levels of unemployment are to be reduced significantly, another 1.5 to 2 million jobs must be found. Since the current labor force is approximately 14 to 15 million, the implications are stark: during the 1990s, roughly 40 percent more jobs must be created simply to prevent unemployment from rising. To reduce unemployment significantly, the number of jobs must rise by about 50 percent. These calculations assume that the current very low participation of women in the labor force (about 12 percent) remains unchanged.[11] Increasing women's market activities typically raises the opportunity costs of children and contributes to reduced fertility rates. These important long-run beneficial effects will be foregone unless still more jobs can be created.

It is important to realize that these simple calculations focus on the need to create jobs at the same real wage. To reduce poverty, real wages need to rise, which means a still more rapid outward shift in the demand for labor. Of course, poverty is a very serious problem in Egypt. Unfortunately, the last national Household Budget Survey to have had its results published was conducted in 1981-82. Predictably, different analysts give alternative figures for the number of households in poverty, but a few generalizations are still possible. Between 1974-75 and 1981-82, rural poverty certainly, and urban poverty possibly, declined.[12] Poverty probably began to increase after the end of the oil boom in the mid-1980s. Not only was the rate of per capita income growth negative for several years in the late 1980s, but data on real agricultural wages show a decline of over 40 percent from 1985 to 1990. Because most farm workers are close substitutes for unskilled urban laborers, similar trends have very likely prevailed in the cities. And real wages of civil servants have plummeted. Only a massive surge of job creation can hope to dent this gnawing social and human problem. The need for employment creation is the greatest political-economic challenge facing the government today. Its dimensions are such that it has become a problem of security as well as of economic development.

This looming crisis was predictable at least 15 years ago when today's entrants to the labor force were born, but since the challenge lay in the future, little was done. Instead, government payrolls ballooned, spawning artificial jobs at ever lower levels of real remuneration. Government effectiveness was sacrificed at the altar of tired Nasserist formulas for distributive justice and social stability. Over half (55 percent) of all jobs created from 1976 to 1986 were in the public sector.[13] Such a system, together with other labor laws, actually *created* unemployment by making the labor market rigid. Available evidence suggests that roughly half of all unemployed are new entrants to the labor force holding intermediate degrees.[14] The educational system is perceived as a "ticket to security," that is, to government employment. Unemployed young men (and young women) holding higher degrees (another 18 percent of the unemployed) are "waiting for the mugama'a (bureaucracy)." But it has not and, because of budgetary constraints, will not arrive. By the mid-1980s, the unsustainability of the "mugama'a strategy" of coping with unemployment was obvious, but only marginal changes were made.

Before the mid-1980s crisis, the other source of employment creation was emigration to the Gulf States, especially to Iraq. Because these jobs were either dependent on the oil boom or upon the course of the Iran-Iraq War, they, too, soon flagged. Emigration had already decelerated by the mid-1980s. A consequence was that real unskilled wages began to fall.[15] Although remittances rebounded strongly after the Gulf War, the impact on employment has been less evident. Egyptian migration experts do not believe that those who left Iraq (over 232,000) are the ones who have found new jobs in Saudi Arabia and Libya.[16] One half of all returnees from Iraq and Kuwait were from Sohag, Dakhaliyya, Gharbiyya, Cairo, and Asyut (and there is some correlation with areas of insurgency, particularly in Asyut). The collapse of the "Iraqi safety-valve" for

Egyptian rural labor, particularly in Upper Egypt, was one of the most unfortunate consequences of the Gulf War for Egypt.

In summary, the old sources of employment creation cannot be relied upon. The employment problem is compunded because the agricultural sector, which used to act as a "shock absorber" by releasing labor during booms and absorbing labor during recessions, can no longer play this role because of mechanization and a severely limited land base. Structural adjustment and the shift to a strategy of labor-intensive manufacturing for export are the only ways out of the employment crisis.

Food Security

The problem of food security has long been recognized in Egypt as a national security issue. Indeed, had the problem of employment creation received the kind of attention food security did, the current scene in Egypt might look very different. However, despite considerable agricultural progress, Egypt must export in order to eat. The growth of the demand for food depends upon the rate of population growth, the growth of income per capita, and the income elasticity of the demand for food. During the 1980s, Egypt "added a Cairo" to its population, about 12 million additional mouths to feed. By the year 2,000, there will be at least 65 million Egyptians, yet another Cairo. In the 1990s, the rate of growth of demand for food is expected to be over 2.5 percent a year.

Domestic farm supply response was far better during the 1980s than in the 1970s. From 1979 to 1990, Egyptian agricultural output grew at 4.1 percent per year, while food production rose by 6.8 percent per year.[17] Even the growth rate of cereal production (3.0 percent) exceeded that of population. Agricultural and food production per capita in 1990 were some 13 percent and 23 percent, respectively, above that of 1979-81.[18] In 1992, total agricultural production was some 145 percent greater than in 1979-81.[19] This is an impressive performance, and it is partly explained by reform of price policies and by the payoff from foreign technical assistance, especially plant breeding. The Ministry of Agriculture was a leading force for economic reform in the 1980s; the sector's performance shows what can be achieved with reform.

Unfortunately, there is no room for complacency. Despite the impressive expansion of wheat production, which more than doubled from 1986 to 1990, the cereal self-sufficiency ratio remained essentially unchanged during the decade. Continuing population increase, revived income growth, and above all the water constraint will doom any plans for national food self-sufficiency.

Water Supply

Egypt's total water supply for the coming decade is essentially fixed at 55 to 56 billion cubic meters per year. Whatever developments may occur with improved storage and sharing of water among Nile riparian states, they are unlikely to have much positive effect for at least 10 years. Indeed, it is easy to foresee negative developments, if there is increased Ethiopian utilization of Blue Nile water resources or greatly expanded Sudanese irrigation projects. Prudence dictates assuming a fixed supply of water in Egypt for the foreseeable future. It follows that more sophisticated demand management will be essential. This is overwhelmingly the responsibility of the agricultural sector, because about 85 percent of all Egyptian water is used in farming. The impact of ongoing agricultural price reforms, a critical component of structural adjustment, may have perverse effects on water use unless water is priced by increasing the production of water-intensive crops. Much more sophisticated demand-management strategies will be necessary to deal with the water problem in Egypt.

One thing is clear: water constraint means that Egypt will have to look to trade rather than to self-sufficiency for its food security. Egypt's only road to food security lies through diversified, competitive exports of farm and factory products. The same strategy needed to ameliorate one security problem (employment creation) can, indeed must, also be used to address a second (food security).

Improving Human Resources

Any viable strategy of export-led growth, or any other growth strategy, must include investment in upgrading the quality of the one resource Egypt has in abundance, human beings. One of the most serious deficiencies in Egyptian public policy during the past generation has been the failure to provide all Egyptians with basic literacy—only half of all adult Egyptians are literate. Only in the later 1980s were all, or nearly all, Egyptian boys enrolled in primary school; nearly one-fourth of Egyptian girls are still not enrolled.

This legacy will haunt Egypt in the 21st century. Nobel Prize winner Theodore Schultz aptly characterized human capital as the "ability to deal with disequilibria" and to respond to shifting technological and market conditions.[20] If Egypt must export in order to employ and feed her citizens, she must be able to compete in the international market place. Egyptians must produce quality articles and market them successfully. They must be aware of new technologies and utilize them effectively. An illiterate workforce is poor material from which to craft an export-led growth strategy.

What sort of competition does Egypt face? If Egypt must produce labor-intensive commodities, it must compete with other low-wage countries. And what do their literacy rates look like? Consider that in 1985, when roughly 56 percent of adult Egyptians were illiterate, corresponding figures for some Asian countries were: Thailand, 9 percent; Vietnam, 10 percent; Sri Lanka, 13 percent; China, 31 percent; Malaysia, 27 percent; and Indonesia, 26 percent.[21] These countries (not Taiwan or Korea, who have long since far surpassed Egypt) are the competition in labor-intensive manufactures in the 21st century. Closer to the Mediterranean, the Eastern European countries currently undergoing radical structural adjustment and reform typically have universal literacy and a high level of skills, comparared to less-developed countries. By the 21st century, competition will be very intense; past underinvestment in human capital places Egypt at a disadvantage. This is an admitted weakness in the "break for the market" strategy. It should be noted that Egypt's policy makers have some real achievements to their credit in the area of human capital development during the 1980s. Infant mortality rates fell from 120 per 1,000 in 1980 to 83 in 1989, and primary school enrollments rose swiftly.

The problem is two-fold: the legacy of decades of past underinvestment, and the current conditions of budgetary stringency that magnify the difficulties of raising the quality of education at all levels. During the 1980s, for example, education's share of total government spending remained roughly constant. However, this hopeful statistic conceals the ever-rising share of teachers' salaries at the expense of materials, books, libraries, and labs. Only if students can learn to think for themselves can education truly produce "the ability to deal with disequilibria" and only if students have some materials other than their teachers' inputs can they learn to think for themselves. The only conclusion is that *in a context of austerity, more funds must be found for education.* This implies still deeper cuts elsewhere; and inefficient, state-owned enterprises are an excellent candidate for the knife. A re-orientation of state activity in the economy is a necessary component of "making a break for the market" as a development-cum-security strategy.

How Economic Policy Reform Can Alleviate Security Problems

The Reform Program of 1991

The short-, medium-, and long-run challenges to the Egyptian economy all point toward the same conclusion: a process of export-led growth must be launched. The role of the private sector must greatly expand; the effectiveness of the government in providing public goods (irrigation maintenance, health, and education) must markedly improve; and prices must reflect social scarcities. Egypt signed Stabilization and Structural Adjustment Agreements with the IMF and the World Bank in May 1991. These agreements provided some, but not all, of what is required to overcome the legacies of the past and to ameliorate their deleterious security implications and comprised six components:

- A stabilization program, which contained the usual macroeconomic measures. The program mandated a banking reform, which made the Egyptian pound a convertible currency; created new financial instruments (in effect, "treasury bills" issued by the Central Bank); and raised nominal interest rates.
- A Structural Adjustment Loan, which provided for a privatization program. This covered the sale of government

assets and the establishment of legal and institutional mechanisms for better management of public corporations. The Central Bank's regulatory functions were also strengthened.

• Price liberalization measures, which included raising the price of cotton in steps so that it would equal the world price in 1995, except for a small export tax on extra-long staple cotton, an area where Egypt has some market power. Cotton marketing and trade were to be liberalized as were subsidies on fertilizers and pesticides. Energy prices were to rise to international levels by 1995, rail tariffs were to be raised, and price guidelines for intercity bus transport removed.

• Trade liberalization, to be achieved by cutting import bans and licensing requirements, eliminating import deposits and lowering tariffs. Export restrictions were to be reduced and then eliminated.

• The abolition of investment licensing by December 1993. Trade in fertilizer and cement was to be privatized, and labor laws were to be reformed so that private companies could more easily lay off or fire workers.

• The establishment of a Social Fund, with a capital of some $600 million, largely provided by European donors. The fund was to reinforce the social safety net by providing labor-intensive public works to generate employment; offering loans to small and micro-enterprises; and retraining public sector workers.

Economic Changes Since the Gulf War

So where are we now? The first component of reform, macroeconomic stabilization, has done very well. Debt relief and banking reform are the keys to this success, although there are also other factors. The United States forgave the roughly $7 billion of military debt up front. Some 15 percent of the debt was forgiven in May 1991 following IMF approval of an 18-month stand-by arrangement, which was extended another 6 months. A further 15 percent was forgiven in September 1993, when the IMF concluded that the first set of reforms had been successful, and agreement was reached on an extended fund facility.

There is consensus that macroeconomic performance has been strong. Tourism has boomed. Remittances and other private transfers have surged strongly upward. Thanks to the banking reform package, Egyptians have been turning dollar holdings into Egyptian pounds, generating a current account surplus. International reserves have soared, rising from $6.8 billion in June 1991 to $20.5 billion in June 1998. The country now has roughly 12 months of import cover. The savings and investment gaps are now being filled with private capital inflows. Price reforms in the agricultural sector are also largely proceeding according to plan, and the government has increased its real revenue by replacing indirect taxation with sales taxes.

Fiscal reform has also been very successful: government deficits have been slashed, falling from over 20 percent of the GDP before the War to under 1 percent in 1998. Fiscal discipline has combined with tight monetary policy to cut inflation from over 25 percent in 1990 to 3 percent in 1998. The contrast between the situation in 1996 with that prevailing before the Gulf War is striking. The macroeconomic performance has been very good indeed.

The bad news is that reforms have so far been largely limited to macroeconomic. The real economy continues to lag. The growth of nontraditional exports has slowed, as local costs have risen and the exchange rate stayed up. The banking system is awash with cash, but the public's holdings are mainly in very short-term (1- to 3-month) instruments. Any shock to confidence could lead to rapid conversion of pounds to dollars, precipitating a sharp, sudden devaluation. It is notable that despite Islamist violence, this has not happened. It is a sign that wealthy Egyptians are betting on the government.

More fundamentally, the problem is that these short-term liquid savings have yet to be translated into investment in the real economy. Only such investment can generate sustainable employment growth. There is consensus among observers that reforms of the real economy are proceeding sluggishly. In particular, there has been little progress on privatization. High interest rates, and especially the general lack of public confidence in the stability of a "level playing field" for private and public enterprise, have so far stymied private investment in traded goods production. In other words, little has been done to correct the fundamental weakness of the Egyptian economy—the absence of private investment in labor-intensive traded goods production. Structural adjustment, as opposed to stabilization, has only barely begun.

Further, the government clings to the industrial dinosaurs of the Nasser era and has failed dismally to provide an adequate social safety net. Implementation of the Social Fund has been greatly delayed as diverse ministries and public personalities have fought for access to the Fund's very considerable resources.[22] While the government dithered, the Islamists continued to move in and win support by providing their own assistance.

What Next?

Three Models of Change

Like any reforming regime, the Mubarak government faces the problem of how to survive the short-run costs so as to reap the long-term benefits of change. This is essentially a problem of the *time horizon* of the political leadership. There is ample evidence of the short time horizon of Egypt's political leaders. We can identify three basic models of coping with Egypt's economic difficulties in the face of this problem:

- Continuation of dilatory reform
- An Islamist takeover
- Accelerating economic reform

The third offers the best chance of averting the second; it is also the only option that offers any real chance of meeting the economic challenges of the 21st century.

Dilatory Reform

The "dilatory reform" model has two components. First, Americans are all too familiar with the classic blockages to meaningful economic reform vested interests create: witness U.S. struggles with its own budgetary deficit. In Egypt, past policies of import-substituting, state-led growth have created powerful vested interests who will lose from structural adjustment. They naturally oppose such changes. However, although such vested interests are a necessary component of policy stasis, their existence is not a sufficient excuse. In both the U.S. and Egyptian cases, inaction leads to mounting economic problems, which would force reform unless foreigners come to the rescue with financing. From the early 1970s to the mid-1980s, petroleum rents performed this "bail out" function in Egypt; thereafter, strategic rent did the job.

The "dilatory reform" model raises questions about the current Egyptian leadership's commitment to reform. After all, the Egyptian Government in 1998 is the same as the one that agreed and then reneged on the IMF agreement of 1987. The credibility of the reform process is vital; only if private Egyptians believe that the government is truly committed to reform (rather than simply manipulating foreign donors) will private investment in traded goods production increase. Private actors' decisions to date suggest that they remain skeptical. Private Egyptian businessmen often point out that the Mubarak Government has been very cautious. Although they believe that this is generally desirable, many feel that the current crisis demands bolder action. They are also disturbed by the continuity of decisionmakers, believing that too many representatives of the "old order" are still in the cabinet. Although there has been some improvement in attracting foreign and domestic investment since 1995, there is still concern that the dance of dilatory reform, particularly on privatization, could begin again. This raises the disturbing prospect of another "window of opportunity," like that of the 1970s oil boom, being squandered to protect special interests.

Islamist Victory

The lateness of reforms and their continued weakness raise fears of "too little, too late." As Samuel Huntington rightly stresses, people tire of any government and they are ill disposed to tolerate economic failure for very long.[23] The problem for the Mubarak Government is the same as that of other authoritarian regimes:

opposition to the specific government becomes opposition to the system itself. The government has been trying to change the system, but the difficulty may be that political as well as economic reform has been dilatory and that by now widespread popular disgust may translate into increasing support for extremist Islamists. The problem is compounded by governmental ineffectiveness, itself a product of dilatory reform. An often incompetent state with diminishing legitimacy has been implementing unpopular economic reforms. The government has done little to explain the logic and necessity of reform and continues to drag its feet on facing the deeper problems. The legacy of dilatory reform looks increasingly baleful.

The Islamist opposition has the advantage of being relatively untested (although the experiences of Iran and Sudan hardly inspire confidence). Two points should be made about this alternative:

- "Cultural politics" dominates their program; all other considerations (including economic ones) are secondary. It is very difficult to know what, if any, economic program they actually have.
- Insofar as they have any economic strategy, it seems to be a private-enterprise, market-oriented one. This is especially true of the more moderate wing of the movement, the Muslim Brotherhood. Their strict interpretation of the Islamic injunction against usury (which they understand to forbid paying interest on loans) really is simply a demand that all capital be equity rather than debt. Although this introduces some inefficiencies into financial and macromanagement, it need not be an insuperable barrier to development. The Islamist tent is large enough to contain sensible bankers as well as wild-eyed young extremists. The quality of their economic governance would depend on precisely *who* actually ran things.

No one believes that the "Iranian" model is apposite for Egypt. Perhaps the only way in which Islamists could gain major influence would be through a "Pakistan" scenario: a weak and discredited government is replaced by a military leader, who restores order and popular legitimacy, partly by forming a coalition with more moderate Islamists. From an American perspective, this would be the "least bad case" for an Islamist takeover, because the military would probably want to continue cooperation with the United States and businessmen with links to the Muslim Brotherhood would be strong.

Nevertheless, it is unlikely that Islamists of any stripe will succeed where the dilatory reformers have failed. First, they would forfeit the strategic rents that have kept the Egyptian economy afloat for the past half-decade. A militant Islamic regime would have difficulty raising foreign exchange. Iran may be able to bail out Sudan; it cannot also bail out Egypt. This would not pose an immediate problem, because of the country's large foreign exchange reserves; these would quickly be dissipated, however, and the capital outflow would be massive. An Islamist Egypt would also face much tougher conditions from the international lending community and would forfeit American food aid. How would a regime without strategic rent find the resources to buy the 50 percent of the food that it imports on the open market? If the money could be found, how would the country pay for the rest of its imports (largely intermediate and capital goods needed to keep industry running)? The chances of economic disaster under the Islamists are reasonably good.

Second, any attempt of an Islamist government to solve the economic problems of Egypt is likely to "trip on the Dome of the Rock." By pursuing the doomed and quixotic regional political agenda of confronting a better armed, better organized, and better connected enemy (Israel) without significant Great Power protection, such a regime would either have to eat its own rhetoric or face a potentially catastrophic military confrontation with the region's only nuclear power. But there are many uncertainties here. The fact that such a course of action would be disastrous does not mean that it cannot happen. There is no reason why the examples of Sudan, Somalia, Lebanon, and Bosnia cannot be repeated on the Lower Nile. If the disaster unfolds, historians will be able to trace some of its roots back to the anodyne yet deeply destructive game of dilatory reform.

Successful Reform

There is, of course, an alternative to both business-as-usual and victory of the extremists. There are some reasons for optimism about the government's commitment to reform. First, the international climate has changed dramatically. The end of the Cold War, combined with increasing domestic concerns, implies that the United States is less likely to lobby IMF or the World Bank to "go easy" on Egypt. (Indeed, there are some signs that the United States is now more impatient than the World Bank with the pace of economic reform.) Second, Egyptian leaders have had long connections with Eastern Europe. The events there have demonstrated (at least to some of them) that the old, centrally planned model is simply not viable and that the political penalty for waiting too long to change can be very severe indeed. Third, and perhaps most important, several decades of professional training in the West are now making their mark, as the recipients of such training mature and move up the bureaucratic ladders within important ministries. These men (and they are mainly men) understand clearly the necessity of sweeping economic reform and are committed to its implementation. Finally, no political leadership likes to have its "back to the wall," to run out of significant options— but that is precisely what happened to Egyptian policy makers on the eve of the Gulf crisis. Although the outcome of the war permitted the Egyptian leadership to reap important gains, there is a sense that such a sharp narrowing of options could be repeated if reform is not successfully implemented.

If the government is committed to reform, then it must be willing to dispense with the short-run rents that accrue from large-scale interference in the economy. Such rents can be allocated to reward friends and punish enemies; they are a vital resource for staying in power. Taking the longer view means that the government would be willing to give up at least some of these discretionary resources, because it can find others. If reducing government interference will considerably enlarge total economic benefits, as economists believe, the government must calculate that it can capture enough of the gains so that the its total revenues will rise. From the government's perspective, however, there are two problems with this model:

- The benefits must actually materialize in the longer run, and the government must believe that this will happen. However, although economists believe that there is no other way out of Egypt's current impasse than the path of economic reform, there is and can be no guarantee of success. After all, exogenous international events could derail export-oriented growth: a regional war, a collapse of GATT, sudden unfavorable terms of trade, and the like. Recently, international economic conjunctures have indeed been unfavorable, with low oil prices combining with the collapse of Egypt's traditional export markets in Eastern Europe. The "future benefits of reform," however persuasive to economists, may look quite uncertain from the perspective of the national political leadership. Economic outcomes are rarely unambiguous; economists do not agree on the probable success of structural adjustment. Political leaders often find themselves bewildered by conflicting advice, which reduces their credulity on the future benefits of reform. Such uncertainty can reduce the utility of reform to current leaders. Egyptian policy makers may well be "generally incredulous, never really trusting economic reform until tested by experience."
- The leadership must have considerable confidence in its own political longevity. Even if the benefits do materialize, the leaders must still be in office to reap them, or they gain little (politically speaking) from their far-sighted strategy. This means that the government will persevere with reform only if it can manage the (mounting) opposition. But here there looms an apparent dilemma. If reform demands sacrifice and imposes hard times, will extremists be the only beneficiaries? Any government's first priority is the maintenance of order; is it possible that economic reform will make this goal more difficult? Although these are good questions, the answer to both is not necessarily. There is a way out of this dilemma.

The Twin Prongs of Accelerating Reform

Accelerating economic reform must be a political as well as an economic strategy. The strategy has two prongs; both are crafted to alleviate the unemployment problem, and thereby to undercut much of the Islamist appeal. On the one hand, privatization and deregulation must be accelerated, in order to send the clear signal to Egyptian private wealth holders that the government is serious about change. Only such bold action will entice the necessary investment in job-creating industries. Because of the government's past record (rather spotty), large-scale, reasonably dramatic moves need to be made. On the other hand, the government must aggressively reassert control over the social safety net. This means that the Social Fund must become fully operational as quickly as possible and that the government must accelerate its reforms and upgrade its activities in health, education, and housing.

The first prong of the strategy may be called "making a break for the market." The benefits of genuine, credible, visible privatization are obvious. The costs are often exaggerated. First, much of the pain of reform has already been felt. The recession, which is typically necessary to achieve macroeconomic stability, has come and gone. Although continued fiscal discipline will be required, the economy has already started to experience growth rates of 5 percent (1997). Second, opponents of privatization grossly exaggerate the amount of unemployment privatization will create even in the short run.[24] Total employment in Law 203 companies (public companies eligible for privatization) is 1.07 million. The worst-case scenario would be that 25 percent (about 250,000) of these workers are redundant, so that they all lose their jobs over, let us say, a 5-year period. But not all these would become unemployed. Some would be retrained through the Social Fund, and some receive early retirement or severance packages. Such circumstances should cover more than half of redundancies. Even under the worst case scenario, then, only about 100,000 unemployed workers would be added over 5 years. Contrast this number with the approximately 2.5 million young people who will join the labor force during the same period. And, of course, there are ways to reduce the costs still further. The worst-case scenario is not the only way to privatize rapidly, but even then the amount of unemployment created by massive privatization is only 4 percent of the additions to the labor force! Privatization will reduce, not increase, unemployment. One cannot help thinking that the "unemployment bugbear" blocking privatization is simply a smoke screen for the defense of vested privilege, at the expense of Egypt's national security, as well as its economic interest.

Of course, there are transitional costs, and there are many Egyptians whose skills are very limited and who will need protection. The second prong of the strategy is "grabbing back the social safety net." This is both an economic and a political strategy. It supports the break for the market and undercuts the Islamists both directly (by depriving them of organizing tools) and indirectly (by enhancing governmental legitimacy).

The 1992 earthquake dramatically demonstrated government incapacity, which is the fruit of past policies. After decades of spreading the state too far and too thin and grossly underpaying civil servants, the rot of indifference, lethargy, and malfeasance have spread so far that they are paralyzing the state. Such poor administration is hardly new in Egypt. However, the traumatic aftermath of the earthquake dramatized political incompetence and corruption in a destabilizing way, as in Nicaragua in 1978.

There is evidence that the government is beginning to move in this area. The Social Fund has finally begun to operate, and governors have been instructed to focus on housing construction. Much more remains to be done. As in the case of privatization, policies and programs have been formulated. The problem is implementation—that is, political will at the top. The twin prongs of making a break for the market and grabbing back the safety net have been forged. It remains for the Government of Egypt to weld them together and wield the instrument.

Notes

1. *Poverty Alleviation and Adjustment in Egypt* (Washington: The World Bank, 1990), 17.

2. Heba Handoussa, *The Burden of Public Sector Employment and Remuneration: a Case Study of Egypt* (Geneva: ILO, 1989), 118, and Alan

Richards, *Higher Education in Egypt* (Washington: The World Bank, 1992), 8.

3. Ishac Diwan and Lyn Squire, *Economic Development and Cooperation in the Middle East and North Africa* (Washington: The World Bank, November, 1993), 4.

4. Handoussa, 119.

5. Diwan and Squire, 5.

6. Bent Hansen, "A Macro-Economic Framework for Economic Planning in Egypt", in *Employment and Structural Adjustment: Egypt in the 1990s,* eds. Heba Handoussa and Gillian Potter (Cairo: American University Cairo Press for the ILO, 1991), 193.

7. Handoussa, 121.

8. *Structural Adjustment Loan Document: Egypt* (Washington: The World Bank, 1991), 52.

9. *Poverty Alleviation and Adjustment in Egypt* (Washington: The World Bank, 1990), 21.

10. "Egyptian Economic Trends" (Cairo: U.S.Embassy, 1990), 3.

11. There are serious problems of under counting women's work activities in agriculture. The official 12 percent figure is a gross understatement. However, the beneficial fertility consequences of womens' employment on population growth are probably limited to urban work.

12. *Poverty Alleviation and Adjustment;* Karima Korayein, *The Impact of Economic Adjustment Policies on the Vulnerable Families and Children in Egypt* (Cairo: Third World Forum and UNICEF, 1987), 50-53.

13. Handoussa, 126.

14. *Trends in Developing Economies* (New York: Oxford University Press, 1993), 29.

15. Alan Richards, "The Egyptian Farm Labor Market Revisited," *Journal of Development Economics*, no. 43 (1994): 239-261.

16. Nader Fergany, *Arab Labor Migration and the Gulf Crisis* (Cairo: unpublished paper, 1992), 3.

17. Growth rates are calculated from *Food and Agricultural Organization (FAO) of the United Nations Production Yearbooks.* Continued price disincentives for cotton production largely explains the differential between food and agricultural growth rates.

18. *FAO Production Yearbook 1990* (Rome: U.N. Food and Agriculture Organization Headquarters), 238.

19. *FAO Production Yearbook 1992,* 239.

20. Theodore Schultz, *Investment in Human Capital* (Glencoe, IL: The Free Press, 1971).

21. *World Development Report, 1991* (Washington: The World Bank, 1991), 162

22. The Social Fund itself constitutes a continuation of strategic rent. Its size testifies to the importance of Egypt. Other reforming states, like Turkey, have had to generate more of their compensatory resources internally. The result has been a tight rope act, balancing government deficits to obtain votes with an export oriented program. The Egyptians perform this act, but the international community seems willing to give it a longer balancing pole. John Waterbury, *The Egypt of Nasser and Sadat: the Political Economy of Two Regimes* (Princeton, NJ: Princeton University Press, 1983), 346.

23. Samuel Huntington, *The Third Wave: Democratization in the Late Twentieth Century* (Norman, OK: The University of Oklahoma Press, 1991), 18.

24. I am thankful to John Waterbury for quantifying the issue for me.

ECONOMIC REFORM AND INTERNAL STABILITY

Hanaa Kheir el-Din

Despite its economic problems, Egypt is likely to remain a force for stability in a volatile region. It may not become a model of economic efficiency or of exemplary financial management, but it is likely to remain at peace with all of its neighbors. And it may well succeed in facing its economic problems, particularly if there is an increasing public conviction that these are due . . . to economic mismanagement.

Because of adverse external developments and the cumulation of distorted economic policies, since the mid-1980s Egypt has suffered from a number of negative economic factors. These include an unsustainable external debt, rising budget and balance-of-payments deficits, and an increasing rate of inflation. Worse, there has been a gradual erosion in its standard of living, which had steadily improved through the 1970s and early 1980s.

Dr. Hanaa Kheir el-Din is Chairperson of the Economics Department, University of Cairo. She has been an advisor to the Egyptian Government and was recently appointed a council member for the U.N. University in Tokyo. Dr. Kheir el-Din has published extensively on economics.

Since 1990, the Egyptian Government has responded to these developments with a comprehensive program of structural reform and stabilization, the result of a standby agreement signed in May 1991 with the IMF and by a structural adjustment loan agreement signed with the World Bank in November 1991, both with the aim to:

- Stabilize the economy, restore its creditworthiness through a better macroeconomic balance, and reduce inflation
- Stimulate efficient resource mobilization and allocation through structural adjustment
- Alleviate the potentially adverse economic effects of such a program on the poor.[1]

The stabilization effort has succeeded on a number of fronts. It has achieved a substantial reduction of the fiscal deficit, a sharp decline in inflation, and an improvement in the balance of payments outlook. In fiscal year 1992, Egypt realized a surplus on the current account, excluding official transfers, for the first time in two decades. Exchange rates were stabilized despite the removal of foreign exchange controls on Egypt's currency. Egypt's creditworthiness also improved because of the reduction in its external debt and its ratio of debt service to exports.[2]

However, although macroeconomic indicators have shown undeniable improvements, the stabilization effort has had a number of negative effects, principally increased unemployment and rising evidence of poverty. These negative developments have raised several questions about the sustainability of the reform program; the optimal path to stability; and the future of the Egyptian economy and the implications of these economic trends for Egypt's domestic and foreign policy.

This paper will examine three issues that bear on these questions:

- The short-term impact of the economic reform and structural adjustment program (ERSAP) on internal security and stability
- The sustainability of the program and vulnerability of the Egyptian economy to external shocks

- The main challenges facing the Egyptian economy in the longer term.

Negative Short-Term Effects of ERSAP

ERSAP has created or led to the following negative phenomena:

- *Lower rates of GDP growth.* The government's stabilization plan may have been over ambitious; as a result, the Egyptian economy underwent a deep recession. In the early 1990s, the real GDP growth rate slowed from 2.5 to 3 percent per annum during the 1989-91 period (before ERSAP) to 0.4 percent in 1992-93 (after ERSAP),[3] because of its adverse effect on demand and supply factors. On the demand side, budget deficit adjustment caused sharp increases in real interest rates, and a sharp contraction of demand for Egyptian exports from the former USSR, Eastern Europe, and Iraq. There was also a decline in tourist revenues because of repeated terrorist acts. On the supply side, the general uncertainty about future economic prospects, the slowness of structural adjustment, the weak performance of the private sector, the reduction in input subsidies (energy, transportation, fertilizers, etc.), and increased taxation also contributed to slow growth.[4] However, by the mid-1990s, the economy showed considerable improvement in growth rates, reaching 5 percent in 1996-97.
- *Increased rates of unemployment.* Unemployment has become a major problem. The rate of open unemployment increased from an average of 7.5 percent in the late 1970s to more than 14 percent in the 1990s. There are now 2.2 million unemployed. The structure of unemployment is equally alarming—some 75 percent of the unemployed are new entrants to the labor force with intermediate or high school degrees; 25 percent are less educated, less skilled, and predominantly male (90 percent).[5]

Continued pressure on the job market comes from ongoing reduction in government recruitment of the new entrants to the labor force. The mismatch between the skills of new entrants and the requirements of the productive sectors in the economy is a major problem that can be solved only by a drastic revision in Egypt's education system.

· • *Increased incidence of poverty.* Increased poverty and a deterioration in social conditions have resulted from increases in the price of essential consumer goods, such as flour, sugar, rice, and edible oils, and to a rise in the cost of basic services following government reduction in subsidies. Prices of nonsubsidized goods and services have also increased, as government controls have been lifted. The availability and quality of basic services such as education and health have been reduced, because of a reduction in public expenditure. All these factors have produced a reduction in real wages and possibly a transfer of income from wage earners to property earners.[6] These have all increased the incidence of poverty. The lively "informal" economy has helped in part to cushion the negative impact of the reform program.

Thus far, the Social Fund, set up for the purpose of alleviating poverty, has not been effective. One reason is the limited availability of its financial and administrative resources. Another is the goal of the fund itself, which is to find new employment for those displaced by privatization. However, the privatization effort has not yet been seriously undertaken.[7]

• *Slack response of the private sector.* Although ERSAP aims at boosting the private sector, it contains a number of measures that can depress commodity producing activities in general, and industry in particular. These include provisions for raising domestic interest rates, devaluation of currency, raising energy prices, a general sales tax, and trade liberalization. For example, high after-tax yields on treasury bills have drawn capital away from private investment. In addition, taxing the equity on income and the exemption on interest on bank deposits have discouraged real investment. Last, but not least, inefficient bureaucracy is often a handicap to private investment. Private investors have also been wary of possible reversals in reform measures. A deepening of reforms will enhance investment incentives, restore credibility in the system, and may even call forth a stronger response from the private sector.

These negative economic impacts from the ERSAP were predictable, but they nevertheless could be politically dangerous. Violent acts against government officials and tourists intermittently threatened Egypt's stability and internal security; these in turn adversely affect the investment climate. Decreasing proceeds from tourism contribute to a delay in fulfilling reforms. Declining popular support for the program can be explained by increased public conviction that Egypt's problem is not that of resource scarcity but rather of *economic mismanagement, bureaucratic red tape, and distorted priorities.* This perception, in turn, constrains the government from moving more quickly to implement reform measures for fear of increasing social unrest, as the impact of reform measures continues to take its toll on the poor.

The opportunity for long-term improvement in Egypt's quality of life may be substantial. But the short-term political risks cannot be discounted. If these risks are not addressed, they could hamper the sustainability of the reform program itself.

The Medium-Term Sustainability of the Reform Program

The ongoing reforms, as well as debt forgiveness and rescheduling, have led to a rapid accumulation of Egypt's international reserves; these have enhanced Egypt's ability to absorb temporary external shocks. However, the economy remains vulnerable to external shocks and dependent on foreign financial support. The following are among the most important examples:

- Egypt has several sources of foreign exchange earnings: workers' remittances, Suez Canal dues, tourism receipts, and oil exports. Most of these are positively correlated with each other. At the same time, all are highly sensitive to regional and international economic and political developments.
- As a net importer of agricultural products, Egypt is expected to suffer from deterioration in terms of trade that will follow reduction of food export subsidies following the Uruguay Round. Food production will become more competitive, both

domestically and internationally. However, Egyptian consumers will incur higher prices on imported agricultural products.
- Under the Multi-Fiber Arrangement (MFA),[8] Egyptian textile and clothing exports are subject to import limitations in major markets, such as the European Union (EU) and the United States. Egypt would benefit from elimination of the MFA quotas; constraints on exports of textile and clothing would be relaxed and demand for raw cotton would likely expand. However, elimination of these constraints is conditional on Egypt's undertaking appropriate policy measures to increase the efficiency of the textile industry, which, in fact, is hindered more by domestic supply limitations than by import restrictions abroad.
- Nontraditional exports, especially engineering products and cotton manufactures, have responded positively to the exchange rate devaluation since 1987. However, the prevailing inflation rate of about 10 percent (subsequently reduced by the late 1990z), combined with the stability of the exchange rate against the U.S. dollar, led to an appreciation of the Egyptian pound. Egypt thus lost competitiveness in the commodities trade sector. This points to the need for Egypt to increase export incentives within the framework of the General Agreement on Tariffs and Trades, 1994 (GATT).
- Egypt does not enjoy the same degree of preferential access to the EU market as other Mediterranean and East European countries. As a result, Egypt is unlikely to benefit from multilateral trade liberalization under GATT, which is gradually reducing the tariff preferences between the EU and other countries.

Medium-Term Prospects for Reform

In spite of some bright spots in the reform program, its medium-term prospects appear to be fragile, because of its dependence on:

- External economic developments beyond Egypt's control, to include petroleum and other export markets and import prices.

- Domestic economic policy in the areas of revising the structure of incentives; raising the efficiency and competitiveness of domestic industries; upgrading living standards in poor areas; and revising the pattern of regional investment away from Cairo and the Delta toward Upper Egypt and the frontier governorates. [9]
- Continued external financial support from creditors and other donors.

Both political and economic considerations suggest the necessity of creating new job opportunities. This requires economic growth that, in turn, implies a *substantial increase in investment* and a corresponding improvement in investment efficiency and export prospects.

Over the medium term, real output growth is expected to rise by more than 5 percent a year. The ratio of gross investment to the GDP should rise to no more than 20 percent. While these ratios would contribute to employment creation, they will not be sufficient to absorb all the unemployed. Labor market imbalances will continue unless and until macroeconomic policy encourages the adoption of labor intensive techniques or stimulates more rapid economic growth than projected. This situation involves real risks of reversal in reform measures and dangers for Egypt:

- With continued unemployment and rising poverty, popular support for economic reform is declining. Rising opposition to the reform from domestic industry is developing among groups that fear foreign competition. A significant outflow of capital could result.
- The economic effects of terrorist acts against foreign tourists have been severe, although those threats have since declined. Tourism revenue declined by 42 percent in 1993.[10] While this abated in the mid-1990s, continued attacks on tourists, such as that at Luxor in November 1997, could result in increased capital outflows and reduced private investment.
- Any adverse development in the external environment, such as a decline in oil prices or a reduction in donor support, would

hamper the sustainability of the program. Continued donor financial and technical support for the reform program is crucial to its success.

Long-Term Challenges and Prospects

The main long-term challenge faced by the government is how to make the adjustments to the public investment program necessary to maximize Egypt's growth prospects while minimizing their adverse impact on the country's vulnerable groups. The following factors make this challenge doubly difficult:

- *Rapid population growth is Egypt's most important economic problem.* Rising population contributes to the very high increase in the labor force and thus to high unemployment; to unmanageable urban problems; to environmental degradation; and to an aggravation of poverty. The continuous decrease in mortality, combined with a much slower decline in birth rates, has led to a doubling of the Egyptian population from 26 to 60 million between 1960 and 1996. This population lives on less than 3 percent of Egypt's total area. Egypt's population is also increasingly young, because of reduced infant mortality and an outflow of adult workers to Arab countries. Although annual growth rates have decelerated from 2.6 percent in 1981 to 2 percent in 1991, population is still growing by more than one million a year.[11] These rates will continue to strain available resources for many years to come.

- *The need for land reclamation for expanding communities.* In spite of its high priority for long-term development and stability, international donors have been reluctant to invest in land reclamation. However, this is the only way Egypt can productively employ its growing population. Reclamation also poses the longer term problem of water scarcity. The search for additional water resources is another area of priority for investment. Undertaking large-scale irrigation projects in the New Valley and Qattara depressions[12] and finding new sources of underground water call for technical and external financial support. Both are essential for sustainable, long-term growth in Egypt.

● *Environmental degradation.* The Nile provides more than 95 percent of Egypt's water requirements. The Nile is becoming increasingly polluted from industrial wastes, with serious consequences for the health and productivity of Egypt's population. In urban areas, where about half the population lives, the air has also become severely polluted. Water and air pollution is also affecting Egypt's coasts and its antiquities, which are major attractions for tourism. Water and soil pollution is reducing agricultural productivity.

● *A decline in productivity.* The actual performance of both the industrial and the agricultural sectors has been below the potential output. Over the past three decades, the two sectors combined accounted for only about 20 percent of GDP growth. Worse, their total productivity has declined sharply over the past 15 years.

● *Continued poverty and shortfall in human resource development.* Egypt's social welfare system, in place for the last 40 years, has helped reduce poverty and improve basic social welfare. However, Egypt has major deficiencies in its basic infrastructure in education, health, and social services. This is true in nearly every part of the country, but especially in rural areas, particularly in Upper Egypt. In the face of budgetary constraints, these services have deteriorated markedly in availability and quality. Egypt is no longer providing even the minimum basic requirements in health and education.[13] Social programs and transfer mechanisms (pensions for widows, the elderly, and the disabled) do not provide an adequate safety net to protect the most vulnerable from the adverse effect of the structural adjustment program. Nor are there employment adjustment services, unemployment benefits, or retraining programs to assist the unemployed or those to be displaced by privatization programs.

● *Unemployment and labor market imbalances.* These will remain for the next several years until new resources are added to the economy and more rapid economic growth can provide employment to the growing labor force. Shifting the education system toward vocational training is essential to match the skills of additional workers to the demands of the productive sectors.

Conclusions

Over the long term, Egypt can succeed in opening up its economy and reforming, as long as it receives outside economic assistance and significant direct foreign investment. Among external sources of finance, private foreign investment, especially equity financing, has the greatest potential for growth. It is superior to development aid and commercial lending. For this reason, Egypt has little alternative to improving its investment climate. It must encourage repatriation of Egyptian capital and attract direct foreign investment.

Over time, Egypt has become increasingly aware of the need to adopt appropriate economic policies and to reform its legal and institutional framework. It must develop an atmosphere conducive to business while maintaining an adequate infrastructure and ensuring that qualified human resources are available to business. The government also seems to be gaining a greater understanding of the limits of its own intervention in the economy and the need to encourage private initiative.

However, Egypt now faces a dilemma. It must reform its economy to achieve economic stabilization and sustainable growth, but the implementation of the reform program, in the short and medium terms, will impact negatively on vulnerable groups, increasing the incidence of poverty. This deteriorating situation has contributed to terrorist acts that are threatening internal security and the sustainability of the reform program itself. To make its way out of this situation, the government must deepen and accelerate its reform effort; improve the incentive system; increase the efficiency of the public sector, and raise the scope of private sector participation. These actions would all enhance productivity growth. At the same time, however, greater emphasis must be put on alleviating poverty and improving the social safety net.

Notes

1. "Egypt's Economy in the 1990s: Challenges and Opportunities Ahead" (Washington: The World Bank, June, 1991), unpublished paper.
2. Central Bank of Egypt, *Annual Report*, 1992-93.
3. The World Bank, unpublished material, 1992 and 1993.
4. Hanna Kheir el-Din and A. el-Dersh, "Foreign Trade Policy of Egypt, 1986-1991," in *Foreign and Intratrade Policies of the Arab Countries*, ed. Said el-Naggar (Washington: International Monetary Fund, 1992), 206-241.
5. *Population Census* (Cairo: Government of Egypt, Central Agency for Public Mobilization and Statistics, 1986).
6. H. el-Laithy and Hanna Kheir el-Din, "Assessment of Poverty in Egypt using Household Data," in *Economic Reform and its Distributive Impact*, eds. G. Abdul Khalek and Hanna Kheir el-Din, Proceedings of the Conference of the Economics Department, November 21-13, 1992, Cairo University.
7. A. Abdul Latif, "An Assessment of the Egyptian Social Fund for Development in the Light of the Bolivian Experience," in *Economic Reform and its Distributive Impact*, 193-213.
8. Introduced in 1974, the Multi-Fiber Arrangement (MFA) restricted imports from developing countries. The agreement is to be phased out by 2005 due to free trade agreements under the World Trade Organisation.
9. El-Laithy and El-Din.
10. The World Bank, unpublished material, 1994.
11. *Population Census*.
12. Plans were approved in 1980 to build a canal from the Mediterranean Sea to the Qattara Depression in the desert of northwest Egypt. The New Valley project is a massive effort to irrigate a million acres in the Western Desert by pumping water through a canal from Lake Nasser.
13. *Egypt, Human Development Report, 1994* (Cairo: Institute of National Planning, 1994), 18-42.

THE MILITARY IN EGYPTIAN SOCIETY

Stephen H. Gotowicki

The Egyptian military has established itself as a positive and effective institution in Egypt's domestic society with the potential for increased value. There are currently no significant indicators of displeasure by the corporate military over the course the nation is pursuing or its role in that course.

S. E. Finer says that an army is a purposive instrument, rationally conceived to fulfill certain objectives; its central purpose is to fight and win wars in defense of the state.[1] Throughout the world, with few exceptions, armies represent professional, highly structured, hierarchical organizations characterized by high levels of discipline and motivation. By virtue of their function and training, armies also acquire highly prized skills and values, such as the capacity for intercommunication, an *esprit de corps*, and self-sufficiency. A

Lieutenant Colonel Stephen H. Gotowicki, USA, is a Middle East Foreign Area Officer and is currently the U.S. Defense and Army Attaché to the Republic of Yemen. Previous positions include Strategic Plans and Policy Directorate, Joint Chiefs of Staff, and Middle East Desk Officer, Headquarters, Department of the Army.

military's unique structure facilitates rapid decision making and efficient execution of these decisions. These institutional character- istics provide military organizations with the potential to undertake social action well beyond the defense function, to include conducting affairs of state and resolving political chaos. The military also comes to serve as the corporate representation and defender of a state's nationalism.

In Egypt, these political capabilities were demonstrated by the 1952 overthrow of the Egyptian monarchy by Gamal Abdul Nasser and elements of the Egyptian military. After seizing power, senior military officers served as Egypt's president and prime minister, while military officers dominated the cabinet and senior governmental positions.

However, modern Egypt has evolved since the 1952 military putsch. From 1952 until the mid-1970s, the Egyptian military was the strongest institution within the Egyptian polity. But, as Egypt has liberalized, the military's involvement in national politics has declined as has its interference in matters of state. At the same time, the military's role in Egypt's domestic society and economy has expanded. As a result, it is not altogether impossible that the Egyptian military could once again become a dominant player in Egyptian politics—through circumstances beyond its control or by conscious intent. Thus it is necessary to examine the role of the Egyptian military in domestic society, addressing the potential of the military as a socializing agent; its expanding involvement in the economy; and its role in domestic politics. The Egyptian military, by design and chance, has evolved into an entity that is supportive of national goals, is responsible to civilian control, and has no overt interest in political dominance.

Military Structure and Roles

Egypt maintains a large, professional army of 440,000, comparable in size to the armies of Syria, Iraq, and Iran.[2] Given the status of Egypt's peace treaty with Israel, the size of Egypt's military greatly exceeds that of its most likely opponents—Libya (70,000) or Sudan (118,500).[3] Although this force exceeds Egypt's realistic defense needs, Egypt maintains such a large posture in part because it believes it provides deterrence, prestige, and credibility to Egypt's putative regional leadership. Also, it is clear that under Egypt's constrained economic conditions, it would not be wise to add several hundred thousand individuals with military training and experience to the unemployment lines. While providing a major source of national employment, Egypt's large military is not without costs. Between 1966 and 1994, Egypt's military expenditures averaged around 23 percent of Egypt's total government expenditures (excluding the wartime peaks in 1973 and 1974).

Egypt remains concerned over Israel's military strength and its reputed nuclear capabilities, which serves as another justification for maintaining such a large force. With an active military force only about a third of the size of Egypt's (136,000), Israel still effectively eclipses Egypt's military capabilities. Despite the peace between Israel and Egypt, most of Egypt's ground forces remain permanently stationed between Cairo and the Suez Canal.[4] Historically, this has been a measure taken to safeguard the Suez Canal and Cairo from an Israeli invasion. While the continued stationing of forces in this area reflects Egypt's continuing concern over the Israeli military, it also takes account of the reality that the housing and infrastructure for these forces have long been located in this area.

Beyond the central objective of national defense, the Egyptian Armed Forces have other important goals: deterrence of potential adversaries, support for Egypt's regional role, effective employment of soldiers idled by diminished defense requirements in an era of peace, and providing an engine for economic growth and development.

The Socialization Role of the Military

The Egyptian Armed Forces comprise less than 1 percent of Egypt's population of 64.8 million.[5] A more meaningful measure of its potential to exert social influence over the population is its percentage of the labor force. The male working-age population (15 to 64 years) in Egypt is 18.6 million;[6] the Armed Forces comprise 2.4 percent of this number. Approximately 650,000 males reach military age each year; of these, approximately 80,000 are conscripted into the Armed Forces.[7] Within this group, the Armed

Forces will have trained 12.3 percent of Egyptian males entering the work force annually, a not insignificant figure. However, the reach of the military may still be modest when compared with that of the mosque attended, over a lifetime, by many more Egyptians.[8]

Figure 1. Egyptian Military Expenditures as a Percentage of Current Government Expenditures, 1962-94

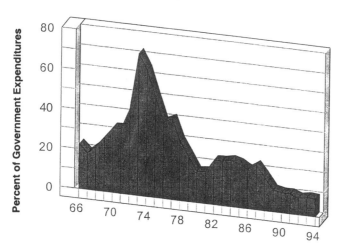

Source: *World Military Expenditures and Arms Transfers*, U.S. Arms Control and Disarmament Agency, various issues, 1965-95 (Washington: Government Printing Office).

The service length for conscripts varies with education level. Conscripts who have completed high school serve 2 years; those without a high school diploma serve 3 years. Conscripts live in military barracks and are trained in military specialties with some remedial instruction given in basic skills such as literacy. Conscripts are paid only £E 32 a month (about $10). After about a year they are promoted to the next higher grade and their pay increases to about £E 140 (about $40). Conscripts identified as lacking basic skills are given full-time vocational training in skills convertible to civilian employment for the last 6 months of their conscripted service. This vocational training appears to be an instrument designed to support national economic development. Reportedly, many of the conscripts leave the military at the end of their term of service and take their newly acquired skills into the civilian economic sector.

Egyptian military service is an important socialization agent in Egyptian society. In the military, a new recruit coming from a traditional background is placed in an egalitarian environment that provides the soldier with the prospect of social mobility through the system of promotion based on merit rather than through class or kinship factors and, in addition, is provided with a relatively satisfactory standard of living. Conscripts receive a monthly salary, adequate food, medical care, uniforms, and living accommodations. From a political perspective, recruits learn of a world beyond their rural, agrarian origins and of a larger political identity as part of a national community. This tends to be a politicizing experience that provides soldiers with a sense of "civic" duty and loyalty to the state—a world view much expanded beyond their previous exclusive reference to family, village, and religion. Military service is thus a chief purveyor of a sense of citizenship, responsibility, and national identity—all especially important in the Middle East, where the credibility and legitimacy of a central government usually diminish rapidly as distance from its capital increases.

Coupled with this experience in national identity is an exposure to modern technologies and life styles. By its nature, an army constantly looks abroad to compare its strengths to possible enemies and to correct deficiencies.[9] It is thus more aware of the importance of technology and its own weaknesses and is, therefore, willing (even driven) to modernize and to utilize needed technologies. The soldier is exposed to and trained to use technologies that run the gamut from modern weapons, communications systems, manufacturing processes, and management systems not available in the other sectors of the state.

The Egyptian military's socializing influence is expected to continue as long as the Egyptian Armed Forces remain at their present strength levels. However, as economic pressures rise, it may become increasingly difficult for Egypt to maintain these high force levels. For the last several years, the U.S. Department of Defense has been attempting to persuade the Egyptian Armed Forces to downsize and accept the combat efficiencies enabled by their new Western weapons systems. Specifically, the United States would prefer that Egypt discard its large inventory of nearly obsolete Eastern Bloc military equipment, which is expensive to maintain, manpower intensive, and of only marginal military capability. This would allow much needed funds, previously spent on maintaining these aging inventories of Eastern equipment, to be diverted to the more useful purposes of training and sustainment. Under these circumstances, Egypt would require significantly fewer soldiers to man its equipment effectively. As noted previously, Egypt has resisted downsizing its force because of the value it places on a robust military and because Egypt does not want to add thousands of individuals to the unemployment lines. A smaller military would have less effect as a socializing force, but the cost savings might provide additional funding for military modernization and other nonmilitary national priorities. These trade-offs need serious consideration. Arguably, no other institution in Egypt is as effective as the military in providing a work ethic, egalitarianism, social mobility, exposure to technology, civic responsibility, and nation building. But, Egypt also needs infusions of resources in its service sectors as investment in productive facilities.

The Military and the National Economy

A military establishment comes as close as any human organization can to the ideal type for an industrialized and secularized enterprise.[10]

Since the 1970s, the Egyptian military has had an expanding role in Egypt's economy, playing a primary role in four sectors of Egypt's economy: military industries, civilian industries, agriculture, and national infrastructure. Both Egyptian President Husni Mubarak and former Egyptian Minister of Defense Field Marshall Abdul Halim Abu Ghazala (1980-89) shared a vision of the beneficial role the military could play as an engine for economic growth and development.[11] According to Robert Springborg, this led to a horizontal expansion in the role of the military into the national economy.[12] This shared vision is probably due to a number of factors: a widely held Egyptian belief that the organizational attributes of the military could provide an effective spur to economic growth and development; the potential to exploit the comparative economic advantages of the military (low salaries, heavy equipment infrastructure) in fostering economic growth; the military's goal of self-sufficiency; and a need to employ large numbers of soldiers in meaningful activities during a period of low defense requirements.

It should be noted that there are counterarguments to these considerations. Some scholars, such as William Quandt, claim that these activities may not be helpful to the Egyptian economy as a whole because the military, with its low-cost subsidized labor and exemption from taxes and licensing fees, undercuts private entrepreneurs.[13] Others, such as Robert Springborg, argue that the relationship between the military and civilian sectors has been characterized by cooperation; private entrepreneurs have benefitted from the millions of dollars awarded by the Army for associated contracts as well as cooperative efforts in technology sharing.[14] An argument can also be made that Egyptian society benefits from this compensation because the military's profits (if, in fact, there are any) can be used to offset declining military budgets. These activities also create a trained workforce that migrates out of the military into the private sector. Robert B. Satloff believes that if the Army failed to assume many of these economic roles, Islamic institutions would be in a position to do so—a situation the government would prefer to avoid.[15]

Military Industries

To paraphrase Yezid Sayigh, Egypt is the veteran Arab arms producer.[16] Military production began in Egypt in the 1820s under Mohammed Ali, who created Egypt's fledgling arms industry to support his regional military conquests. With foreign help, his industries reportedly produced high-quality small arms, artillery, warships, and ammunition.[17] Egypt's initial arms production efforts essentially ended in the 1840s, under pressure from the European powers, and did not resume again until the 1940s. In recent years, Egypt's arms industry has produced or assembled a wide variety of products, including artillery, mortar, and small-arms ammunition, indigenously produced armored personnel carriers, the U.S. M1A1

Abrams tank, British Lynx helicopters, Aerospatiale Gazelle helicopters, European AlphaJet aircraft, Chinese F-7 fighter aircraft, aircraft engines, and a wide variety of military electronics, including radars and night-vision devices.

One of the principal goals for the defense industrial sector is the pursuit of self-sufficiency, which means military autonomy and self-reliance. There have been numerous instances where the West has refused to provide or even embargoed arms needed by Egypt. The Soviet Union did the same after the 1973 war, when it refused to rearm Egypt or provide repair parts or overhaul assistance to the Egyptian military. It also discouraged cooperation with Egypt by its other client states. Self-sufficiency permits Egypt a greater measure of independence in security matters and allows the Egyptian military to fight longer without foreign resupply. Other goals for the defense industry include import substitution, increased employment, increased export earnings, upgrading worker skills, economic development and modernization, regional power, acquisition of industrial and military technology, and encouraging Pan-Arab cooperation.

Egyptian defense production involves some 30 factories and companies that reportedly employ up to 100,000 people. The value of production in the industry was estimated at an average of $400 million a year in the 1980s.[18] Egyptian military industries also exported an annual average of $191 million in the 1980s. The amount earned from exports ranged from $30 million in 1981 to $550 million in 1988.[19] The majority of exports consisted of arms sales to Iraq during the Iran-Iraq War. Figure 2 shows that once this war ended in 1988, Egyptian arms exports fell precipitously. Reportedly, the profits from these exports were returned to the military coffers with no governmental accounting or taxes (that is, they were "off-budget").[20]

In April 1975, Egypt, Saudi Arabia, the United Arab Emirates and Qatar formed the Arab Organization for Industrialization (AOI)—an arms production consortium. The Gulf countries provided the funding ($1.04 billion) and Egypt provided the manpower and

Figure 2. Egyptian Arms Imports Compared with Arms Exports

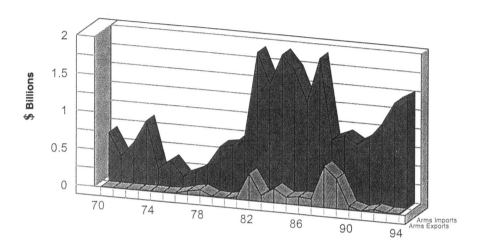

Source: *World Military Expenditures and Arms Transfers,* U.S. Arms Control and Disarmament Agency, various issues, 1965-95 (Washington: Government Printing Office).

infrastructure. The intention was for the AOI to produce weapons for its charter members and to export surplus production to other Arab, Islamic, and Third World countries. The goals of AOI were to provide the partners with a measure of self-sufficiency in conventional military hardware, reduced military production costs, a basis for advancing Arab industrialization, a source of export earnings, and a means to promote Arab cooperation. Four Egyptian production facilities were immediately turned over to the AOI and production began through licensed manufacturing arrangements with Western firms. In 1979, after President Sadat signed a peace treaty with Israel, the other members of AOI left the organization and withdrew their funding. Despite its short life, the AOI provided Egypt with the basis for its rapid expansion in assembly and manufacturing operations. Egypt continues to maintain the AOI, which serves as the chief agency responsible for aerospace, missiles, electronics, and avionics production. Since returning to the Arab fold in the late 1980s, Egypt has not been able to convince any other Arab states to rejoin AOI.[21]

In the coming years, Egypt's military production sector will probably decline. As a whole, Egypt's manufacturing sector suffers from low productivity and a lack of adequate funding and external markets. Egypt's largest consumer during the 1980s, Iraq, has been removed from the market place as a result of U.N.-imposed sanctions. Egyptian military products also face increased competition from abroad. The cash-strapped Russians are offering highly advanced weapons at bargain prices. The affluent Gulf Arab States, a traditional focus of Egyptian marketing efforts, prefer advanced U.S. military systems, relying on their military superiority to provide effective deterrence and using their purchases to provide a political insurance policy for continuing U.S. security involvement. As illustrated in figure 2, Egypt's military industries have not been effective in promoting import substitution or sustaining export earnings. Despite ambitious goals, the real technological benefit of the Armed Forces' military industrial endeavors has proven to be only marginal to Egypt's economic development. While Egypt does assemble sophisticated military weapon systems, the facilities to do so are provided by Western businesses as turnkey operations. The Egyptians receive kits for assembly, but the technology involved is closely guarded by the Western partner. Hence, little technology that would allow independent Egyptian development of systems has been transferred. For Egypt, technology is a conundrum. High-technology industry is a capital-intensive endeavor, while Egypt has a labor-intensive economy with little capital. Finally, it would also appear that Egypt's military industries have done little to enhance its regional power.

Civilian Industries

In the late 1970s, plagued with over capacity, falling oil prices, rising government deficits, declining per capita income,[22] and a need to offset the military's diminished role resulting from peace with Israel, the Egyptian military converted large portions of its military production capacity to the manufacture of civilian goods.[23] This initiative was taken under the auspices of the National Service

Project Organization (NSPO), a Ministry of Defense subsidiary established to control projects in the exclusively civilian sectors of the economy.[24] Its task was to incorporate the military into national economic development efforts.[25] Military facilities now manufacture a wide variety of products such as washing machines, heaters, clothes, doors, stationery, pharmaceuticals, and microscopes. Most are sold to military personnel through discount military stores, but a significant percentage also reaches commercial markets. Profits from these activities are, like military export earnings, "off budget."

The Military in Agriculture

Under the auspices of the Food Security Division of the NSPO, the military has set a goal of 100 percent self-sufficiency in foodstuffs. As in the case of weapons, the government believes that national security will be bolstered by military self-sufficiency in food.[26] In the early 1980s, the NSPO began to develop a broad network of dairy farms, milk processing facilities, cattle feed lots, and poultry and fish farms. For example, the military produced 18 percent of the nation's total food production and 60 percent of the army's required consumables (food, uniforms, footwear, etc.) in 1985.[27] Again, while the military consumes most of the products, the surplus is sold through commercial outlets, and the profits are returned to the military's coffers "off-budget."

The Military in National Infrastructure

The military has also been involved in a significant number of major infrastructure projects, such as construction of power lines, sewers, bridges, overpasses, roads, schools, and installation and maintenance of telephone exchanges. These projects involved associated contracts to civilian businesses, although there are no data on how significant civilian involvement was. Some have argued that such military activity is harmful to civilian commercial activities, competing with and denying opportunities to private firms. Others claim that infrastructure development benefits civilian enterprise; such development was affordable only to the government through military resources. Some military officers have criticized the economic role because it detracts from the military's focus on national security, while others claim that it improves the military's image with the Egyptian people. There are not much data available to resolve these issues, but the arguments indicate that the military's economic role is controversial.

Overall, the performance of the Egyptian military's civilian sector economic activities has been fairly impressive in terms of production and the achievement of some measure of self-sufficiency for the military. The activities will probably continue to expand because of their reported profitability[28] and because they maintain military productivity and enhance self-sufficiency.

The Domestic Political Process

Military participation in the domestic political process in Egypt has been in decline since 1967. The overthrow of the monarchy in 1952 by the Free Officers movement made the Egyptian military one of the most important political institutions in Egypt. President Nasser appointed many senior military officers to this cabinet and senior positions in order to implement the social revolution. Toward the end of his rule, and as a result of the military's poor showing in the 1967 war, the number of senior military officers in government and cabinet positions began to decline.

The decline accelerated under President Sadat (1970-81). Sadat removed most of the senior cabinet officers likely to challenge his policies and replaced most of them with civilians. This "demilitarization" of the Egyptian cabinet is detailed extensively by Mark N. Cooper, who points out that since Sadat's "purge" of the military from the cabinet, the military has routinely come to occupy posts that are technical in nature or directly related to the military, such as ministries of defense, military production, transport, communications, maritime transport and civil aviation, and occasionally interior.[29]

As part of his effort to reduce the military's influence in government and stave off political threats from that quarter, Sadat manipulated the senior military command positions, frequently removing incumbents before they could amass any relevant political support. From 1971 to 1980, President Sadat had seven ministers of defense. In lieu of the military's political involvement, Sadat insisted on a program of greater military professionalism. The benefits of this drive for professionalism were realized in the greatly improved performance of the Egyptian military during the 1973 war, compared to the debacle of 1967. Sadat was also committed to reducing the military budget. As can be seen in figure 4, military expenditures declined significantly from 1977 until President Sadat's assassination in 1981.[30]

Figure 3. Number of Egyptian Military Officers Serving in the Cabinet, 1951-81

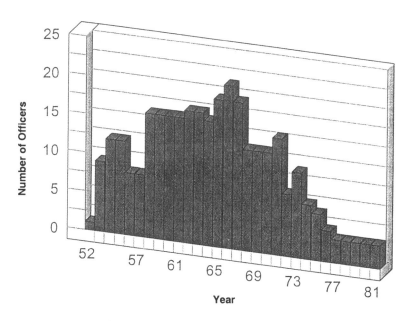

Source: Mark N. Cooper, "The Demilitarization of the Egyptian Cabinet," *International Journal of Middle East Studies* 14 (1982): 206-207.

Unlike Sadat before him, President Mubarak embraced the Egyptian military as a partner in the economic development of the country. However, while expanding the military's economic mission, Mubarak was careful to restrict the influence of the officer corps on political decisions.

Figure 4. Military Expenditures (Milex) Against Current Government Expenditures (CGE)

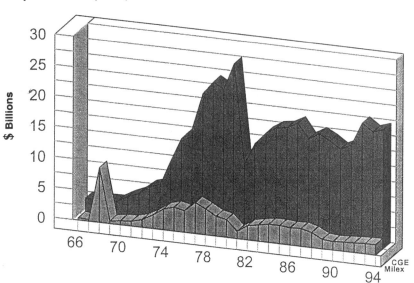

Source: *World Military Expenditures and Arms Transfers*, Arms Control and Disarmament Agency, various issues, 1968-95 (Washington: Government Printing Office).

The Egyptian military seems to have accepted its declining role in the political process. It has turned its attention to military modernization and economic activities that, in fact, seem to have offset its diminished political role. Senior military officers removed from the cabinet or the government have usually been able to establish parallel domiciles in military sectors. Likewise, upon retirement, many senior officers find important niches in military-related commercial sectors. One recent example: in 1995, Lieutenant General Saleh Haliby, retired chief of staff of the Egyptian Armed Forces, was appointed director for the Arab Organization for Industrialization.

Available evidence indicates that Egyptian military officers, as a group, harbor no extraordinary political ambitions. Probably as important, there have been no major cuts in the Egyptian military budgets, with the exception of the years following 1977 when President Sadat was committed to reducing the military budget by

50 percent. Since then, available data show no major declines in allocations to the Egyptian military. Figure 5 charts central government financing of several major economic sectors. While the military represented a dominant proportion of government spending during the 1980s, it was not overwhelming. The 1990s data indicate that defense generally parallels education and social services. It is difficult to determine, with any assurance, whether high military expenditures were a function of the dynamic Minister of Defense, Abu Ghazala, or the hesitancy of the president to risk the military's displeasure by reducing its budget. While there have been some recent declines in the military budget (generally correlated to declines in the national economy), "off budget" profits achieved in the military industries may have been significant enough to offset their effects.

Figure 5. Funding Comparison of Major Public Sector Categories

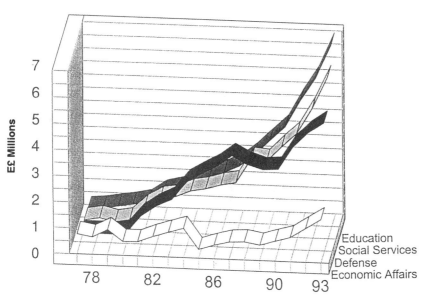

Source: *Government Finance Statistics Yearbook, 1995* (Washington: International Monetary Fund, 1996).

During his tenure in the 1980s, Field Marshall Abu Ghazala encouraged a program of "perks" for the military to maintain the Egyptian officer corps. One such program was the construction of military cities, such as Nasr City in Cairo. These developments provided military personnel with what Robert Springborg refers to as "relatively sumptuous flats"[31] at highly subsidized prices in communities virtually isolated from civilian society. These self-contained military cities include schools, nurseries, and military consumer "cooperatives" selling a range of domestic and imported products at discount prices. Abu Ghazala reportedly financed the construction of these military cities by selling valuable army-owned land adjacent to Egypt's largest cities.[32] In the face of recently declining military budgets and poor economic conditions, these military cities have probably been an important factor in maintaining the prestige and self-esteem of the military's officers and protecting their salaries from inflation.

Figures 1, 4, and 5 do not include the $1.3 billion in Foreign Military Financing (FMF) and the $800 million in Economic Support Funds (ESF) provided Egypt annually by the United States. In fiscal year 1997, Egypt received 40 percent of worldwide U.S. security assistance monies, second only to Israel (56 percent).[33] FMF funds, committed exclusively for military procurement, primarily fund Egypt's military modernization. ESF funds are not committed to the military. While there is an expectation that these monies will begin to decline in the next few years, they should affect only Egypt's ongoing military modernization program and not Egypt's military industries or payroll.

There are two central myths regarding the Egyptian military and politics in Egypt. One is that the Army is Egypt's kingmaker, and the other is that the Army is the ultimate guarantor of regime security. There is certainly some credence in the later, but no longer much in the former. Every president of Egypt since the revolution has come from the ranks of the military; this fact owes much to the character of the 1952 revolution as a military putsch. As Egypt's political institutions have matured and political participation has broadened, the role of the military as kingmaker has probably come to an end, absent conditions of dire national crisis. The Egyptian Government is no longer focused exclusively on national security in its international and domestic affairs (as it was at the time of the revolution); hence, there are fewer demands for military leadership. Moreover, the military is no longer the dominant interest group in the country. Significant interest groups now include a large bureaucracy and public sector, a large group of unionized workers, a relatively large group of urban commercial businesses, a small group of wealthy industrialists, and professional associations. To these must be added intellectuals, clerical as well as secular. Another important factor in reducing the political importance of the military is the emergence of trained, experienced, professional civilians, such as Osama al-Baz, political advisor to President Mubarak, and Foreign Minister Amr Moussa, who are both close to the president. These and similar individuals are probably better positioned than the senior military officers to emerge in a future succession, particularly since the government's central focus is now on international politics and domestic economics.[34] Futhermore, there are no indications that military loyalty to the regime or to the president depends on the succession of a military officer.

What of the second myth, that the military is the ultimate guarantor of the regime? In two instances, the military has been called into the streets to respond to a domestic threat, which could have endangered the government. The first occasion was the 1977 food riots, which broke out when the Sadat government proposed the elimination of various subsidies that would have raised the price of many common food items. Perhaps reflecting a corporate concern for Egypt's citizens, the Army reputedly refused to intervene in the riots unless the subsidies were reestablished.[35] Sadat restored the subsidies. The second was the uprising of Central Security Force (CSF) conscripts in 1986. The conscripts rioted, setting fire to tourist hotels and nightclubs, when a rumor spread that their mandatory term of service was to be extended from 3 years to 4. Such an extension would have meant a significant hardship, considering that CSF conscripts were paid much less than those in the Army. In both instances, the Army responded in a professional and efficient manner and returned to their barracks immediately upon conclusion of the crisis. The military's performance in these crises has led to the public perception that the Army is the ultimate safeguard of the regime. However, despite the effectiveness of the military in these crises, the Ministry of the interior retains primary responsibility for domestic security.

The Egyptian military will maintain a monopoly on firepower to respond to future threats to domestic order if needed, yet it is clear that the Army does not relish these duties. Senior Egyptian military officers have been disinclined to volunteer the army to control increased extremism but would undoubtedly do so in a crisis.

Military Loyalty to the Regime

Scholars of civil-military relations present various motives and incentives for military intervention in political processes. These range from domestic circumstances to the existence of overt or latent crises, the popularity of the military, the level of the political culture, governmental corruption, and the dependence of the regime on the military. S. E. Finer proposes several possible intervention scenarios that may be relevant to Egypt. The first hinges on the principle of civil supremacy. According to Finer, the military's consciousness of their professionalism may lead them to see themselves as servants of the state rather than the government in power. The military may become reluctant to coerce the government's domestic opponents. Military leaders may also feel that only they are competent to make decisions on military size, force structure, mission, and modernization. Another scenario that Finer proposes concerns the corporate interests of the military. A motive for intervention is raised when the military comes to feel that its status, privileges, or autonomy are threatened or that its organizational goals and objectives are being thwarted.[36]

With respect to the principle of civil supremacy, there are strong indications that the Egyptian military supports the 1971 civilian control constitutional clause specifying that the Egyptian Army "shall belong to the people." However, this acceptance has not been tested since Sadat's assassination, because there have been no significant popular challenges to the rule of President Mubarak. The military has shown its willingness and capability to oppose direct threats to the government during the food and CSF riots. However, the question is still open as to how the military would respond to a mass popular challenge to the regime, such as a major protest over government corruption or a wider Islamic challenge.

With respect to the corporate interests of the military, decisions on military issues have been left predominantly in the hands of senior officers. U.S. security assistance to Egypt has provided the means for its much needed modernization despite declining national budgets. The military has been the driving force in the decisions on how these American funds are spent. Some have warned that the military's declining status, coupled with declining living standards for its officers, could raise the level of military dissent. The military's involvement in economic activities appears to have allowed the military to preserve its status and, for the most part, its privileges. These derived prerequisites have, thus far, been sufficient to prevent major dissent within the ranks.

In summary, the Egyptian military has established itself as a positive and effective institution in Egypt's domestic society with the potential for increased value. There are currently no significant indicators of displeasure by the corporate military over the course the nation is pursuing or its role in that course. It remains strongly loyal to the current government. While the military does have systematic shortcomings and weaknesses (an emphasis on mass over quality, highly centralized, inflexible command structures, outdated choreographed Soviet military doctrine, and too little emphasis on sustainability), these problems are not insurmountable. The Egyptian military should remain a reliable and positive agent of modernization and stability in the coming years.

Notes

1. S. E. Finer, *The Man on Horseback: The Role of the Military in Politics* (Boulder, CO: Westview Press, 1988), 6.
2. *The Military Balance 1994-1995* (London: Brassey's, 1994), 125.
3. Ibid., 125.
4. Helen Chapin Metz, ed., *Egypt: A Country Study* (Washington: Library of Congress, 1991), 307.

5. *The World Factbook 1997*, Central Intelligence Agency (Washington: Government Printing Office, 1997), 125.

6. Ibid., 126.

7. Metz, 320.

8. Egyptians as a whole tend to be more pious than many of their Arab counterparts. Hence, the influence of clerics and of religious practice over a lifetime, can be assumed to have more weight than the impact of civic training received over a period of several years in military service, albeit during a formative period.

9. Lucian W. Pye, "The Process of Political Modernization," in *The Role of the Military in Underdeveloped Countries*, ed. John J. Johnson (Princeton, NJ: Princeton University Press, 1962), 79.

10. Ibid., 75.

11. General Mohammed Abdul Halim Abu Ghazala was selected as minister of defense in late 1980 by President Sadat while serving as the Chief of Staff, Egyptian Armed Forces, a position he had been assigned only early in 1980. Abu Ghazala, an army artillery officer, was considered very pro-American, having attended the U.S. Army War College and served as the Egyptian defense and military attache to the United States from 1976-80.

12. Robert Springborg, *Mubarak's Egypt: Fragmentation of the Political Order* (Boulder, CO: Westview Press, 1989), 107.

13. William Quandt, *The United States and Egypt* (Cairo: The American University in Cairo Press, 1990), 355.

14. Springborg, 117.

15. Robert Satloff, *Army and Politics in Mubarak's Egypt* (Washington: Washington Institute for Near East Policy, 1988), 14.

16. Yezid Sayigh, *Arab Military Industry: Capability, Performance and Impact* (London: Brassey's, 1992), 45-46.

17. See R. Väyrynen and T. Ohlsohn "Egypt: Arms Production in the Transnational Context," in *Arms Production in the Third World*, eds. Michael Brzoska and Thomas Ohlson (London: Taylor & Francis, 1986), 105-124, and Mohammed El-Sayed Selim, "Egypt," in *Arms Production in Developing Countries: An Analysis of Decision Making*, ed. James E. Katz (Lexington, MA: Lexington Books, 1984), 123-156.

18. Sayigh, *Arab Military Industry*, 45.

19. *World Military Expenditures and Arms Tables*, Arms Control and Disarmament Agency (Washington: Government Printing Office, various issues, 1976-91).

20. See Springborg, 108, and Satloff, 21.

21. See Sayigh, 48-51; Springborg, 107; Väyrynen and Ohlson, 109-113; and Selim, 142-146.

22. External debt rose from $5.4 billion in 1975 to $50 billion in 1993. Total debt as a percentage of the GDP rose, in the same time frame, from 47.9 percent to 103.2 percent. The average annual growth of GNP per capita fell from 5.9 percent in 1975 to -1.3 percent in 1993. See *Claiming the Future: Choosing Prosperity in the Middle East and North Africa* (Washington: The World Bank, 1995), 92-93.

23. Estimates of the proportion vary greatly from 40 percent of capacity to as much as 60 percent.

24. Springborg, 109.

25. Metz, 325.

26. Ibid., 325.

27. Metz, 327, and Springborg, 112.

28. There is an assumption of profitability, but without the availability of cost data this may not truly be the case.

29. Mark N. Cooper, "The Demilitarization of the Egyptian Cabinet," *International Journal of Middle East Studies* 14 (1982): 209.

30. Figure 4 demonstrates a significant decline in military expenditures beginning in 1971; figure 1 shows a significant decline in the percentage of military expenditures immediately following the war in 1973. This difference can be explained by the fact that the military expenditures remained fairly flat from 1974-77, while government expenditures increased dramatically (figure 4), thus lowering the percentage of military expenditures.

31. Springborg, 105.

32. Ibid., 105.

33. *Congressional Presentation for Foreign Operations—Fiscal Year 1997* (Washington: Department of State, 1996), 159.

34. See John Waterbury, "Whence Will Come Egypt's Future Leadership?" in this volume. In his article, Professor Waterbury discusses the balance between the *technicos* the *politicos* in elite recruitment and proposes four scenarios for the future sources of Egyptian leadership. One of his possibilities (number 2) proposes an engineered democratic opening allowing "real" politicians to replace nominally apolitical technocrats similar to that proposed in this paper.

35. Metz, 279.

36. Finer, 20-76.

II. Egypt's Regional Role

Northern Africa and the Middle East

North Atlantic Ocean

Azores (PORT.)

Madeira Islands (PORT.)

Canary Islands (SP.)

PORTUGAL — Lisbon
SPAIN — Madrid
FRANCE
GIBRALTAR (U.K.)
MOROCCO — Rabat
Western Sahara — El Aaiún
MAURITANIA — Nouakchott
SENEGAL — Dakar
THE GAMBIA — Banjul
GUINEA-BISSAU — Bissau
GUINEA — Conakry
SIERRA LEONE — Freetown
LIBERIA — Monrovia
MALI — Bamako
CÔTE D'IVOIRE — Yamoussoukro
BURKINA — Ouagadougou
GHANA — Accra
TOGO — Lomé
BENIN — Porto-Novo
NIGER — Niamey
NIGERIA — Abuja
CAMEROON — Yaoundé
EQUATORIAL GUINEA — Malabo
SAO TOME AND PRINCIPE — São Tomé
GABON — Libreville
CONGO
ZAIRE
CENTRAL AFRICAN REPUBLIC — Bangui
CHAD — N'Djamena
ALGERIA — Algiers
TUNISIA — Tunis
LIBYA — Tripoli
ITALY — Rome
MALTA — Valletta
Sardinia
Corsica
Sicily
Balearic Islands
Mediterranean Sea
Crete
GREECE — Athens
ALBANIA — Tiranë
F.Y.R.O.M. — Skopje
SERBIA — Belgrade
MONT. — Podgorica
BOSNIA — Sarajevo
CRO. — Zagreb
SLOV. — Ljubljana
BULGARIA — Sofia
ROMANIA — Bucharest
Black Sea
UKRAINE
RUSSIA
GEORGIA — Tbilisi
ARMENIA — Yerevan
AZERBAIJAN — Baku
TURKEY — Ankara
CYPRUS — Nicosia
Caspian Sea
KAZAKHSTAN
TURKMENISTAN — Ashgabat
UZBEKISTAN
TAJIKISTAN — Dushanbe
AFGHANISTAN — Kabul
PAKISTAN
IRAN — Tehrān
SYRIA — Damascus
LEBANON — Beirut
ISRAEL — Jerusalem
JORDAN — Amman
IRAQ — Baghdad
KUWAIT — Kuwait
Tigris
Euphrates
Persian Gulf
BAHRAIN — Manama
QATAR — Doha
Abu Dhabi
U.A.E.
OMAN — Muscat
Gulf of Oman
SAUDI ARABIA — Riyadh
YEMEN — Sanaa
Gulf of Aden
Socotra (YEMEN)
Indian Ocean
Equator
SOMALIA — Mogadishu
DJIBOUTI — Djibouti
ETHIOPIA — Addis Ababa
ERITREA — Asmara
Red Sea
SUDAN — Khartoum
Blue Nile
White Nile
Nile
EGYPT — Cairo
KENYA
UGANDA — Kampala
Lake Victoria

Tropic of Cancer

Niger
Senegal
Gulf of Guinea
Benue

Scale 1:42,300,000
Azimuthal Equal-Area Projection
500 Kilometers
500 Nautical Miles

Boundary representation is not necessarily authoritative.

802409 (546325) 9-95

CAPITALIZING ON DIPLOMACY

Rosemary Hollis

Egypt is aiming for a regional role which combines centrality for Cairo in the quest for Middle East peace with a prominent position for Egypt in the new economic climate.

Since the beginning of the 1990s, Egypt has been in a process of reinventing its regional role. For decades that role was determined by the logic of the Cold War and the Arab-Israeli conflict. From the mid-1970s, Egypt opted for alignment with the United States and peace with Israel. This resulted in some 15 years of relative isolation from the rest of the Arab world, while also guaranteeing U.S. support for Cairo as one of Washington's most important strategic allies in the region. Then came a series of events that posed new problems, as well as opportunities, for the Egyptians, and by 1998, it seemed that Egypt had succeeded in regaining for itself a position of first among equals in the Arab world.

The end of the Cold War, the 1990-91 Gulf War, and breakthroughs in the Arab-Israeli peace process brought a big shift in Egypt's strategic position. Participation in the Gulf War coalition

Dr. Rosemary Hollis is Head, Middle East Programme, Royal Institute for International Affairs, London. Previously Dr. Hollis was Head of the Middle East Programme at the Royal United Services Institute for Defence Studies, London, and a lecturer at The George Washington University, Washington. She is the author of numerous publications on the Middle East.

enabled Egypt's reintegration into the Arab fold. Israel's 1993-94 peace deals with the Palestinians and Jordan, as well as moves to normalize relations with the Jewish state by Arab governments in the Maghreb and the Gulf, meant that Egypt was no longer an isolated advocate of peace. The special importance of Egypt for the United States was thus reduced, at a time when Washington was inclined to re-examine all its foreign commitments. Still conscious of Egypt's place in the region, however, U.S. officials and analysts have suggested certain courses of action to Cairo that, from a Washington perspective, represent the best way for Egypt to adapt to the new international and regional environment. Yet, what makes sense in Washington may not seem feasible or even desirable from a regional perspective.

As some U.S. analysts would have it, the imperatives for Cairo are clear and pressing. In order to stand a chance of having an impact beyond its borders, Egypt must adapt its economy, its political and legal arrangements, and its military capabilities to the new global realities. Attempting to encourage regional economic integration as a corollary to Arab-Israeli peace, U.S. analysts have urged progress toward economic liberalization in Egypt to enable the country to survive and compete without external aid. Economic adaptation implies deregulation and more political pluralism. On the military front, Egypt's Armed Forces and equipment require rationalization if they are to be effective on the modern battlefield.

Viewed from Cairo, however, the situation looks rather different. The social consequences of rapid economic liberalization threaten to aggravate political unrest on the one hand and upset vested interests on the other. In the name of stability, therefore, Cairo is inclined to take a cautious and gradual approach to economic restructuring. Meanwhile, as depicted by a number of Egyptians, the country's chances of taking a leading role in regional economic development have been overshadowed by the possibility of Israel becoming the economic and financial powerhouse in the Middle East, progress toward peace permitting.

The imperatives for Egypt, therefore, have been to concentrate on preventing movement toward normalization of Arab-Israeli economic relations from running ahead of progress on the political and strategic front. Egypt, as is the case with other Arab states bordering Israel, is not ready to compete and needs time to introduce a more liberal economy.

Meanwhile, as viewed from Cairo and other Arab capitals, Israel still represents a potential military threat, pending a comprehensive peace, and it is not yet time to reduce Arab military strength, even in the name of rationalization. Also, as is evident in Egypt, Arab governments face threats from within. Islamic militants who challenge the legitimacy of Arab regimes on the grounds of corruption are also vocal in their condemnation of peace moves that appear to sell the Arabs short to benefit Israel. Since Egypt claims for itself the role of principal coordinator and mediator for the Arabs in the quest for peace, its task is to keep the channels to Israel open while talking tough on the behalf of the Arab cause. This task has become particularly onerous as the peace process has stagnated.

Egypt's posture at the Middle East and North Africa (MENA) Economic Conference of November 1996 provides a valuable indicator of the direction in which Cairo is headed. The Egyptian Government decided to go ahead with the hosting of the conference, bringing together Arabs and Israelis to discuss regional economic development and potential business ventures, despite the fact that the Arab-Israeli peace process had suffered a number of setbacks since the election of Israeli Prime Minister Binyamin Netanyahu. He and his Likud-led cabinet regard the Oslo accords, negotiated by the previous Labour government with the Palestinians, with extreme distaste and are set against the emergence of a Palestinian state in the West Bank. This posture aggravated tensions and violence there, and belligerence entered the rhetoric of Syrian-Israeli relations after Netanyahu came to power. By going ahead with the conference in this atmosphere, President Husni Mubarak found a useful platform from which to send a stern warning to the Israeli Government about the potential penalties of backsliding on the peace process. The occasion also allowed the business community of the region to emphasize the vital importance of peace for economic survival, not to mention prosperity, and Egyptians used the conference to showcase changes underway in their own economy.

In sum, Egypt is aiming for a regional role that combines centrality for Cairo in the quest for Middle East peace with a prominent position for Egypt in the new economic climate. It was perhaps fortuitous for Egypt that the Arab-Israeli peace process ran into difficulties when it did. This afforded Cairo another chance to demonstrate its skills as a power broker and mediator. Also, the prospect of Israel gaining economic hegemony in the region took a jolt, as investor confidence in Israel's prospects receded.[1] The importance of peace for economic growth was thus demonstrated, while Egypt gained a little extra time to make more headway with its own restructuring plans.

Egypt's Weight as a Regional Power

Egypt's size and geostrategic location make it the linchpin linking the Maghreb and the Mashriq and Africa and Asia, as well as the communications link between the Mediterranean and the Indian Ocean, Europe, and East Asia. Since Israel and Jordan signed their peace agreement in 1994,[2] direct air and land routes from the Mediterranean, via Israel to Jordan and beyond, have opened up and pipelines for energy supplies could follow. In the future, therefore, Egypt's importance as a strategic communications route may diminish somewhat but will certainly not cease altogether.

Egypt's weight in regional affairs also derives from its historical tradition of prominence and leadership in the regional setting. Of course, precedent does not assure Cairo continued influence, but no other Arab state can rival Egypt's accumulated diplomatic expertise and connections, which are manifest in the active role Egypt plays in an array of international and regional organizations, from the Arab League to the United Nations. Egypt also has advantages of access to all players in the region, which neither other Arabs nor the non-Arab powers—Israel, Turkey, and Iran—can match.

In the multilateral talks on arms control and regional security, which parallel bilateral Arab-Israeli peace negotiations, Egypt is at the forefront of Arab thinking on the complex technical issues concerned. In 1994-95, as discussed below, this translated into Egypt taking the lead in the debate about Israel's nuclear capability and questioning whether other Middle Eastern States should be expected to sign the new Non-Proliferation Treaty in light of Israel's refusal. As it turned out, the treaty was adopted, but not before Egypt had made its point.

Egypt can also boast more solid foundations for its statehood and national identity than most other countries in the region. It does have serious problems on the domestic front, as will be discussed, but it does not face separatist or irredentist movements or external claimants to sovereignty over its territory. Most other countries in the region have to cope with such problems.

The sheer size of the Egyptian population, over 64 million and growing, is a source of strength as well as difficulties. Representing about one-third of the whole Arab world, Egyptians constitute a powerful influence on Arab intellectual and popular opinion: it has a huge media and film-making industry, much of which is Cairo based; traditionally, it supplies the teachers and texts for Arab schools across the Middle East; and it is also a cultural center and favorite holiday resort for other Arabs. All in all, what happens in Egypt resonates well beyond the borders of the country.

In part because of its large labor force, Egypt can also claim one of the biggest regular armies in the Middle East, matched only by the Iraqis and Iranians, and Egypt has the most reserves. Equipped and trained by the United States over the past several years, the Egyptian forces would benefit from more modernization and rationalization, but, as the Egyptians themselves argue, quantity can still carry more weight than quality in the regional prestige stakes.

Egypt is also by far the largest single Arab market. It also possesses both skilled and unskilled laborers and a highly educated elite, elements of which have been recruited for work abroad. At home, Egyptian potential has yet to be realized on the industrial and business fronts, pending greater economic liberalization and improved regulatory practices. However, since the beginning of 1996, with the appointment of a new prime minister dedicated to market reforms, there has been a palpable change in mood on the Egyptian economic front. Even before that, Egypt was proceeding with the implementation of the economic restructuring program agreed with the International Monetary Fund,[3] but progress has been mixed. Notably, between 1991 and 1996, the budget deficit was dramatically reduced—from 20 to 1 percent of the gross domestic product—and Egypt's foreign reserves were built up from nearly nothing to $18 billion.[4] However, plans to privatize elements of the enormous Egyptian public sector remained a promise until 1996, when a number of enterprises were put up for sale and the government decided to invite equity participation in others. The reluctance to move ahead on reducing the state sector has apparently stemmed from fears of lost jobs, at least in the short term. After all, the extensive role of the government in employment has been one of its strengths, in that it has ensured the loyalty of a sizable proportion of the population, beholden to the government for their livelihoods.

This points to the kind of difficulties facing Egypt, notwithstanding its strengths. For the foreseeable future, Egypt faces problems overcoming the pressures of rapid population growth and limited natural resources. Currently, the population is increasing by about 1.3 million a year, and efforts to curb the birth rate cannot significantly reduce the mounting demands for health care, housing, education, and jobs from the high proportion of young people. In terms of natural resources, perhaps the most serious problem for Egypt is limited water supplies, which derive almost exclusively from the Nile River and the delta. Available water is insufficient to sustain simultaneous expansion in agricultural, industrial, and domestic usage without a radical change of orientation away from wasteful farming practices and reconstruction of the aging infrastructure, especially in the cities. Egypt's oil reserves, never great, have been drawn down to the point where there would no longer be any left over from domestic consumption to export, were it not for the development of gas as an alternative source of energy for the home market.[5]

Along with oil exports, Egypt's foreign currency earnings derive principally from worker remittances, tourism, and Suez Canal dues. With the oil boom years over for the Gulf region, employment opportunities for Egyptians are not what they were, and the Gulf War totally disrupted the labor market. Tourism was also affected by that war and, having picked up thereafter, was blighted anew by fears of terrorist attacks on tourists by Islamist militants. Toward the end of 1994, the Egyptian Government claimed to have curbed the rise of Islamic activism, through persistent suppression. However, the factors contributing to the appeal of militant Islam,[6] including poverty, lack of housing and jobs, bureaucratic inertia, and corruption, remain in place.

Pending greater rewards from economic restructuring, Egypt still relies on foreign aid, which continues to flow partly in recognition of Egypt's regional role. Latterly, though, Egypt's traditional supporters, whether the Gulf States or the United States, have been facing their own financial constraints, and subsidies to Cairo cannot take for granted the indefinite continuance of their assistance. Herein lies one of the reasons for U.S. urgings that Egypt speed up reform of its economy and compete in the global market. The problem, of course, is that Egyptian industries and services are not likely to compete effectively unless and until they are supported through a difficult transition period. Yet, ever resourceful, the Egyptians have turned their sights to the European Union (EU) to provide a new source of capital and support, through the EU Euro-Mediterranean Partnership Program.

Formally launched at Barcelona in fall 1995, this is a scheme to turn the Mediterranean into a free-trade area involving concluding partnership agreements between the EU and its Mediterranean neighbors. The EU, already a source of some aid to the poorer Arab economies of North Africa and the Middle East, is making new grants and soft loans available to Mediterranean partner countries with viable projects to stimulate indigenous enterprises and job creation.[7] Egypt, in company, not to say competition, with Morocco and Tunisia, is pursuing such possibilities with notable determination.

In sum, Egypt is not about to transform itself overnight into an economic powerhouse for the region, and economic strength will not be the principal explanation for its regional significance. However, Egypt is not going to fall by the wayside, either, and its restructuring program is gradually producing some results. Meanwhile, the country and its economy are simply too big a presence in the Arab world and region generally to be ignored. Also, because the prospects for the Egyptian Government at home depend in part on its ability to shape regional economic, political, and strategic developments to its advantage, Egypt can be expected to play its regional role accordingly.

Regional Agendas

Now that the Cold War has ended, the Middle East is no longer subject to superpower rivalry, which once underlay the Arab-Israeli confrontation. Peace moves, although faltering, have nonetheless reduced fears of a catastrophic war between Israel and its neighbors. However, other sources of tension and instability have come to the fore. Against this backdrop, Egypt's potential as a regional power lies in its capacity to take a lead in resolving the new problems.

With the peace process in serious trouble in 1998, the possibilities of a return to armed confrontation loom large. Meanwhile, politics and international relations have become permeated by religious issues, with militant Islam the new vehicle for dissent within Arab States and with Arab governments under pressure to defend the rights of Muslims caught up in nationalist struggles abroad, as was seen in Bosnia and Chechnya. On the strategic front, the military balance in the Middle East has been profoundly altered as a result of the demise of the Soviet Union, the unrivaled power of the United States, and the consequences of the defeat of Iraq in the Gulf War. Lastly, the international economic environment has changed, leaving the Middle East and North Africa lagging way behind other parts of the developing world in terms of inward investment and growth rates. The collapse of Asian economics may temporarily affect this equation, but it is too soon to evaluate the long-term implications of the Asian economic downturn.

In the Arab-Israeli peace process, Egypt has found two basic roles: to facilitate progress in the bilateral negotiations and to play a part in multilateral talks on regional economic, security, environmental, water, and refugee issues. Technically, Egypt is not directly involved in the bilateral peace negotiations. Jordan and

Israel certainly did not involve Cairo in the discussions that led to their peace treaty of October 1994. In the Syrian-Israeli negotiations there is only one mediator, the United States, and Lebanon follows Syria's lead. Meanwhile, on the Israeli-Palestinian track, the Oslo Agreement was concluded between Israel and the Palestine Liberation Organization (PLO) directly, with Norwegians the only facilitators. Nonetheless, Egypt is not without a part to play in the bilaterals, especially when trouble looms.

Specifically, Egyptian involvement has proved essential to keeping the Palestinian-Israeli negotiations in play on a number of occasions. Of all the Arab leaders engaged in bilateral talks with Israel, it is PLO leader Yasser Arafat who has paid greatest heed to Egypt, consulting with Egyptian President Mubarak regularly. Following the signing of the Israeli-Palestinian Declaration of Principles (DOP) in September 1993, Egypt hosted numerous rounds of negotiations on its implementation and mediated the Cairo Agreement of May 4, 1994,[8] including helping to overcome Arafat's last-minute reluctance to sign it. Thereafter, Egypt stood by Arafat during the painful period preceding extension of Palestinian autonomy from Gaza to towns and villages in the West Bank, when the Palestinian leadership looked as if it might be holed up in Gaza indefinitely.

By the time of the Palestinian elections in January 1996, it seemed that the extension of Palestinian self-rule was well underway. Since then, Egyptian-Israeli relations have soured over Israel's settlement policy and lack of progress on the Oslo Agreement. In addition, as it turned out, much greater problems were to come. The bus bombings in Israel, carried out by Palestinian Islamists still implacably opposed to Israel and at odds with the Palestinian authority, prompted Israel to institute a "closure" policy on the Palestinian territories of unprecedented severity. Plans for a road link between Gaza and the West Bank, allowing free passage for Palestinians between the two, were put on hold. Only because of Egyptian assistance, including helicopter transport, was it possible for Arafat himself to make the journey on certain occasions.

Egypt has reason to fear the consequences if the divide between the West Bank and Gaza becomes a permanent fixture. With access to Israel for Palestinians from the Gaza Strip limited and frequently closed altogether,[9] Egypt could end up as the only exit route for Gazan people and commerce. Having no interest in becoming the lifeline for Gaza, for this reason as well as broader security interests Cairo is not going to give up its efforts to promote a viable Israeli-Palestinian peace.

Exemplifying the kind of role Egypt can and does play in the peace process as a whole, in early February 1995 Cairo hosted the first four-way summit among Egypt, Israel, Jordan, and the PLO, to overcome the persistent obstacles on the Israeli-Palestinian track.[10] Prior to this, at the end of December 1994, Egypt convened a summit with a rather different purpose, when Mubarak held talks with King Fahd of Saudi Arabia and President Assad of Syria. The aim, it appears, was to coordinate the Arab position and agree to ensure that normalization of relations with Israel by faraway states, like Oman and Qatar, could not overtake progress in bilateral negotiations between Israel and its immediate neighbors.[11]

This Egyptian initiative triggered much critical comment in Israel, with some foreign ministry officials allegedly advising punitive measures against Egypt for seeking to slow down or hinder the peace process.[12] From Egypt's perspective, however, the summit was a necessary intervention to ensure that the fundamental requirements for a lasting peace, namely peace among the states at the heart of the Arab-Israeli conflict, could not be sidelined. Since the arrival of Netanyahu and his hardliners at the Israeli helm, Egypt has taken an even more forceful position. This has been all the more pronounced because, in the first instance, Mubarak counseled against hasty condemnation of the new Israeli Prime Minister. When Netanyahu then insisted on trying to renegotiate deals already done between Israel and the Palestinians, the peace process atrophied and Mubarak was personally affronted. In September 1996, Netanyahu sanctioned the extension of an archaeological tunnel into the Muslim Quarter of the Old City of Jerusalem, which triggered violent clashes between Israeli forces and Palestinian demonstrators, including Palestinian police, and resulted in heavy casualties. Attempting to calm the crisis, President Clinton called an emergency summit in Washington. Arafat and King Hussein answered the summons, but President Mubarak studiously stayed away. For this he gained renewed criticism in Israel and acclaim in the Arab press.

In the multilateral talks that paralleled the bilateral Arab-Israeli peace negotiations in 1991 in Madrid, Egypt was bound to be an important player in the discussions about regional economic cooperation, water, and environmental issues, by virtue of its sheer size. If the problems to be overcome can be tackled effectively in Egypt, then the value of the whole endeavor will have been demonstrated. With Egypt on board, regional cooperation stands a chance of genuinely transforming the whole area. Conversely, if Egypt is not central to the endeavor, neither economic integration nor conservation programs could be considered truly regional or effective. On the commercial side, without the huge Egyptian market, the rewards for trade and industrial development would be relatively limited.

Egypt's role has been most prominent, however, in the conduct of the arms control and regional security talks,[13] because, of all the Arab states, Egypt has made the most progress in developing expertise and formulating negotiating positions in this field. As was apparent from the behavior of the Gulf Cooperation Council (GCC) states, at the multilateral talks in Doha in 1994, regional security is about local border disputes. Syria and Lebanon, meanwhile, have refused to enter into the debate at all, pending progress on the bilateral negotiations. Iraq and Iran are for the time being excluded. Consequently, Egypt has led the way in tabling Arab proposals to match Israeli suggestions for regional arms control.

The fact that Egypt takes a view at odds with that of Israel on this matter has again led to criticism of Cairo for raising difficulties.[14] However, the Egyptian perspective on arms control reflects not only its own but broader regional concerns about Israel's assumed nuclear capability. It recognizes that as long as Israel has a "bomb in the basement," other powers in the region will have an incentive to acquire nuclear weapons (or chemical or biological capability) as a deterrent. For this reason, Egypt has called for the inauguration of a zone free of weapons of mass destruction in the Middle East. Israel, by contrast, has preferred to focus on arms control to address imbalances in the conventional sector. Egypt's refusal to participate in the multilateral Arms Control and Regional Security Working Group since 1995 has suspended operations of that committee. Also, while Israel is concerned about the military capabilities of all potential protagonists from North Africa to the Gulf, Egypt advocates concentrating first on the balance within the inner circle of Israel and its immediate neighbors.

Egypt's readiness to take a lead on regional arms control issues has surfaced outside the multilateral talks, and also in the discussions preceding the renewal of the Non-Proliferation Treaty (NPT) in April 1995.[15] The United States and other nuclear powers have argued in favor of an indefinite extension of the treaty. While lobbying signatory states, such as Egypt, to agree to go along with this, the United States has recognized that it is unlikely to persuade Israel to sign up, presumably because that would have obliged them to admit their capability and submit to formal strictures accordingly. Egypt's initial response, namely that it would not support an indefinite extension of the NPT, unless Israel either signs up or promises to do so by a specified date, won support among other Arabs, some of whom have followed the Egyptian line in the pre-renewal debate.[16] As some cynics would have it, Cairo may have decided on its bargaining position as a tactic to pressure Washington to continue aid to Egypt, despite arguments in favor of a cutback. Others have countered that it is the United States that has pressured Egypt to cooperate or face a possible diminution in U.S. good will and support. Either way, the whole episode has served to demonstrate Egypt's capacity for diplomatic brinkmanship.

The Egyptian Government's outspokenness on the nuclear issue also won it public support at home.[17] This, as well as President Mubarak's decision not to attend the Washington summit at the end of September 1996, serve as a reminder that standing up to the United States and Israel can help to ameliorate criticism of a regime that has otherwise enjoyed little popular acclaim for its domestic policies, especially economic liberalization measures that have apparently further widened the gap between the rich few and the poor majority.

The Egyptian leadership is not alone among Arab governments in facing general criticism for corruption, lack of accountability, and a poor economic record over the years. Egypt is also in the forefront of the Islamic debate, in so far as its security forces are at war with Islamist militants, while the establishment is trying to steal the thunder of the dissidents by espousing a more overtly Islamic line on various issues at home and abroad. Other Arab governments would feel the shock waves if the Egyptian regime fails to hold the line against its radical opponents. Conversely, if the Egyptian Government can show the way to overcome the Islamist challenge, it will enhance its regional stature.

The point here is that Egypt may end up steering a course that keeps Islamist militants at bay on the one hand, but on the other does not conform to Western remedies for such sources of instability. As discussed, U.S. analysts foresee a general trend toward regional economic integration and advocate economic and structural reform in Egypt to enable it to keep pace. In fact, Egypt may opt instead for a more nuanced path. The economy is being liberalized, but slowly and cautiously. Meanwhile, Cairo is bolstering its political standing by criticizing Israeli actions antithetical to peace, such as settlement building in the West Bank and counseling against rewarding the Israeli Government with more economic cooperation, unless and until it shows more readiness to implement the Oslo Agreement and make some progress on the Syrian track.

Quite apart from the Arab-Israeli divide, relations among the countries of the Middle East and North Africa remain distrustful, if not actually hostile. Since the 1991 Gulf War, Saudi Arabia and Kuwait are still bitterly opposed to the regime in Baghdad and deeply suspicious of the monarchy in Amman. The border dispute between Saudi Arabia and Yemen awaits resolution. Meanwhile, the alignment between the Islamic republican regimes of Iran and Sudan has compounded Saudi fears of being surrounded by hostile powers. Egypt, too, is wary of Iranian and Sudanese mischiefmaking beyond their borders, in support of Islamic militants.

Egyptian fears of external threats from militants may now be exacerbated by the bombings of U.S. embassies in Nairobi and Dar es-Salaam, reputedly masterminded by the Saudi dissident Usama bin Ladin, and the U.S. military responses in Afghanistan and Sudan, unpopular in the Middle East. The fighting between the military and the Islamists in Algeria worries not only Algeria's immediate neighbors, Morocco and Tunisia, but also the states of the Middle East as a whole, for fear of overspill or the effects of an Islamist victory.

Against this background, conflict prevention is an important item on the regional agenda. Given its pivotal position, diplomatic standing, and military weight, Egypt has the potential to facilitate the containment of regional disputes. By itself, Egypt cannot act as regional policeman; yet, as demonstrated in the Gulf War, Egyptian military participation in multilateral operations can be politically important.

According to U.S. commentators, Egypt's capacity to undertake regional peacekeeping or enforcement operations could be enhanced, if the Egyptian forces were better organized for force projection. As it is, however, Egypt seems still to think in terms of needing a large standing force in the name of home defense and bolstering the Arab side of the regional military balance overall. In sum, Egypt's importance for regional stability lies in its intrinsic role in the regional power balance, and it does not look poised to detach itself sufficiently to adopt instead the role of neutral arbiter on the sidelines.

Egypt's Geographic Reach

For present purposes, there are four main geographic areas of interest: North Africa, the Horn of Africa, the Levant, and the Gulf. Egypt's role in these areas is in part a function of tradition, size, and proximity, but it is also a function of deliberate efforts by Cairo to make Egypt matter. Whereas for the past decade or so Egypt has acted as a linchpin for U.S. involvement in the region, it is now furthering its own alliances to enhance its influence and standing on its own account.

To summarize, in the Maghreb, Egypt is a partner to the governments of Morocco, Algeria, and Tunisia on internal security concerns and has pursued cooperation with them in this sphere. The Egyptian Government also has a special relationship with the Libyan regime, which actually puts it at odds with Washington, because Cairo would rather ease the pressure on the Libyan leader than see him further isolated.[18] In contrast, Egypt's cautious approach to Sudan has had some impact on Washington thinking. It is not clear how this will be affected by Washington's 1998 bombing of a Sudanese pharmaceutical plant (alleged to have been manufacturing chemical weapons) in response to terrorist attacks on two of its African embassies. In the Levant, Egypt is Israel's longest standing partner in the peace process. It is Arafat's closest Arab ally and enjoys good access in Syria. With Jordan, Egypt's relationship is less close, but as demonstrated by Cairo's capacity for summitry linking the Israeli, Palestinian, and Jordanian leaders, it can claim a useful working relationship with all the players in the peace process. In the Gulf, meanwhile, Cairo maintains an ongoing rapport with the Saudis. Further, by early 1995, Egypt had managed to repair its previously tense relations with Iran and adopted a low-key approach to the issue of Iraq's ostracism from the Arab fold, talking of the need to envisage Baghdad's reintegration in due course. Cairo placed Arab solidarity above pleasing Washington in August 1996, when the United States sent cruise missiles into southern Iraq to demonstrate disapproval of Iraqi military support for the campaign of the Kurdistan Democratic Party to oust its rivals in the Patriotic Union of Kurdistan from the town of Irbil in northern Iraq. Egypt, as other Arab states, denounced the U.S. action.

In the case of the Maghreb states, Egypt's interest in expanding ties has been prompted by its observation of developments between North Africa and the European Union. The Barcelona initiative of 1995 was designed by the EU to bolster development on the southern shores and thereby stem migration flows and curb security risks. With an eye to benefitting from EU economic assistance and investment, and to playing a role at the center of this new scheme for north-south cooperation in the Mediterranean,

Egypt is aiming to expand its relations with both the Maghreb and the EU. Having posited and then apparently thought better of the idea of seeking membership in the Arab Maghreb Union (UMA), Egypt has requested observer status with this organization.[19]

Egypt has something to offer the Maghreb in terms of its access to and influence in Libya, which languishes in isolation because of U.N. sanctions. According to Cairo, the Libyan regime of Muamar Qadhafi is a bulwark against Islamic militancy and warrants preservation. Cairo is essentially saying that it can contain Qadhafi's maverick tendencies given the chance, and in the interests of ending Libya's isolation, Egypt advocated a compromise on the issue of where the two wanted Libyan suspects should be tried for their alleged role in the bombing of flight Pan Am 103.[20] (They are currently on trial in Scotland.) Much also depends on how far the troubles in Algeria can be contained. Broadly, Egypt is to the Maghreb as Turkey is to Europe—a partner on security issues, but not part of the same political and economic bloc.

As have other states on the southern shores of the Mediterranean, Egypt has been negotiating a partnership agreement with the EU.[21] In its quest to derive economic benefits from the relationship, Egypt faces some of the same constraints as the Maghreb countries, in that its bargaining power with the EU depends in part on convincing the Europeans that it is potentially dangerous for them to ignore Egypt's needs, for fear of destabilization. At the same time, to attract investors and economic cooperation, Egypt must demonstrate low security risks. This makes for a dilemma and requires a complicated balancing act on Egypt's part, which is more apparent in its dealing with the United States. Aid from Washington has been a valuable source of income, and even if the intention is to do without this eventually, the chances of the United States cutting aid increase to the extent that Egypt appears not to warrant its continuance. With the EU, however, Egypt's prospects of attracting more investment are enhanced the greater its commitment to economic reform.

Looking at the Horn of Africa, Egypt's primary concern in Sudan and further south is a matter of security. While the ideology and objectives of the Sudanese regime remain so much at odds with those of the Egyptian Government, there is little room for development of economic ties. In fact, the Sudanese Government is in dispute with the United Nations for refusing to extradite three suspects wanted in connection with an assassination attempt on President Mubarak in Ethiopia in June 1995. Yet, Egypt has insisted that the United Nations adopt a gradual approach to putting pressure on Khartoum, rather than move straight to an air embargo.[22] Also, Egypt has held somewhat aloof from a U.S. scheme to assist rebels and Sudanese neighbor-states committed to overthrowing the Sudanese regime.

It is in the Levant, or Arab-Israeli sector, that Egypt's role has been and will continue to be the most extensive and comprehensive. In the near term, Egypt is an essential source of support for Arafat and a valuable interlocutor with President Assad of Syria. On the Palestinian leader's behalf, Egypt has repeatedly made the case for channeling more aid to the Palestinian community; in this Cairo has echoed the line of the erstwhile Labour government of Israel, if not its Likud successor. On behalf of the Syrians, meanwhile, Egypt has stated publicly and often that peace requires a full Israeli withdrawal from the Golan Heights, and in this respect Egypt can be assumed to have a sense of what the bottom line is for Damascus. Since Likud took over from Labour in Israel, however, the chances of Syria gaining all its demands seem to have receded.

Egypt's future role in the Arab-Israeli sector will depend on how the peace process evolves. If it delivers a comprehensive array of political and security agreements, Egypt may be expected to play its part in a new regional economic configuration, even if it is not in the forefront. Much has been said about the cool nature of the Egypt-Israel peace and the disappointing absence of Israeli-Egyptian business collaboration. However, Egypt presents a better model for how peace would likely pan out for Syria than does Jordan, which faces different imperatives in terms of its needs for access to the Mediterranean through Israel, resolution of water problems in conjunction with Israel, and development of relations with the Palestinians, in cooperation with Israel.

If the peace process were to collapse on the Israeli-Palestinian and Israeli-Syrian tracks, and Lebanon to continues being a battlefield between the protagonists, the ramifications could destabilize Jordan. That Egypt would renounce its peace with Israel seems unlikely, unless militant Islamic rejections of the peace attain predominance. For fear of this, and to hold out against the tide of Arab opinion antithetical to Israel—and by extension the United States—the Egyptian Government would have to revert to the coolest of relations with the Jewish state and might want to distance itself from the United States, too.

In the Gulf, Egypt's role is somewhat circumscribed. Unlike in the Levant, in the Gulf sector Egypt is not a central player geographically, politically, or diplomatically. Also, Cairo is not in a position to play the honest broker among the three main protagonists in the Gulf: the Gulf Cooperation Council (GCC, or more specifically, Saudi Arabia), Iraq, and Iran, because for now the U.S. alignment with the GCC and containment of Iraq and Iran define the power balance and allow little play for regional initiatives. In any case, Iran has stated publicly and repeatedly that Egypt has no business in Gulf affairs. Meanwhile, the impetus to build economic ties between Egypt and the GCC is not as it was during the oil boom years. Egypt's military contribution in the Gulf War coalition could represent a precedent, but only as part of a multilateral effort, and the GCC states have declined ongoing Egyptian involvement in their defense. There is room, though, for Egyptian-Saudi cooperation in Red Sea security.

New Challenges and Egypt's Prospects

As the foregoing review of Egypt's current regional standing and involvement indicates, the country does have weight and influence, but the key to its importance lies not only in what it is doing and may continue to do under its present leadership, but also in what it would mean for the region if Egypt devolved into disorder or was overtaken by radicals opposed to the prevailing regional order. That order, characterized by the partnership between the United States and its regional allies, stands for containment of Iraq and Iran in the

Gulf and pursuit of the peace process in the Arab-Israeli sector—but on all of these issues the United States has been having difficulty retaining Arab support for its approach.

Arabs in the region are increasingly unhappy about the suffering of the Iraqi people under continued sanctions. Many believe that Iraq no longer poses a serious military threat, except potentially to Kuwait, and that if it grows any weaker it will cease to act as a bulwark against Iran. There is also a distaste for U.S. military actions against Iraq, such as the cruise missile attack of August 1996. On the peace process, meanwhile, the Clinton administration is depicted as biased in favor of Israel and therefore not a neutral peace broker. In addition, as new tensions between Israel and the Arabs overtake the peace process, the prospect of regional economic integration recedes.

For Egypt there is no possibility of returning to the status quo before Madrid. It can no longer rely on being pivotal to U.S. involvement in the region, and the United States is not in a position to distribute largess in the way it did to underwrite the Egyptian-Israeli peace. Egypt thus has to worry about the continuance of U.S. support for itself, let alone soliciting new U.S. aid to bring others on board in the peace process. The Gulf States, meanwhile, cannot make up the difference, because they are feeling the pinch of new budgetary problems themselves. Admittedly, the European Union is inclined to make a larger contribution to regional economic development, in its own security interests, but the price of European investment and soft loans for the would-be recipients is adoption of IMF-inspired economic reforms. Three scenarios serve to illustrate the range of possible developments to which Egypt must accommodate:

- The scenario preferred by optimists and the most ardent supporters of the Middle East peace process is the advent of a new era of economic and political restructuring across the region. According to this vision, the oil-producing states will respond to the challenges facing them and undertake the political policies necessary to sustain support for economic restructuring. As a result, the Islamist agenda for radical change will be overtaken by the introduction of strict legal accountability, facilitating investment and long-term growth in Algeria, Saudi Arabia, Iran, and Iraq.

Under this optimistic scenario, oil prices, at relatively low levels today, will be accommodated and turned into a challenge to stimulate other sectors of the oil-producing economies. Overall, the Middle East and North Africa will integrate into the global economic order and keep pace with general trends in world economic development. Israel and its neighbors, meanwhile, will complete their peace agreements and become integrated into the regional economic order.

• By contrast to this rosy scenario, the gloomiest prognosis for the region is widespread turbulence and fragmentation. In the oil-producing states and others there will be no radical adjustment, and government policies will be characterized instead by retrenchment, inertia, corruption, and increased repression of opposition forces. In Iraq, crime and the breakdown of social structures will accelerate, with Iraqi Kurdistan in the north devolving into civil war, the authority of government diminishing in the predominantly Shia south, and security at the center taking the form of protection rackets.

In Iran, according to this worst-case scenario, the government will be immobilized by factionalism and indecision at the center, with a dissipation of its control at the periphery. Minorities within Iran, such as the Baluch and the Sunnis, will feel obliged to look to their own. Economic recovery will simply not happen. In Saudi Arabia, avoidance of structural reform will make for instability and increased U.S. involvement in protection of the Kingdom's assets.

Meanwhile, in the Arab-Israeli sector, turbulence is postulated to overtake order between the Palestinians and Israelis, halting progress in the peace process and affecting stability in Jordan. At the same time, in North Africa, Algeria is predicted to descend into a protracted civil war.

• The third scenario lies somewhere between the worst and the best cases just described. According to this scenario, some of the regional states muddle through, while others collapse. At the two geographical extremes, Algeria and Iran are paralyzed by internal strife or dissipation of government control. Saudi Arabia and Iraq, meanwhile, manage to make significant structural reform and attain stability.

In the Arab-Israeli sector, Palestinian autonomy is expanded, within limited confines, but the West Bank and Gaza Strip are disconnected and dependent on Jordan and Egypt, respectively. Israel and Jordan maintain their peace, though without much warmth, while Israel and Syria fail to make full peace, although they do avoid war.

As will be evident, these three scenarios are designed to depict alternative directions for the Middle East and North Africa: the first means peace, economic adjustment, and regional integration; the second postulates limited if any economic restructuring, widespread unrest, and the breakup of some states; and the last one foresees a mixed picture, with some states managing a measure of economic restructuring, a limited outcome for the peace process, and pockets of serious conflict.

Egypt's fortunes as a regional power will vary, depending on the comparative fortunes of others. In the context of the first scenario, Egypt could be expected to benefit from increased regional prosperity and stability but would not be a leading player in developments or regional political affairs, because other states, notably the oil-producing countries and Israel, would more likely make the running in the economic power stakes.

In the context of the worst-case scenario, Egypt would likely be powerless to halt the trend toward fragmentation and instability across the region and would have to concentrate its efforts on protecting and insulating itself from being caught up in the disorder.

Last, in the case of the third, or mixed, scenario, Egypt would stand to play a prominent regional role in maintaining as much order as possible and limiting the spread of disorder from the most troubled states. In this endeavor, Egypt would likely be aided by both the United States and Europe.

In sum, if the Middle East and North Africa were overtaken by turbulence and fragmentation, then by definition, Egypt would have failed, as others have, to exercise sufficient regional influence to prevent serious and widespread instability and conflict. If, however, a new era of peace and prosperity dawns, Egypt would benefit but, by virtue of its own difficulties, would not lead the way. The most likely scenario presents a mixed picture, and it is in this context that Egypt's regional role will likely be of most significance. The line Egypt could be expected to take would probably be in keeping with the direction it has been adopting since the signing of the Israeli-Palestinian Declaration of Principles in September 1993. What this means when the peace process falters is a line similar to the one Egypt adopted concerning the 1996 MENA conference.

Conclusion

Egypt's standing in the Middle East will likely remain high because the economic fortunes of the region are probably not going to be radically transformed and Egypt will keep pace. The peace between Israel and the Arabs will be patchy and troubled. Old animosities among the Arabs themselves, and between them and Iran, will continue to stall regional integration. Meanwhile, Egypt and its immense internal problems are part and parcel of the regional reality. The problems besetting Egypt—resource constraints, rapid population growth, the rise of militant Islam in reaction to corruption in high places, and bureaucratic inertia—are not peculiar to Egypt, but if it slides into greater poverty, unrest, and extremism, it will become a vortex in the middle of a troubled region.[23] This, ultimately, is why Egypt cannot be ignored.

Egypt's highly trained and talented diplomats have been credited with managing Cairo's foreign relations so skillfully as to save the country from the miserable fate that could otherwise befall it because of the incompetence and inertia of its home civil service. Since the 1991 Gulf War and subsequent developments in the Arab-Israeli peace process, it is evident that Egypt has been as active as ever on the diplomatic front to protect and promote its regional role in a new setting. The thrust of Egyptian endeavors has been to keep the peace process afloat and synchronize the pace of regional economic change with political developments and security imperatives.

Notes

1. Judy Dempsey, "Israel waits for Nethanyahu to deliver," *Financial Times*, November 22, 1996.

2. Treaty of Peace Between the State of Israel and Hashemite Kingdom of Jordan, October 26, 1994, *Journal of Palestine Studies* 24, no. 2 (Winter 1995): 126.

3. Digby Larner, "Currency Factors Key to Egypt's Growth," *International Herald Tribune*, March 4, 1995.

4. Thomas Friedman, "Egypt Set to Join the Global Economy and 'Live by Its Rules,'" *International Herald Tribune*, November 14, 1996.

5. "Egypt," *Middle East Monitor* 5, no. 3 (March 1995): 12.

6. Paul Witter, "Tackling Egypt's Islamist Insurgents," *Middle East International*, November 4, 1994, 19.

7. Council Report on Relations Between the European union and the Mediterranean Countries, in Preparation for the Conference on November 27-28, Barcelona, *EUROPE Documents*, no. 1930/31, April 27, 1995, 5.

8. See Chronology, *Journal of Palestine Studies* 23, no. 4 (Summer 1994): 154-75.

9. Robert Fisk, "Cairo Puts Faith in Bullet and Bulldozer," *The Independent*, February 10, 1995.

10. David Makovsky, "Common Ground Found in Tense Cairo Summit," *Jerusalem Post,* February 11, 1995.

11. Robert Satloff, "The Egyptian-Syrian-Saudi Summit: Implications for the Peace Process," *Peacewatch*, no. 44, Washington Institute, January 3, 1995.

12. David Makovsky, "Egypt: An Unfriendly Ally," *Jerusalem Post,* January 28, 1995.

13. Joel Peter, *Building Bridges: The Arab-Israeli Multilateral Talks,* (London: Royal Institute of International Affairs 1994), 21.

14. Dore Gold, "One Step Forward, One Step Back," *Jerusalem Post* April 20, 1995.

15. Julian Ozanne and Shahira Idriss, "NPT under Middle East Cloud," *Financial Times*, March 10, 1995.

16. Michael Sheridan, "Third World Challenge to Nuclear Treaty," *The Independent*, February 20, 1995.

17. See Robert Fisk, "PLO Second Thoughts Chill Mid-East Peace," *The Independent*, February 21, 1995.

18. Jonathan Bearman, "U.S. Questions Aid to Cairo As Egyptians Help Out Libya's Oil Industry," *Oil Daily, Energy Compass*, January 9, 1995.

19. George Joffe, "Looking to Maghreb," *Middle East International,* December 2, 1994.

20. Ibid.

21. Inas Nour, "Bridging the Mediterranean," *Al Ahram,* January 19, 1995.

22. Jules Kaglan, "U.N. Ups the Ante," *Middle East International,* November 22, 1996, 13.

23. David Hirst, "Poised between control and chaos," *The Guardian,* February 11, 1995.

FROM GEOPOLITICS TO GEOECONOMICS

Abdul Monem Sa'id Ali

> *Egyptians have come to the conclusion that an ambitious Egyptian role in the area not only invites massive foreign intervention and defeats, as proven by Mohammed Ali and Nasser, but also drains limited Egyptian resources.*

The thesis of this paper has two components. First, throughout most of Egypt's modern history, national security perceptions and geopolitical concerns have defined its regional and international roles. Second, in order to achieve its national interests and preserve its regional and international roles, Egypt needs to redefine its foreign and security policies and to focus on geoeconomic factors that will enable it to adapt to the new world order and to adjust to changing regional realities.

Geopolitics here is understood as encompassing the traditional national security threats that emanate from the geography and history of the nation state. Geopolitics regards the survival of the nation and protection of its territorial integrity as the main objectives of national security policy. Power politics and the balance of power have been the chief means to achieve these objectives.

Dr. Abdul Monem Sa'id Ali is Director of the Al-Ahram Center for Political and Strategic Studies, Cairo.

Geoeconomics, on the other hand, is a much more complex concept. In this construct, the survival of the state and its territorial integrity is not so much challenged by external threats as safeguarded by its economic well being, its social cohesion, and its ability to withstand economic competition. In the new geoeconomic order, national security is ensured by raising productivity, economic reform, integration into regional and international markets, and protecting sources of income.

Egyptian national security goals should undergo a fundamental change from the traditional geopolitical perspective to the more complex geoeconomic perspective.

The Victory of Geoeconomics

The events of the 1990s have unleashed major economic and political transformations in the world and the Middle East. Both have given primacy to geoeconomic considerations in the formulation of national security policies.

In terms of its power structure, the "new" world order is not simply a change from a bipolar world to an older multipolar (or unipolar) world, but a fundamental change in the nature of polarity itself. Traditionally, polarity was defined as the distribution of power among nation-states or blocs of nation-states engaged in the pursuit of hegemony or dominance by force or the threat of force. Now, this definition has been replaced by one characterized by the prevalence of a system of international political-social-economic interactions. The dominant system is a Western, capitalist (and also liberal) order, represented by the powers of North America, Western Europe, and Japan, plus the Pacific rim. This order is highly integrated through a large network of multilateral institutions (e.g., the G-7, the General Agreement on Tariffs and Trade, IEA, the Organisation for Economic Co-operation and Development, International Monetary Fund, International Bank for Reconstruction and Development), multinational corporations, trade, and investments.

Moreover, the third industrial revolution, the revolution in communications, has unleashed a historical process of significant proportions. Economically, it has generated production capacities unprecedented in human history. No state in the world can be satisfied any longer with its internal market, not even the United States. As a result, the search for larger markets has become relentless. Within this new system, power is based not only on military capabilities, but also on the ability to innovate and to market. The United States may have a leading position because of its $6 trillion GNP, but it is by no means assured of hegemony.

Any such change in the world structure means a new agenda. The post-World War II order was dominated by the Soviet-American contest, the arms race, and regional conflicts; the new order is searching for new issues. The new agenda is basically economic, involving issues such as unemployment, inflation, exchange rates, trade barriers, and population growth. Pollution, environmental safety, communications, and air traffic control increasingly command attention in world summits, along with transnational social problems such as drugs, refugees, and AIDS.

This new world order could not have emerged without contingent socioeconomic and political processes in various regions of the world. The socialist bloc, particularly the USSR, could not adapt to the change and, by the 1980s, was on the road to regression. By the 1990s, its failure led to final collapse and disintegration.

In the Western bloc, social-economic-political systems were better able to adjust to the third industrial revolution by creating mechanisms capable of dealing with regional and global economic integration and coping better with political disintegration. As a result, it has emerged, at least temporarily, as dominant.

Transforming the Middle East

How has the Middle East fared in this new world order? The Middle East, too, has witnessed major changes. The most important development in the region has been a change in the dynamics of the Arab-Israeli conflict, precipitated mainly by the Gulf War.

For Israel, the war manifested the result of the arms race in the Middle East. Iraq's missile attacks on Israel's population centers raised fears of another war in which chemical weapons would be used, given added urgency by the discovery that Iraq was developing biological and nuclear capabilities. The fact that the American-Arab coalition minimized Israel's strategic value to the United States was also worrisome as was Washington's growing ties with Saudi Arabia, Egypt, and even Syria. Israel preferred to start a peace process while its standing with the United States was still high.

For Arab parties to the multinational coalition, the war brought risks and opportunities. Saddam's accusation of "double standards" raised against the United States and its coalition partners worked well with the Arab masses. Fearful of losing credibility, Egypt, Syria, and Saudi Arabia found it imperative to establish a "consequential linkage" between the Iraqi withdrawal from Kuwait, peaceful or otherwise, and a resolution of the Arab-Israeli conflict. Meanwhile, the defeat of Iraq left the pro-Iraqi Arabs, particularly the PLO and Jordan, weak. They turned to the Arab-Israeli peace process as an avenue to return to the Arab fold.

For the United States, the major mediator in the Middle East, credibility was at stake. The resolution of the Arab-Israeli conflict became a test case for American leadership, a strategy to fight radicalism, and a means to cap the arms race, especially in the field of mass-destruction weapons. The collapse of the Soviet Union also played its role in spurring the peace process. Syria and the Palestinian Liberation Organization (PLO) lost an important ally, a factor that narrowed their options and compelled them to look to the United States for help in launching peace initiatives.

All these factors accomplished a gradual shift in Israeli public opinion. In the wake of these changes, the second Gulf War and the end of the Cold War created an opportunity no one wanted to miss. And the opportunity was not missed. Through active American mediation efforts, the Madrid peace process was started in October 1991 and by 1994 a Palestinian-Israeli agreement and an Israeli-Jordanian peace treaty were in place. Equally important, the new Arab-Israeli reconciliation process has introduced a geoeconomic dimension to its traditional geopolitical concerns of territory and security. In addition to the bilateral political negotiations, there is another layer of multilateral negotiations to discuss five issues of interest to the parties: arms control, water, refugees, economic development, and the environment. Multilateral negotiations, begun in January 1992 in Moscow, have incorporated 35 states, including 13 Arab countries and Israel. Although the results are still limited, the multilaterals have inspired a host of initiatives for development and economic cooperation in the Middle East, the most notable of which has been a series of economic summits in the Middle East.

In the bilateral agreement, the economic dimension was even more concrete, with provisions for a socioeconomic link between the Palestinians and Israel. Likewise, the Jordanian-Israeli peace treaty lists seven areas for economic cooperation: water, refugees, natural resources, human resources, infrastructure, economic fields, and tourism. Thus, a recognition of the new geoeconomic realities has already been built into the geopolitical structure of the peace process. Despite recent setbacks in that process, these issues will have to be addressed and a structure for doing so has now been put in place.

Transforming Egypt's Regional Role

Throughout its long history, Egypt's regional role has been based on its geopolitical and strategic significance and its ability to act as a regional pace setter. In the 19th century, Egypt was first to industrialize, to establish secular education, and to experiment with parliament (1866). From Egypt, these institutions and practices spread to the Arab world. In the 20th century, art, literature and broadcasting, in addition to a more modern press, made Egypt the Mecca of the Arab intelligentsia. These factors—in addition to Egypt's leading role in modernization and nation-building, its large, modern army, and a significant and growing middle class—have put Egypt in the position to exercise Arab world leadership.

Egypt's Arab Role

Under Nasser's regime (1954-70), Egyptian influence in the Arab world reached its apogee. During the 1950s and 1960s, Nasser nurtured Egyptian leadership in the Arab world through an innovative package of domestic and foreign policies inspiring to all

Arabs. Domestically, Nasser embarked on an ambitious development program that resulted in an important shift in the socioeconomic structure of the country. Externally, Nasser's support for national liberation movements in Algeria, Tunisia, Sudan, Palestine, South Yemen, and the Gulf caught the imagination of the Arab masses. His ideology of "Arab nationalism" created a sense of purpose for the Arab world, while his nonalignment policy successfully manipulated a largely bipolar world in the interests of Egypt and other Arab countries. For better or worse, Arab states followed the Egyptian lead in nonalignment, Arab nationalism, independence from foreign domination abroad, and "Arab socialism."

The death of Nasser in September 1970 marked a change not only for Egypt but also for the Arab world. His successor had a different point of view, less ideological and more pragmatic. The defeat of Egypt in the 1967 war; the need to liberate Sinai from Israeli occupation; the declining economic fortunes of the country; waning Egyptian support for Nasser's politics; and the emergence of détente in the early 1970s had led to Sadat's new agenda for Egypt. This agenda had four points: peace with Israel, alliance with the West (particularly the United States), economic liberalization, the infitah, or opening, and a degree of political pluralism.

Unfortunately, this agenda was not yet acceptable to the Arab world. Although Sadat was successful in forging the largest Arab coalition ever against Israel in the October 1973 war, he was isolated from the Arab world when he signed the Camp David Accord in September 1978 and the peace treaty with Israel in March 1979. As a result, Egypt lost her Arab leadership position for most of the 1970s and 1980s, but her agenda continued to be debated. In November 1987, the Amman summit allowed Arab countries to resume diplomatic relations with Egypt; in 1990 the Arab League returned to Cairo; and by 1991 the Egyptian agenda for the region had been accepted by the Arab states.

This stunning reversal of the Arab position was due to three interrelated factors: security, economic development, and culture. In security terms, Egypt's withdrawal from the Arab fold had increased the security threat, especially from Israel, for all Arab countries, including Egypt. Meanwhile, the Iranian revolution and the outbreak of the Iran-Iraq war created security problems in the Gulf.

Gradually, the Arab world came to realize that Egypt's demographic and geographic weight made it essential to any balancing strategy in the Middle East. Egypt was important, not only because of its military weight, but also because of its influence in international forums and its Islamic credentials. In a conference in Amman in November 1987, Crown Prince Hasan of Jordan said that the Arab world without Egypt was like NATO without the United States. While something of an exaggeration, this statement has a large element of truth.

Economic forces also pointed to the region's need for Egypt. After the October 1973 war, the Arab oil-producing states were able to double their revenues to unprecedented levels by restricting production and increasing prices. Despite a 1986 dive in oil prices, two decades of accumulated oil revenues have created a massive industrialization drive in these countries. For the first time in their history, Arabs were not simply producing raw materials but also refining oil and manufacturing petrochemicals, aluminum products, iron, steel, cement, construction materials, and home appliances. Egyptians supplied these developmental plans with human resources, skilled and unskilled. Thus, in spite of Egypt's ostracism from the Arab world in the 1980s, Egyptian-Arab economic interdependence continued to grow.

Lastly, in the cultural arena, Egypt plays a leading role. The oil era intensified personal interactions between Egypt and the rest of the Arab world through tourism and labor migration, while increasing cultural ties, and also saw an increase in education, books, periodicals, magazines, and newspapers, all with a large pan-Arab market. The same is true for Arab writing on art, politics, economics, and religion. In the mid-1980s, the Arab world had 250 broadcasting stations covering most of the Arab world. In addition to providing the human and intellectual resources for the communications revolution, Egypt today provides one-third of all intra-Arab television programming and has almost a monopoly on cinema and videos.

Constraints on Leadership

The previous discussion of Egypt's regional role should not lead to the conclusion that Egypt has finally become *the* leader of the Arab world. What it does show is that Egypt is important to the Arab world and has a potential for leadership. Above all, Egypt has the capability to work as an "agenda setter" for the Arabs, defining their goals and priorities.

However, Egypt's potential to lead the Arab world faces serious constraints. Chief among these has been the discrepancy between Egypt's weight in the Arab world (its geopolitical role) and its domestic capabilities (its geoeconomic base). Egypt's demographic size among Arab countries (out of 230 million Arabs, 26 percent are Egyptian) has been a factor in Egypt's leading position, but at the same time, demography acts as a restraint on Egyptian capabilities. Until the end of the 1960s, Egypt was the wealthiest, best educated, and only industrial Arab country; today, it lags behind the wealthy Arab oil-producing countries. This shift in Egypt's economic position has lost Egypt some of its prestige among the Arab masses.

Even more important, because of its declining socioeconomic conditions, for the first time in its modern history Egypt faces major domestic political turbulence in the form of radical Islamic movements that resort to violence. Since summer 1992, the level of terrorism practiced by groups such as the Islamic Liberation Party, the Society of Muslims, al Takfir wal-Hijra, al-Jihad, and al-Najun Min al-Nar has reached new heights. Attacks have been made on the liberal political writer, Farag Fouda, on Egyptian Christians in villages of Upper Egypt, and on tourists in order to cause serious damage to the Egyptian economy. Early in 1994, extremists attempted to assassinate Atif Sidqi, the prime minister. Although Islamic radicalism has been sharply reduced since 1994, it remains a threat to the socioeconomic fabric of Egypt. In fact, it is increasingly considered a national security concern to Egypt, reflecting the upgrading of internal domestic troubles to the level of a national security threat.

These economic factors have made Egyptians wary about any leadership position in the Arab world. At the same time, Egypt has lost some of its value to the Arab world. As Arab countries have become independent, each has begun to look out for its own national interests. The economic development of the Arab world and the spread of education have reduced the Egyptian edge in technology and know-how. Finally, as Arab countries become linked to the new world order, increasingly they look to the United States for support and protection, rather than Egypt. Finally, there is an element of fear of Egypt in the Arab world, particularly in the conservative countries of the Gulf, where memories of previous Egyptian intervention in the Arabian peninsula (Mohammed Ali, 1811-23, and Nasser, 1962-67) are not forgotten. Egypt, like other regional powers (Iran, Turkey, Iraq) may be cause not only for admiration but also for anxiety.

The Case for Geoeconomics

In the past two decades, this discrepancy between Egypt's leading regional role and its declining domestic power base has been resolved by an active foreign policy. By using its geopolitical position and its historical and cultural assets, Egypt has been an influential international and regional actor. It has been assisted in this by four factors: the Cold War, the Arab-Israeli peace process, the need for Gulf security, and the continuing crisis in the Horn of Africa.

Equally important, Egypt has gained considerable economic aid from its diplomacy. Financial returns from the Arab Gulf States have been considerable. Between 1975 and 1992, the United States contributed over $18 billion in economic assistance in addition to an even greater amount in military aid. Europe, Japan, and major industrialized countries have been no less generous to Egypt. The second Gulf War reduced pressures on the Egyptian economy by canceling Egypt's debts ($6.7 billion from the United States, $7.1 billion from the Gulf), thereby reducing Egypt's foreign debts by 50 percent. Meanwhile, world politics has been transformed by the primacy of economics and increased international interdependence. The Arab-Israeli peace process, although not completed, has reduced the threat of war and paved the way for normalization of relations and regional economic interdependence. All these factors emphasize the primacy of geoeconomics over geopolitics. Gulf security has finally come to rest in U.S. hands, while the crisis in the Horn of Africa has become irrelevant in the wake of the Cold War.

These changes have resulted in a relative decline in Egypt's regional and international status. As geoeconomics gains primacy in regional and world politics, Egypt appears less capable of dealing with the new situation. All economic measures indicate that Egypt is less able to compete in regional and international markets than many of its rivals. In Egyptian national security circles, this reality has been translated into a growing anxiety over the future, one in which the Egyptian market will be dominated by foreign powers, particularly Israel. It has even been claimed that Israel will achieve by economic means what it failed to achieve by military means. Egypt is finally confronting its weak domestic situation that for too long has been overshadowed by its geopolitical position and concerns. Economic as well as political reforms are not only essential to Egypt's welfare and progress but fundamental to its national security. So far, however, Egyptian efforts to reduce the rising fears of the future have been insufficient, as have been efforts to address their causes.

To address these fears, Egypt must redefine its regional position in a way that takes account of major international transformations. It must also address the Middle East subsystem, which includes not only the Arab world but also Israel, Turkey, and Iran. Egypt cannot succeed in this without a major political and economic transformation in the direction followed earlier by the newly industrialized countries of Latin America and the Asia Pacific Rim. Fortunately, the time needed to catch up with the developed world has been progressively shortened, thanks to the faster spread of technology and ideas and the rapid movement of capital across borders. Since the mid-1970s, Egypt has adopted economic and political reforms with some successes in infrastructure and physical policies, but Egypt's economic growth has been limited and, in many years, stagnant.

The New Regional Agenda

For Egypt to maintain and expand its regional role, it has to set a new agenda for the region, just as it has done in the past. This new agenda must involve a package of domestic and foreign policies that harmonize with the rising trend toward geoeconomics as the major determinant in national policies. To this end, Egypt has to overcome the bureaucratic lethargy, intellectual hesitation, and visionary reluctance that to a large extent have been due to traditional geopolitical concerns. Instead, Egypt must move at high speed toward a major domestic economic and political reform and a significant regional reconstruction of its role abroad. The new Egyptian agenda should include four elements:

- Completing the current geopolitical agenda by actively working to reach a just and comprehensive Middle East peace
- Building a regional strategic structure based on a geoeconomic posture
- Upgrading Egyptian regional capabilities
- Encouraging the United States and other major powers to support and consolidate these goals.

Completing the Old Agenda

Although the Arab-Israeli peace process has achieved noticeable progress, three factors highlight continuing geopolitical concerns that threaten to reverse the process: delay in the implementation of the Palestinian-Israeli agreement, now set back by the election of a new hard-line leadership in Israel; slow progress on the Israeli-Syrian (and hence Lebanese) front; and the current arms race in the area, particularly in weapons of mass destruction (WMD).

Egypt is already making a great effort to solve the first problem by consolidating the evolution of Palestinian self-rule. However, more needs to be done to raise the political base of support for Yasir Arafat and the PLO. Egypt should initiate a new agenda to generate support for the Palestinian cause to encourage peace with Israel, Palestinian development, and ultimately, statehood. At the same time, Egypt should encourage Israel to remain faithful to the letter and timetable of its agreement with the Palestinians.

On the second issue, the Egyptian role has thus far been subsidiary to American mediation efforts. However, American diplomacy has shown limited ability to mobilize mediation at the highest levels of government. Egypt should fill this vacuum through direct mediation by President Mubarak. The Egyptian initiative, including an active presidential shuttle diplomacy, should include the following guidelines:

- Reaffirmation by Israel of Syrian sovereignty over the Golan Heights and a commitment to full withdrawal during an acceptable period of time.
- A commitment to recognize Israel and its right to security. Syria should pledge its commitment to a full peace, including the establishment of full diplomatic relations, an end to the economic boycott, and the development of economic and cultural relations with Israel.
- Israeli withdrawal from Golan and Syria's steps to normalize relations with Israel should move in parallel stages in accordance with a schedule negotiated by the parties. These phased steps should be simultaneous and interdependent and accompanied by mutual security measures.

With respect to the arms race, Egypt should continue to seek a Middle East free of WMD by means of multilateral negotiations. These efforts should be accompanied by incentives to Israel and an education campaign to convey to the Israeli public the Egyptian and Arab threat perceptions. The initiative should have two parts: to link arms control measures to a political timetable for the overall settlement and to eliminate the most devastating weapons from the area.

The latter cannot be achieved without transparency on WMD in the inventories of both sides to the conflict. Transparency is also important for negotiations on conventional weapons. Both sides should provide information not only on the existing inventory of weapons, but also on those under development. A moratorium on the acquisition and development of high-technology weapons should be implemented during the negotiating process. Failing this, an alternative would be to put a moratorium on the deployment of such weapons, important for long-range ballistic missiles (over 150 kilometers) and antiballistic missiles, such as the Israeli ARROW. A ban on exporting long-range ballistic and cruise missiles should be arranged among arms-exporting countries. The present Israeli plans to expand its sea-projection capabilities, particularly sea-launch, long-range conventional and nuclear missiles and advanced submarines, should be halted during Arab-Israeli negotiations. This step would prevent triggering a new naval arms race that might make future arms-control measures difficult. Confidence-building measures, such as notification of naval movements and cooperative sea operations against drug smuggling and terrorist actions, would enhance both the possibilities of arms control and the mutual trust necessary for peace in the Middle East.

The New Geoeconomics

Historically, Egypt has built its regional and international influence by forging alliances with Islamic, African, and Third World countries to serve Egyptian and Arab geopolitical goals. As the global and regional settings change, so should Egyptian foreign policy, to emphasize stability and economic development. This new direction in Egyptian foreign policy should involve strategic understandings with the major regional powers progressing in the same direction.

The first of these countries should be Saudi Arabia. For the foreseeable future, the combination of Egypt and Saudi Arabia could provide the Arab world with the leadership it needs. It was the Egyptian-Saudi coalition that curtailed Israeli ambition in the October 1973 war, defeated Iran in the Iran-Iraq war, and finally Iraq in the second Gulf War. The geopolitical Egyptian-Saudi connection played such a role in the past, and it could do even more in the future. In geoeconomic terms this alliance can anchor Egyptian-Gulf interdependence and foster the importance of the Gulf region in regional development and even in the world economy. An innovative agenda would look to consolidate the peace in the area, secure the Gulf, reintegrate Syria and Iraq into a region with a moderate developmental outlook, and cooperate with other major regional powers to enhance regional economic cooperation. An activated (or even reinvented) formula along the lines of the Damascus Declaration should give this framework the necessary underpinning.

Israel and Turkey will be very important for any such regional understanding. Western European integration projects were built on the shoulders of France, Germany, Italy, and Britain; in the Middle East, Egypt, Saudi Arabia, Turkey, and Israel should do the same. This is not an easy task for Egypt, which has long conceptualized its foreign policy around the idea of Arabism in its political and cultural dimensions. Egypt's cool reaction to growing Israeli-Turkish military ties illustrates the difficulty. Reconciling both is necessary for an active Egyptian regional role in a postpeace era. If Britain could reconcile its Anglo-Saxon heritage with its European Latin connection, Egypt should be able to do the same. The new agenda for the four regional powers can be based on the old geopolitical idea of consolidating the peace, as well as the new geoeconomic agenda of promoting different forms of interdependence; integrating the Middle East into the world economic system; and reincorporating the still radical states into an ambitious regional economic development plan. Fortunately, the four countries mentioned have close associations with the West, albeit for different reasons; they should thus be able to provide a bridge between the Middle East and the new emerging world order.

Building regional institutions would be a major function of the new regional structure. Currently, Middle Eastern countries belong to different regional institutions, including the Arab League, the Organization of Islamic Conference, and the Organization of African Unity, but Israel does not belong to any. In fact, these institutions tend to take an anti-Israeli stand as a part of Arab efforts to balance the strong Israeli association with the West. Integrating Israel into a regional institutional framework could be part of Egypt's new regional effort. To solve these contradictions, Egypt needs to conceptualize a new framework with emphasis on a new socioeconomic order.

Upgrading Regional Capabilities

As the end of the 20th century approaches, Egypt will no longer be able to rely on a daring and courageous foreign policy to cover the gaps in its domestic weakness. To increase its regional power capabilities, Egypt must engage in more speedy economic and political reforms. This will give Egypt important economic assets that could be utilized in regional affairs.

First, with over 60 million consumers, Egypt could be the largest market in the Middle East, *if* the Egyptian economy can improve the slow pace of its growth. In 1994-95, Egyptian imports totaled about $15 billion and exports, $5.4 billion.[1] This does not make Egypt a lucrative trading partner or a seductive investment opportunity. Egypt's growth rates have risen from under 2 percent in 1991-92 to 5 percent in 1996-97. If Egypt could resume an economic growth rate of 7 percent (achieved 1974-84) for the coming 10 years, it would become an increasingly influential economic partner. In addition, Egypt is a tourist attraction no other Middle East country can match. In this case, Egypt would cease to be an arena for terrorism and economic burden on its regional and international partners. Instead, Egypt could restore its power position in economics as well as politics.

Second, an end of the Arab-Israeli conflict and economic development of the Israeli-Palestinian-Jordan triangle should create a new, vibrant economic area. Egypt could take an active part in the development of the Palestinian economy and energize economic relations with the other parties in the triangle. The development of north Sinai and the coast of the Gulf of Aqaba, possibly even the whole of the Sinai Peninsula, could act as a developmental bridge between the Egyptian hinterland and eastern Egypt with the rest of the Levant, Turkey, and the Arabian peninsula.

Third, Egypt's geographical position has made it a transportation bridge for three continents. The establishment of the Suez Canal in the 19th century added considerably to these assets. The creation of the Sumed oil pipeline, with the capacity of 1.6 million barrels per day has shown the potential of Egypt as a passage for oil and possibly gas in the future. This transport function could be expanded by sophisticated networks of roads and railways that extend via Israel to the Levant states and the Gulf. The Camp David accords envisioned the establishment of a highway linking Sinai to the city of Aqaba in Jordan via Elat in Israel. With Libya and Sudan integrated into the new Middle East, Egypt could be the transit point, as it was in the past, among the Levant, North Africa, and Africa south of the Sahara.

Fourth, and probably most important, Egypt has no cultural industry equal in the Middle East, but in the past few decades, bureaucratic difficulties have stifled this potential. The liberalization of Egypt politically and economically could give Egypt greatly expanded possibilities in this area. As education and the use of audio-visual material expand, along with satellite transmission, Egypt is best equipped to fill the pages, the papers, and the television hours for the region.

The Role of the United States

The United States has much to gain in enhancing Egypt's regional role. Israel and Syria may have more military power, but they lack acceptance of their leadership from the rest of the Arab world. Saudi Arabia may have the economic muscle, but it lacks population and a social model that can be emulated. Turkey may have better economic credentials and a stronger association with the West through NATO, but it, too, lacks acceptability in the region because of its Ottoman past and its wavering attitude toward the Middle East. Egypt can exercise a leading Arab and Middle Eastern role, but only if it can rise above its economic hardship and see an end to the protracted Arab-Israeli conflict. If this happens, the Egyptian vision and agenda of the past two decades will be vindicated.

As an active partner with Egypt, the United States has provided Egypt with generous economic support. The two countries have cooperated in conceptualizing and implementing the agenda of peace and security in the Middle East and the Gulf. As a new agenda is born, an active American role is needed even more. Of course, the American role is fundamental in completing the geopolitical agenda of the past—consolidating the Palestinian-Israeli agreement, finalizing an Israeli-Syrian peace, and more forcefully encouraging efforts for arms control. It could enhance Egyptian efforts in these directions, but the United States can also support Egyptian efforts to build a new regional strategic structure, using its influence with Saudi Arabia, Israel, and Turkey.

More important, however, the United States can enhance Egypt's new geoeconomic agenda for the Middle East and for Egypt. In the last few years, U.S. foreign policy has concentrated on four areas:

- Consolidation of the world capitalist system by building networks of free-trade areas
- Neutralizing instability that may result from the collapse of the Soviet Union and integrating the ex-Soviet bloc into the world capitalist order
- Developing new giant markets, particularly in China, India, Brazil, and Argentina
- Preventing regional crises from disturbing economic development, as in the Arab-Israeli and Gulf conflicts.

The United States also needs to shift from a geopolitical to a geoeconomic agenda in the Middle East. America should upgrade the Middle East from an area of crisis and concern with conflict management to an area of potential economic development, capable of interdependence and integration into the world capitalist system. This cannot be achieved without laying the foundation for a regional order based on geoeconomic relations over and above geopolitical relations.

In the past, American aid to Egypt has emphasized political, not economic, motives. Out of the massive American aid to Egypt, the Egyptian private sector received a mere 5 percent; the rest went to the public sector consolidating government control. Only 1.9 percent of the aid has gone to science and technology, which represent the weakest link in the Egyptian industrial base. The need now is to support the Egyptian private sector and technological base. More important than aid is investment from the United States and industrialized countries, which, despite two decades of political partnership, is very low. Egypt has been a partner to the United States in setting the Middle East on the road to peace, security, and stability; it should now be a major partner in reshaping the environment for prosperity.   This new type of partnership would not only integrate the Middle East into the new emerging world order; it would also consolidate the political agenda of the region and prevent its reversal by radical Islamic forces.

Note

1.   *The World Factbook,* http://www.odci. gov/cia/ publications/nsolo/ factbook/eg.htm) (Washington: Central Intelligence Agency, 1997).

THE FUTURE OF
THE MIDDLE EAST AND EGYPT

George Joffe

Egypt is today reasserting its regional role, despite the profound geopolitical changes that have swept the Middle East and North Africa since 1990. At the same time, it is unlikely that its old dominant position can be recovered, simply because of the way in which the region is structured. Instead, Egypt will seek to become the core state that links the subregions that now make up the Middle East and North Africa.

The end of the Cold War and the collapse of the Soviet Union in December 1991 have generated profound changes in the geopolitics of the Middle East. Until then, the region had served as a surrogate arena for the interplay of tensions between East and West. As a result, its systemic relationships and institutional structures remained relatively static. The changes introduced by these two events were catalyzed during 1990-91 by the war against Iraq, authorized by the United Nations and fought by a U.S.-led

---

George Joffe is the Deputy Director and Director of Studies of the Royal Institute of International Affairs, London. He is also co-editor of *Mediterranean Politics*, editor of the *Journal of North Africa Studies*, and the author of over 100 articles on the Middle East and North Africa.

multilateral coalition. The present situation is no longer static; instead, the region is now in a state of flux in which new alignments and patterns of interaction are beginning to emerge. This paper points to trends in this pattern and what they may mean for Egypt.

The New Geopolitical Map

Since 1990, the Middle East has been enlarged territorially and politically disaggregated by the institutions, systems, and perceptions that originally gave it a degree of coherence. Up to 1990, the region was essentially defined as the Arab world, together with the peripheral non-Arab states of Turkey and Iran. The Arab world itself was a self-determined area of common culture and language, one that had articulated a set of common concerns that provided political and diplomatic coherence. These included issues such as the Arab-Israeli conflict, the Palestinian issue, and international oil policy. Common concerns were buttressed by transnational institutions, such as the Arab League and its associated agencies, as well as subregional institutions like the Gulf Cooperation Council (GCC), the Arab Cooperation Council (ACC), and the Maghreb Arab Union (UMA). These three factors of common identity and purpose had been welded into a cohesive system by shared ideologies, ranging from Arab nationalism to Islamism.[1]

Within this system, Egypt enjoyed a natural position of political and cultural leadership, certainly up to 1980 when the Sadat regime signed the Israeli-Egyptian peace treaty. Even after this event, Egypt's cultural dominance remained unchallenged while its foreign policy was dedicated to restoring its political and diplomatic dominance as well.[2] It was certainly the case that no other state, whether Arab or non-Arab, had the capacity or opportunity to capture Egypt's previous leadership in politics, diplomacy, or culture.

This Middle Eastern system, however, concealed growing tensions among its member states. These had been contained largely because the region had become an arena for the articulation of the antagonistic balance of power between the super powers and the associative balance of power exercised by regional states.

Iraq's invasion of Kuwait and the subsequent Gulf War destroyed the regional balance, while the end of the Cold War removed its global counterpart, creating instead a situation of hegemonic stability for the United States. The collapse of the Soviet Union, by conferring on the states of the Caucasus and Central Asia a state of formal political independence (even though Russian hegemony continues to be very real), expanded the boundaries of the Middle East eastward. Although the Muslim states of Azerbaijan, Uzbekistan, Kirghizia, Kazakhstan, Turkmenistan, and Tajikistan continue to be heavily dependent on the Russian Federation (in 1992, 50 percent of their trade was still with the Russian Federation; 80 was percent with other members of the Commonwealth of Independent States[3]), they were now able to develop diplomatic and cultural links with the remainder of the Islamic world, particularly in Southwest Asia and North Africa, in ways that had been impossible before.

The Multipolar Middle East

The Middle East today is no longer a politically cohesive region dominated by the Arab world but has become multipolar. It now consists of five subsidiary regions, each with its own political imperatives and dominated by one or more regional hegemons in which the normative concerns of the original region have been forced into the background:

- The Arab Gulf states of the GCC, with a common concern over oil policy and the primordial importance of their relations with the West
- The North African states of the Arab Maghreb Union, now predominantly focused on the Mediterranean and relations with Europe, which provides their geoeconomic environment
- Northeastern Africa and the Horn, where Egypt has an acute interest, particularly with respect to Sudan, as well as a preoccupation with the Mediterranean and the Arab world
- The Levant, now dominated by the uncertain progress of the peace process, both between Israel and the Arab world and between Israel and the Palestinians

- The non-Arab world of Turkey, Iran, and their new Caucasian and Central Asian hinterland, seeking closer economic relations with the West but also establishing new inter- and intraregional political and diplomatic links, some of which involve the old Arab-dominated Middle East, particularly in the case of Turkey.

Before 1990, the Arab world dominated the Middle East demographically and diplomatically; the new situation has altered that balance. Iran and Turkey are now at the center of a new zone of potential cleavage between Arab and non-Arab worlds, with the Persian Gulf as the fault line. Both worlds are now much closer to demographic and economic equivalence than they were before. Furthermore, new hegemonic states have appeared in the subsidiary regions. Turkey and Iran compete for the support of Central Asia, with its population of 56 million, of whom 65 percent profess to being Muslim and 45 percent speak Turkish. Saudi Arabia dominates the Gulf, while Syria and Israel vie for control of the Levant. In North Africa, the crisis in Algeria has removed the state that was the region's traditional hegemon from any significant regional role, while Morocco is not yet able to fully assert its own claims to such a position. In this new configuration, Egypt appears left with the restricted arena of Northeast Africa and the Red Sea.[4] At the same time, it has begun to cast about for a more significant Mediterranean role as compensation for the loss of its traditionally dominant Middle Eastern position. Regional institutions have experienced a similar decline in influence and importance:

- The Arab League, now the subject of an Israeli proposal to replace it by a League of Middle Eastern States, with Israel as a full member, has been eclipsed by the Islamic Conference Organization at the regional level
- At the subregional level, the League's former role is being usurped by organizations such as the GCC and the UMA. These institutions provide a basis for economic integration and the coordination of policies to address the new political and security

imperatives of the subregions formed from the old, more inclusive Middle East.

Outside Encroachment

At the same time, partly because of profound changes beginning to emerge at more global levels in world affairs, neighboring organizations and institutions are beginning to encroach on the political and economic autonomy of what was the old Middle Eastern region:

• The EU is experimenting, at present bilaterally, with a southern extension of the European Common Economic Space. As a result of the Global Euro-Mediterranean Partnership Policy approved at the Barcelona Conference in November 1995, the EU has expanded its bilateral links with Morocco, Tunisia, Turkey, and Israel and now is in the process of doing the same with Egypt and other Mediterranean littoral states. In essence, the policy aims at creating a free-trade area in industrial goods and services with these states and later at encouraging horizontal economic integration amongst them.

• The EU is also contemplating a long-term trade agreement with the GCC. The concept of such an agreement dates back to the 1980s, but it is now being revived as part of the EU extension of its geoeconomic space into the Middle East and North Africa, as well as into Central and Eastern Europe.

• NATO is considering an extension of its responsibilities to the shores of the southern Mediterranean and has already established a permanent low-level consultative group with Morocco, Tunisia, Egypt, and Israel. The Western European Union (WEU) is also considering a similar approach, while the Conference on Security and Cooperation in the Mediterranean, the "Five-plus-Five," and the "Mediterranean Forum" proposals offer alternative security scenarios, some of which may well be integrated into the EU's Global Euro-Mediterranean Partnership.[5]

• Discussions of migration and security issues, normally confined to the European members of the Trevi Group and the

Shengen Accords,[6] are being extended to North African and Middle Eastern states as well. Morocco is already a permanent observer at the Trevi Group, and other South Mediterranean states anticipate similar forms of participation in the future.

• Even in the non-Arab arena, new structures are accelerating centripetal forces, weakening traditional regional cohesion by strengthening new structures and initiatives. Iran and Turkey have linked with Pakistan to revive the virtually moribund Economic Cooperation Organization, creating the potential for a new "Northern Tier" that now includes Central Asian and Caucasian states. Iran has strengthened its economic ties and transport infrastructure links with Central Asia in an attempt to counter American initiatives designed to exclude it from the region. Turkey itself presides over the Black Sea Council, which provides a link among the Balkans, the Russian Federation, and the new non-Arab Middle East. Even the ongoing struggle in Afghanistan has reverberated in the Middle East, involving Iran in attempting to influence the outcome as the Taliban take control of the state and provide a breeding ground for Islamist extremism. The non-Arab Middle Eastern region, in short, is increasingly acquiring its own political dynamic and economic autonomy apart from the traditional, Arab-dominated Middle Eastern region.

The Situation of Egypt

In this radically changed world, Egypt's renewed aspirations for regional leadership increasingly appeared misplaced, at least on the surface. The core foreign policies of Egypt, which appeared in August 1990 when Egypt recovered control of the Arab League and set the Gulf War agenda for the Arab world, seemed in the aftermath of the conflict to be misplaced and irrelevant. The Damascus Declaration security system for the Gulf has collapsed in a welter of mutual recrimination,[7] and Egypt's role in the Middle East peace process has been increasingly marginalized as that process itself plunges into crisis.

In reality, the Egyptian position is far more complex than these appearances suggest. Furthermore, since the Casablanca

Economic Conference at the end of October 1994 and the Amman Economic Conference in November 1995—both part of the economic component of the multilateral track of the Middle East peace process and designed to stimulate private sector regional cooperation—there has been a renewed vitality in Egypt's foreign policy initiatives as new arenas for diplomatic action are sought. Egypt's proposal in November 1995 to join the UMA resulted in the creation of a special observer status to cater to Egyptian aspirations, despite Tunisian and Algerian anxieties and the general decline in the organization's effectiveness because of the crisis in Algeria and the unresolved issue of the Western Sahara conflict. There is also a new UMA awareness of Egypt's Mediterranean interests (the fourth circle of Egypt's new foreign policy, according to Foreign Minister Amr Mousa), toward both Europe and North Africa, based mainly on its concerns over Libya and its common interests with Morocco and Tunisia. Egypt's initiatives to create a new regional understanding with Syria and Saudi Arabia, as evinced by the heads-of-state meeting in Alexandria in December 1995, reflected a reassertion of Egypt's Arab role. This was reinforced both by the March 1996 Conference of the Peacemakers at Sharm al-Shaikh, where Egypt led the regional initiative to counterterrorism and support the peace process, and by the June 1996 Cairo Arab League summit, when Egypt orchestrated a common Arab response, for the first time in 5 years, toward the implications of Likud's electoral victory in Israel.

More specifically, all these moves were warnings to Jordan and Israel that the path toward comprehensive Middle Eastern peace is more complicated and tortuous than both states seemed to suppose and that Egypt will continue to be key to ultimate success, whatever scenario emerges. It is also a warning to the Gulf States that formal peace arrangements with Israel, provided an equitable solution to the Palestinian issue has been found, must precede the normalization of relations sought by countries such as Kuwait, Qatar, and Oman (until the defeat of the Labour Alignment coalition in Israel in May 1996). Similarly, Egypt's leading role in insisting that its signature and that of other Arab states on a renewal of the Non-Proliferation Treaty depended on a prior Israeli commitment eventually to do so as well was an indication of Cairo's determination to reassert itself within Middle Eastern affairs. Even if in the end Cairo's leverage over Tel Aviv on this issue is limited, the tensions that have developed as a result indicate a new independence in Egypt's diplomatic agenda, as did President Mubarak's threat to cancel the Cairo economic summit set for November 1996 unless the new Netanyahu government in Israel made progress in its negotiations with the Palestine National Authority. These actions also portend widening latitude in Egypt's regional relations as a result of the potential widening of the Arab-Israeli peace process to include other Middle Eastern states—provided momentum on the Palestinian issue is maintained, a consideration depending entirely on the policy options eventually chosen by the United States and the Netanyahu government in Israel.

It is too early to state with certainty that this new Egyptian assertiveness will be successful. It does, however, emphasize that Egypt is still a central factor in regional affairs and that the Egyptian Government is seeking new ways of expressing this. At the same time, Egypt's continued support for the Israeli-Palestinian peace process demonstrates its general commitment to regional peace. Notwithstanding this commitment, automatic Egyptian support for all U.S. or European initiatives in the area can no longer be taken for granted. In the future, Egypt will seek to balance its regional ambitions against its long-standing external alliance patterns. Indeed, the degree to which Egypt is apparently sidelined within the Middle East peace process, as seemed to be the case after Jordan signed its own peace treaty with Israel and Morocco and Tunisia established low-level diplomatic relations with the Jewish state, will determine the degree of freedom that Egypt perceives it has in forging new regional linkages.

It therefore follows that for an outside power, like the United States, with hegemonic interests as well as concerns over access to oil and security of communications, Egypt will continue to be a dominant factor in policy formulation. This importance will be increased if Egypt succeeds in forging strategic alliances with Syria and Saudi Arabia and, at the same time, linking itself into North

Africa. Egypt's role will be particularly important if the policy of "dual containment" is sustained. In this case, Saudi Arabia will be unable to maintain Gulf security either alone or in combination with its fellow members of the GCC and will need external allies. Similarly, peace in the Levant, with Syria at its core, would also depend on Egyptian participation and mediation. In any case, Egypt's role in the underlying changes taking place within the region will make it an essential, indeed, a dominant, component in future policy evolution.

The New Challenges

Many of the new challenges facing both Middle Eastern states and their Western partners have already been cited. Challenges can be placed in three categories—political change, economic development, and ideological evolution interlinked with cultural assertion—but it should be borne in mind that it is extremely difficult to make meaningful predictions beyond the immediate future.

Political Change

The likely crisis points for the immediate future in the Middle East and North Africa are already well known. They involve Algeria, Libya, the dual peace process with Israel and the Palestinians on the one hand and the Arab-Islamic world on the other, the future of Iraq, and the issue of Iran. Behind these lie more general concerns—for example, the potential for the democratization of Middle Eastern political systems and for the creation of viable legal structures to minimize arbitrary government. All these concerns involve and affect Egypt, and Egyptian attitudes toward them will affect the evolution of these problems within the region.

The Algerian crisis, now effectively a civil war with little evidence that the level of violence will subside in the near term, has extremely serious implications for the North African region. Its outcome, most likely a compromise between the Algerian army and moderate Islamist forces, will affect regional security. Depending on the degree of success enjoyed by the Islamists, the Algerian denouement may also affect political attitudes and developments in the Middle East itself. Just as the 1979 Islamic Revolution in Iran rendered Islamic radicalism a licit political ideology at the popular level, an Islamist victory in Algeria would have the same effect, forcing governments to take a stand for or against such developments.

Egypt has had its own Islamist problems, although it seems most unlikely that the extremist Gamaa Islamiyya could seriously threaten government stability. More moderate movements, such as the Ikhwan al-Muslimin, however, can affect the political climate quite significantly. Despite being officially disdained, the MB is important because of the popular pressure it can bring to bear on institutions such as the al-Azhar Mosque-University and on the formal political process. Al-Azhar is a major source of government legitimization, and the Egyptian Government pays attention to its attitudes, even though it also controls its activities.

For the Egyptian authorities, therefore, any solution in Algeria that accepts significant Islamist participation in power will be very difficult to accept, unless the groups involved have not been involved in or openly espoused violence. Groups such as an-Nahda and Hamas would not be tolerated. On this issue, Egypt would move closer to Tunisia, which has taken a very hard line over tolerance for Islamists, than to Morocco, which has been more ambivalent. It is most unlikely that the Algerian crisis will spill over the country's borders directly. However, any degree of Islamist success will, like the Iranian revolution in 1979, create an atmosphere throughout the region in which political solutions originally excluded, such as compromise with Islamists, may become political realities.

Egypt will continue to take a very close interest in the domestic affairs of Libya and to act as interlocutor between Tripoli and the West. This will certainly be true while the Qadhafi regime remains in power, and there is little evidence to suggest its imminent demise. Ironically, Libyan dependence on Egyptian protection means that the Qadhafi regime, long seen as a source of instability in the Middle East and North Africa, has now become a force for regional stability, an irony not lost on Cairo even if it is not fully perceived elsewhere. This will be the case, particularly if the incipient Islamist threat to the Qadhafi regime materializes—a development Egypt will actively oppose. Egypt will, however, continue to press Libya to moderate its policies, both at home and abroad. If Egypt's application to join the UMA is ultimately successful and the organization itself eventually recovers from its current moribund condition, Egypt's economic domination of that organization, and thereby of the Libyan domestic market, seems inevitable.

The peace process is now an arena in which Egypt is determined to recover its central role in parallel with but independently of the United States, by demonstrating its ability to moderate Arab responses and its continued influence over Palestinian movements. It is also an arena in which friction between Egyptian and American objectives may emerge more clearly, particularly if the Clinton administration (or its successor) maintains its preferential support for Israel's objectives. The Israeli Government is aware of Egyptian irritations in the peace process, as was made abundantly clear during President Weizmann's visit to Cairo in early 1995 and by President Mubarak's threat to cancel the Middle East and North Africa (MENA) economic summit in Cairo in November 1996. It is not clear to what extent the new Likud-dominated Netanyahu government is prepared to be influenced by this stance, since it seems to believe that intrinsic American support will persist, whatever policy options it adopts. Nonetheless, the West needs to pay greater attention to Egyptian anxieties and objectives in this respect, as the maintenance of a meaningful peace throughout the region—even if a comprehensive agreement is reached between Israel and the Palestinians, as well as between Israel and other Arab states—will depend heavily on Egyptian goodwill.

In the Gulf, Egypt's current attempt to create a strategic alliance with Saudi Arabia suggests a reworking of the Damascus Declaration concept. However, it is not yet clear to what extent Egypt is ready to commit forces to this objective nor, indeed, to what extent Saudi Arabia would be prepared to accept them. In any case, the success of such an alliance also depends on Saudi attitudes toward the peace process and toward the apparent eagerness of other Gulf states to speed up the process, against Egyptian preferences. If the alliance does become meaningful, then

Egyptian attitudes toward "dual containment" could also be significant. At present, Egypt has rejected close relations with Iran because of Iranian links with Sudan and because of alleged Iranian support for Islamist activism in North Africa and Egypt itself. This situation is unlikely to change, particularly in view of Iranian rearmament and suspected nuclear plans. Egypt is prepared for low-level diplomatic contacts with the Saddam Husain regime but is not yet ready to flout the sanctions regime nor Saudi preferences. Popular attitudes in Egypt may modify this policy because of their sympathy for the parlous situation of the Iraqi population— particularly if the operation of U.N. Security Council Resolution 986, "Oil for Food" (which allows for increasing amounts of Iraqi exports of crude under strict international supervision in return for reparations payments, food and humanitarian supplies) is significantly hampered by Western initiatives.

The remaining area of political concern for Egypt will be Sudan and the Horn of Africa. In part, this concern is related to East African water policy. The anxiety will grow if upstream riverine states, such as Ethiopia, introduce major irrigation schemes as they threaten to do, or if Sudan expands the Jongli Canal system and associated irrigation works,[8] thus reducing Nile water flows to Egypt. More importantly, however, Egypt will continue to be concerned over the Islamist domination of the Sudan Government, where relations are unlikely to improve so long as the Bashir regime and Dr. Turabi's National Islamic Front remain in power. Issues such as the Halaib Triangle dispute[9] can always be used by either side to sour relations. This region, however, will be marginal to American policy concerns, despite the recent U.N. Security Council sanctions imposed on Sudan.

With respect to U.S.-Egyptian relations, there are four major potential areas of friction in policy. All four require close monitoring to ensure that they do not exceed manageable limits.

- The danger of a breakup of the Iraqi state, to the advantage of Iran, and popular concerns over the welfare of the Iraqi population, are important to Egypt.

- The Egyptian Government will be under increasing domestic pressure to respond to any renewed crisis in Bosnia if the Dayton Accord fails. This response will manifest itself in ways that run counter both to American and European policy, despite their divergences, because it will seek to restore Muslim hegemony over the Bosnian state, despite Serbian and Croat opposition. In doing this, Egypt will be supported by other Muslim states, but its policies will largely be the result of domestic popular pressure, rather than sophisticated diplomatic calculation. However, the growing popular sense of Western attitudes of double standards with respect to the Muslim world may circumvent diplomacy for the sake of domestic consensus.
- Egypt is unhappy with Western pressure over its chemical and unconventional weapons program. Such pressure is resented because of what Egypt perceives to be Western refusal to apply similar pressure on Israel to liquidate its own nuclear arsenal. If regional tensions increase, Egyptian obduracy over the issue will also strengthen unless Western statesmen seek to redress the strategic balance by trying to rein in Israel's military ambitions.
- There is growing anxiety in Egypt over the future of American foreign aid. If such aid is reduced or removed, as seems increasingly likely, but is maintained for Israel, the Egyptian Government will find itself in a very difficult situation, no matter its success in economic reform. In this case, domestic public opinion is unlikely to tolerate retention of the close diplomatic relationship with Washington as the cornerstone of Egyptian foreign policy.

If American policy makers perceive Egypt as essential to American policy in the Middle East, these matters will require increasingly urgent attention. The Egyptian Government will feel that its own foreign policy initiatives will carry increasingly little domestic conviction unless there is an appropriate Western response. This will be particularly true if the peace process between Israel and the Palestinians falters, as seems likely, so that Israel, while achieving formal peace agreements with surrounding

Arab states, faces a cordon of permanent insecurity around its own borders. It will also apply if Egypt fails to reassert its role as the pivotal state in the Middle East, to act as a link between subregional hegemons such as Syria and Saudi Arabia, and Algeria and Morocco.

Economic Development

Egypt is currently undergoing a major economic restructuring program under IMF and World Bank tutelage. In this it is little different from other states in the region and fits within the general framework of Western economic policy. However, the demographic and social reality in Egypt raises very acute problems over the character and speed of its economic reform. Too much hardship engendered for Egypt's poorer classes could result in destabilization and a growth of Islamic radicalism, permanently damaging prospects for economic growth. Unless attention is paid to this aspect of the process, considerable tension will be engendered between Egypt and its Western partners. In this respect, the experiences of the former Soviet bloc and North Africa should be kept in mind; there is a balance to be found between economic restructuring and political stability.

The nonoil producing countries of the Middle East and North Africa are least likely to benefit from the reforms undertaken by the Uruguay Round of the General Agreement on Tariffs and Trade (GATT). In fact, recent calculations suggest that southern Mediterranean states will suffer a $600 million annual reduction in regional trade as a result—ironically enough, the only region of the world to suffer such adverse effects, largely because of the increased penetrability of its markets and adverse terms of trade for its exports. This is an additional reason for a more sensitive, differentiated approach to the role of economic restructuring in Egypt. The United States must also consider very carefully the implications of removing its annual aid to Egypt, both in military and civilian arenas. The current demands in Congress for such reductions may well harm Egypt's willingness to participate in the process of regional economic reconstruction with Israel and Jordan, if the peace process achieves viable and acceptable permanent results.

There is also a need to encourage regional economic cooperation in such organizations as the UMA or the proposed economic federation in the Levant to be created as part of the peace process among Israel, Jordan, Egypt, and a future Palestinian entity. Egypt clearly must be a key member in these developments. American policy makers should consider whether Egypt should not be encouraged to strengthen its links with the EU, even though this would not be immediately to the advantage of the United States. It would strengthen both regional peace and economic development. These economic links raise the wider issue of what attitude is to be adopted toward two opposed tendencies within the world economy—one for globalization and the other for regionalization. While financial flows have tended to encourage global integration, commercial issues are increasingly dominated by regional considerations, despite the GATT and the new World Trade Organization (WTO).

Indeed, in terms of geoeconomics, Egypt's most likely location will be inside an expanded European economic arena. It seems likely that the EU will extend its own economic umbrella across the Mediterranean in an effort to integrate southern Mediterranean states into the European economic system. The process has already begun with the proposed restricted free-trade area for Israel, Tunisia, and Morocco and the customs union with Turkey; there are promises of a similar arrangement for Egypt in the near future. The possibility exists, however, for similar bilateral arrangements between Egypt and the United States, as already exist for Israel, quite outside any future North Atlantic economic community. Such a proposal was suggested by President Clinton in 1994, but no action was taken. Egypt needs encouragement to exploit new opportunities for economic growth; it was highlighted by the World Bank in 1991 as one of the few middle-income developing countries with the appropriate infrastructure to attract direct adequate private foreign investment to stimulate economic development.[10]

Ideological Evolution and Cultural Assertion

A further consequence of economic restructuring and the integration of Egypt into a globalized and regionalized economy relates to how its population will respond to parallel integration into the increasing globalization of Western demotic and high culture. There is no doubt that Middle Eastern elites, including those in Egypt, are prepared to accept and operate within the underlying assumptions of Western corporate culture. Many of these elites are also prepared to accept the underlying cultural assumptions behind concepts, such as issues of human rights and democratization. Demotic cultural manifestations can capture a wider audience as well, as the spread of Western "pop" and media culture indicates.

However, it must also be recognized that large components of the populations of Middle Eastern states are excluded from the immediate benefits of economic reform and in consequence are often hostile to it. As a result, they are also likely to reject what they perceive as the cultural concomitants, as well as turning to indigenous cultural archetypes instead. This was a problem originally highlighted by the "dependencia" theorists of the 1960s, although they underestimated the complexity of the issue.[11] With the growth of direct private foreign investment as the major vehicle for economic development in the developing world, the issue of this type of cultural dependence and indigenous resistance to it has been put on the political agenda as well. Indeed, the Asian economic crisis has highlighted this political problem. In the Islamic world, this means a spontaneous reference to Islam as the underlying principle of social and political life, as well as of indigenous cultural expression, once other ideological options are perceived to have failed. In short, populist rejection of the concomitants of economic development, particularly if benefits are unevenly distributed, will be legitimized by recourse to Islamic precepts. The consequent confrontation between "westernized" elites and "populist" Islamists is uniquely acute because of the normative assumption of the political and communal role of Islam. This Islamist role has already been rendered politically legitimate by innovative political interpretations of Islamic values and doctrine by modern Islamists since Sayyid Qutb.[12]

The horizontal cultural divisions within Middle Eastern populations created by this process, which mirror the vertical divisions created inside specific national societies as a result of uneven development and the older patterns of elite stratification, present the outside world with a very difficult dilemma. Either the indigenous response is accepted at face value, whether or not it is acceptable in principle, or it is rejected on the grounds of its moral or rational unacceptability. In the latter case, such an approach, whether explicit or implicit, intensifies the danger of alienation between indigenous and Western cultural and political paradigms. This seems to be an issue policy makers have not yet absorbed, except in one respect—the attitude to be adopted toward regional Islamist movements.

Two policy alternatives seem to exist at present: either complete rejection of any dialogue with the representatives of such ideologies (the preferred approach of France, with support from the Algerian, Tunisian, and to a lesser extent, Egyptian Governments), or an expressed willingness to deal with Islamist movements, provided that they eschew violence and terrorism (the American approach in Egypt and Algeria). It is not yet clear, however, whether such movements can completely abandon the option of violence, or whether they can accept, as Rashid Ghannoushi[13] claims, a pluralistic political system that could involve the loss of power through the ballot box.[14] The caution expressed here arises because such movements have a very real ideological problem to face. They must determine the extent to which they are prepared to accept secular, in place of divine, authority and thus allow the operation of effective democratic political systems.

Egypt, because of its ideological history, embodies these dilemmas in a particularly acute form. Both the experience of Nasserism and the widespread traditional pattern of Islamic observance contribute toward this situation. In addition, Egypt's past role as the source of and major arena for the Sunni Islamist movements of the modern Middle East is an additional and significant factor in this respect. The Egyptian Government will require support and encouragement in its attempts to resolve the dilemma involved in this choice. Furthermore, Cairo's success or failure in this endeavor will have considerable repercussions within the region as a whole. One of the major considerations in this respect is that, although informed opinion considers (probably mistakenly) that Islamism is a waning political force, there is also plenty of evidence of the lack of popular support for Egypt's governmental structure and personnel. This reality will also have to be addressed by outside states formulating their own policies toward Egypt. Nor should the latent potential for a revival of Arab nationalism there be ignored, particularly if the peace process fails to advance satisfactorily. Arab nationalism may seem discredited today, but it still has an atavistic appeal for many who may well form the majority and who reject the Islamist alternative. They are to be found among the intelligentsia, as the sudden resurgence of support for Nasserism in Egypt recently makes clear. Nor are they confined to Egypt, for nationalist traditions have a far wider purview throughout the Arab Middle East. Indeed, they are even coopted by modern political Islam as a means of increasing its appeal at a popular level within the petty bourgeoisie.

Conclusion

Egypt is today reasserting its regional role, despite the profound geopolitical changes that have swept the Middle East and North Africa since 1990. At the same time, it is unlikely that its old dominant position can be recovered, simply because of the way in which the region is now structured. Instead, Egypt will seek to become the core state that links the subregions that make up the Middle East and North Africa. To this end, Egypt has been seeking an alliance with Saudi Arabia and Syria and new links with North Africa. Both could be of real importance, particularly to regional security policy, in the Mediterranean, the Levant, and the Gulf regions.

Egypt, because of its demographic and cultural dominance within the Arab world, continues to be a touchstone for major currents now sweeping the region. Indeed, the way in which many critical issues are resolved in the domestic Egyptian arena will determine the way in which they are resolved in the region overall. Outside powers, particularly those concerned with access to Middle

Eastern resources such as oil, or with issues such as regional stability, cannot ignore the importance of Egypt's future role, given its political status and its control of the Suez Canal. Egypt will, as a consequence, be the dominant factor in future Middle Eastern and North African policy formulation, with particular relevance for the Arab world.

This dominant role will continue to apply, even if the current peace process fails to realize its original potential. There is little doubt that Israel will achieve a situation of formalized peace with surrounding Arab states that will permit the initiation of economic relations (insofar as this is of interest to Israel), even if diplomatic links remain limited. The Gulf States, with their energy resources and financial capacities, might appear to be the most appropriate partners for future Western economic cooperation. The potential size of the Egyptian market, however, together with its links into neighboring regions, is bound to make it an essential component of future regional economic development. Even if these limited horizons fail to be achieved, Egyptian attitudes are certain to dominate future attitudes in the Arab world. The United States, therefore, cannot ignore the primordial importance of Egypt as its major ally in the region.

The future relationship, however, may not be based on quite the same degree of trust as in the past, given the likely changes in American-Egyptian relations as the United States seeks to reduce its direct involvement in global affairs. Washington may not be able to count on the kind of automatic support for its policy initiatives that has been the case in recent years. To a large extent, the relationship will depend on the way in which the United States perceives its future interests in the region as a whole, and in turn that perception will depend in large part on the attitude it adopts toward Israel and the future of the peace process.

Notes

1. T. Y. Ismael, *International Relations of the Contemporary Middle East: a Study in World Politics* (Syracuse, NY: Syracuse University Press 1986), 3-13, 41-65.

2. E. G. H. Joffe, "Amman, the Underlying Reality," *Arab Affairs* 5 (Spring 1988): 6-16

3. *World Economic Outlook, May 1992* (Washington:International Monetary Fund, 1992), 35; *Economic Review: Common Issues and Interrepublic Relations in the Former USSR* (Washington: International Monetary Fund, 1992); and *Statistical Handbook: States of the Former USSR* (Washington: World Bank, 1992), 3-417.

4. E. G. H. Joffe, "The Implications of the 'New World Order' for the Middle East and North Africa," in *The Middle East and North Africa, 1993*, ed. S. Chapin (London: Europa Publications, 1992), 6-7.

5. The Conference on Security and Cooperation in the Mediterranean (CSCM) was a confidence-building initiative proposed by Spain and Italy in 1990 based on the experience of the Conference on Security and Cooperation in Europe (CSCE). It was stillborn, partly because of its complexity and partly because of the Kuwait crisis. The "Five plus Five" was an alternative security- and confidence-building proposal made by France in the wake of the collapse of the CSCM initiative, designed to deal only with the western Mediterranean and to involve the Maghreb states of Libya, Tunisia, Algeria, Morocco, and Mauritania—all members of the Arab Maghreb Union (UMA)—together with France, Italy, Spain, and Portugal (Malta was later added to the list). The Mediterranean Forum was an Egyptian initiative, started in Alexandria in July 1994, which widened the "Five plus Five" forum to include Egypt and transferred the initiative itself into southern Mediterranean hands. All these initiatives have now been overtaken by the second basket of the Barcelona Conference proposals and the French proposals for a regionwide "Stability Pact."

6. The Trevi Group is an informal group of European interior ministers who meet regularly to plan Europewide initiatives on terrorism and regional security. It was created in the wake of the Red Brigades campaign in Italy in the 1970s. The Shengen Accords were negotiated by an inner group within the European Union, formed by Germany, France, Italy, and the Benelux countries, to remove physical impediments to free movement within the Union after the Single European Market came into operation in 1993. They came into effect in 1995, but security concerns in some states, such as Britain, have delayed their full application in these states.

7. The Damascus Declaration in March 1991 set up a new security system for the Arab Gulf States, whereby Egypt and Syria would have provided military forces to be paid for by the six Gulf Cooperation Council member-states in the wake of the war against Iraq, hence its alternative designation as the "Six plus Two" agreement. Despite their formal

agreement, the Gulf states chose bilateral defense and security agreements with European states and the United States.

8. The Jongli Canal system was built in the 1970s and early 1980s as a bypass system for the River Nile as it passes through the massive Sudd swamps of Southern Sudan. It was designed to improve Nile water flow, as 60 per cent of the upper Nile is lost through evaporation in the swamps.

9. The Halaib Triangle is the name given to the triangular northern tip of Sudanese territory abutting Egypt and the Red Sea. It is actually Egyptian territory ceded to Sudan for administrative convenience because it forms the traditional grazing ground for a Sudanese tribe. In recent years, Sudan has tried to claim sovereignty over the region and has been warned by Egypt that this will be opposed. The two countries are, in theory, in the process of mediating their differences over this and other nearby pockets of territory.

10. *World Development Report: the Challenge of Development,* The World Bank (Oxford: Oxford University Press, 1991), 24.

11. B. R. J. Jones, *Globalization and Interdependence in the International Political Economy* (London: Pinter Press, 1995), 31, 204.

12. Y. Choueiri, *Islamic Fundamentalism* (London: Pinter Press, 1990), 23-24.

13. Rashid Ghannoushi is the founder of the moderate Tunisian Islamist movement, *An-Nahda*, and one of the three leading ideologues of moderate Sunni Islamism today. He lives in political exile in Britain.

14. N. Ayubi, *Political Islam: Religion and Politics in the Arab World* (London: Routlege, 1991), 139-140.

MANAGING AMBIVALENCE:
Egypt's Changing Regional Environment

Ali Hillal Dessouki

Egypt is not likely to develop either a grand, encompassing strategy or a regional blueprint for action. Both would be premature. Rather, Egypt will develop policies to deal with specific issues and problems as they arise.

The Context of Regional Change

In identifying areas of potential change and their consequences for Egypt, three major factors must be taken into consideration. First, Egypt's new regional security environment, like those elsewhere, is characterized by accelerated change and a fundamental restructuring of its component elements. The result has been a situation of fluidity. The end of the Cold War, the collapse of the Soviet Union, the consequences of the Iraqi invasion of Kuwait, and the ongoing peace process between Israel and Arab states have all contributed to this fluidity. By definition, such an environment contains the features associated with transition and transformation. Such a situation poses new questions and problems for foreign policy elites and decisionmakers in the region. At the same time, it

Dr. Ali Hillal Dessouki is a professor of political science and Dean, Faculty of Economics and Political Science, Cairo University. He has also taught at Princeton University, UCLA, and McGill University and has published extensively.

creates new challenges and potential sources of threat, as well as novel opportunities.

Second, Egypt is a status quo power with an important interest in regional stability. The goal of regional stability is motivated primarily by domestic factors. In the face of population increases and continuing economic difficulties, Egypt is committed to economic development. Regional stability provides an environment conducive to investment, tourism and multilateral economic cooperation. All are essential if Egypt's economic reform program is to succeed.

Third, Egypt has traditionally pursued a regional role in several directions, reflecting its diverse and multidimensional interests. These have extended into the Fertile Crescent, the Gulf, the Maghreb (North Africa), the Nile Valley, and the Mediterranean. From an Egyptian perspective, these directions are not perceived in terms of either/or but rather as embodying different vital interests that complement one another. The degree of Egyptian activism in each sphere depends upon Egypt's resources and its changing priorities at different periods of time.

Given the complexity and ambivalence of the new regional environment, Egypt's multiple interests, and the pace of political change over the past decade, Egypt is not likely to develop either a grand, encompassing strategy or a regional blueprint for action. Both would be premature. Rather, Egypt will develop policies to deal with specific issues and problems as they arise.

In the context of these general considerations, it is now appropriate to identify and analyze some of the major potential regional changes that Egypt may face in the coming decade.

Developments in the Peace Process

The year 1994 was a turning point in the effort to reach a settlement of the Palestinian problem and the Arab-Israeli conflict. The establishment of a Palestinian Authority in Gaza and Jericho, the signing of a Jordanian-Israeli Agreement, and the convening of the First Economic Summit in Casablanca (followed by a second in Amman in 1995, a third in Cairo in 1996, and a fourth in Doha in 1997) were landmarks of progress. At the level of multilateral talks, different committees continued to discuss regional issues such as water sharing, arms control, economic development, and refugee issues in detail in meetings held in Oman, Tunisia, Qatar, and Egypt. Both Tunisia and Morocco opened liaison officers in Israel, a step in the direction of diplomatic recognition. The year concluded with a surprise visit by Prime Minister Yitzhak Rabin to Oman in December 1994.

A major remaining obstacle in the peace process is completion of the Israeli-Syrian track. While both parties have emphasized their commitment to peace, they continue to quarrel over the modalities and timing of Israeli withdrawal, and each endeavors to improve its negotiating position to the maximum. In December 1994, talks between the two countries were resumed in Washington with the participation of high-ranking Israeli and Syrian military officers, and in January 1995, U.S. Secretary of Defense William Perry inspected the Golan Heights from the air. But despite these developments, by 1998 there was little movement forward. Because of the Israeli-Syrian rift, the Israeli-Lebanese track has also remained unsettled.

In the future, as in the past, the peace process is likely to proceed in several different directions. Based on existing evidence, the impact of the process on Egypt is likely to be mixed. On the one hand, Egyptian leadership takes pride in the fact that history has vindicated its strategic commitment to peace. By 1998, all but a few Arab states (Iraq and Libya) had followed Egypt's path; those who had not were isolated. Egypt's position has also been strengthened by its successful diplomacy, which has been instrumental in identifying elements of agreement between adversarial parties and in explaining to different sides the constraints on others. Egypt has also been vocal in identifying potential threats to the peace process. For example, during a visit to a number of European countries in late 1994, President Mubarak highlighted the problems facing the Palestinian Authority and the failure of Western powers to deliver on promises of economic aid and assistance.

On the other hand, Egypt's foreign policy elite, led by Foreign Minister Amr Mousa, has manifested a distinct sense of unease in the face of a phenomenon they are calling "an Arab rush toward Israel." In an interview in July 1996, Amr Mousa stated that he was "concerned about pressures to reach a peace that benefits one party at the expense of the other. This cannot work." The new Middle East cannot precede peace, but must be the reward of peace.[1] At the same time, Mousa has alluded to Egypt's leadership position and the impossibility of marginalizing its role. At a speech at the Casablanca Summit, he referred to the importance of Egypt's role in "regulating regional interactions." Although Israel has sought to ease Egyptian worries, it has had no great success on this score.

Egyptian anxiety over the peace process is related to two sets of concerns, the first being the substance of the peace accord, its potential impact on regional stability, and its requirements. Egypt is trying to achieve a comprehensive and sustainable peace in the region that encompasses military, political, and economic dimensions. The military dimension calls for a true military balance in the region; the political dimension, for Israeli withdrawal from occupied territories and, in the second phase, Israeli-Palestinian negotiations for the final status of the territories; the economic dimension, for regional cooperation and development. With respect to the second two dimensions and their interrelationship, it was Egypt's understanding that regional economic cooperation would take place only after the resolution of political and territorial issues. Egypt feels that Israel is attempting to circumvent this understanding. The Casablanca Meeting and the subsequent summits are evidence of Israel's desire to reap the fruits of peace before making the concessions necessary to achieve it.

The other set of concerns relates to the military balance in the region and more specifically, the issue of Israeli nuclear power and the threat it may pose to Arab states in a postsettlement era. At first, Israel was reluctant to discuss the nuclear issue in multilateral talks. Later, it refused to commit itself on the future of its nuclear arsenal. In 1994, Egypt offered a number of proposals that would allow Israel to declare its intentions after the conclusion of a peace treaty with Syria. None of these met with success. Instead, the Israeli press criticized Foreign Minister Amr Mousa for his position on the issue. Finally, President Mubarak publicly supported his Foreign Minister's position and promised that Egypt would not sign the Non-Proliferation Treaty under the present circumstances.

Egypt's fears over the military balance were intensified by a declaration in January 1995 by Prime Minister Yitzhak Rabin that Israel might resort to war. President Mubarak expressed his sorrow over this declaration, and these differences have put strains on the Egyptian-Israeli relationship, already rather cool. Meanwhile, Egypt began moving in a different direction, attempting to achieve more coordination among a number of key Arab states. In late December 1994, Egypt convened a summit meeting in Alexandria that included Saudi Arabia, Syria, and Egypt. Since that time, stagnation on the peace process has cooled Egypt's relations with Israel even further.

These events have created new Egyptian anxieties and deepened clouds in Israeli-Egyptian relations. They are likely to continue in the next few years, with the potential to impact on U.S.-Egyptian relations in significant ways.

Inter-Arab Relations and Conflicts

In the post-Cold War era, inter-Arab relations have been characterized by diplomatic inconstancy, flexible relationships, and a pattern of shifting alliances. In this uncertain environment, Egypt has had to cope with the vagaries of the peace process and mounting domestic problems, including the rise of violence-prone political groups. Not surprisingly, Egypt has seen Arab state cooperation as important to its security and has acted as a catalyst for consensus. Thus Egypt mediated the Saudi-Qatari border dispute in 1993; sought to improve relations with Jordan and Yemen, two states ostracized for their pro-Iraqi position in 1990; and continues to have good relations with most of the Nile Valley States, particularly Ethiopia.

In the coming few years, this fluidity is likely to persist. A polarization between two blocs of Arab states is unlikely, but might occur if a militant Islamic group should take power in an Arab state, such as Algeria or Yemen, precipitating the establishment of an alliance of Islamic governments (Sudan, Algeria, Yemen) supported by Iran. While such a scenario is unlikely, it would nevertheless impose new constraints on Egypt. The emergence of such a bloc would give a boost to Islamic militant groups throughout the region and within Egypt itself. Given domestic public opinion in Egypt, such a contingency would surely make the Egyptian Government reluctant to cooperate with Israel or the United States. As a result, relations with both could cool considerably.

Precisely because it needs support from outside and a cooperative regional environment for development, Egypt is concerned with putting the Arab house in order. It is paradoxical that Arab States are showing more enthusiasm for reaching a settlement with Israel than for settling their own rifts and petty disputes. Inaugurating a new parliamentary session in November 1994, President Mubarak emphasized the importance of Arab solidarity and cooperation. In December 1994, the declaration of the Alexandria summit once again referred to the need to energize the work of the Arab League and its institutions. President Mubarak made sure to specify that these efforts were not directed against Israel; rather, they constitute another element in Egypt's perception of the kind of regional peace and stability it needs for its own domestic security.

In the context of regional cooperation, the future of Iraq and its role in the region are crucial. Egypt's position toward Iraq includes several components. First, Egypt supports the territorial integrity of Iraq as a necessary condition for stability in the Gulf. Iraq is a regional power that must eventually have a place in the region. Second, Egypt insists that the Iraqi ruling regime must comply with all U.N. Security Council resolutions honestly and sincerely and refrain from posing threats to the Gulf states, particularly Kuwait. Third, in case of a renewed Iraqi threat to Kuwait, Egypt would not hesitate to support Kuwait. Finally, Egypt has an interest in the region to its west. Egypt has close relations with Libya for economic and strategic reasons. The long frontiers between the two countries make cooperation to prevent the smuggling of arms and infiltrators essential. Equally beneficial to Egypt, the Libyan Government plays an active role in combating the activities of militant Islamic groups on its territory. In addition, Egypt has a strong economic interest in protecting the position of Egyptians working in Libya as well as Libyan-Egyptian trade and joint ventures. On the political front, the Egyptian link to Libya has been instrumental in moderating Libyan positions.

Another manifestation of Egyptian interest in this region is its attendance, as an observer, of the Foreign Ministers' Meeting of the Arab Maghreb Union (AMU). The move is symbolic in nature, demonstrating Egypt's role as a "link" between the Arab Mashriq (Levant) and the Arab Maghreb (North Africa).

In the next decade these policy trends are likely to continue with different emphases as different issues emerge. From an Egyptian perspective, inter-Arab relations are neither contradictory to nor a substitute for broader regional and international cooperation. Each set of relationships represents a level of cooperation with its own rationale and dynamics.

Domestic Problems and the Rise of Militant Opposition

One feature of the 1980s was the emergence, in most Arab states, of political groups opposing governments in the name of Islam, a phenomenon loosely called "Islamic fundamentalism," the "Islamic resurgence," or simply "Islamism." While these groups are an indigenous phenomenon par excellence, they have increasingly acquired a regional dimension. They support one another, and the gains of one group provide reflected prestige and encouragement to others. During the Iraqi invasion of Kuwait, leaders from a number of these groups established a common delegation, which visited Baghdad, Riyadh, and Amman.

Because of this new link, a change of government in one Arab state is likely to have broader regional impact than was the case earlier. Algeria is usually cited as a prime candidate for such a change. Nevertheless, such a scenario cannot be predicted with any certainty; rather, the existing stalemate between the military-backed government and the Islamist forces is likely to continue. However, such a regional change is one contingency that would affect Egypt's security, at least indirectly. As a result, Egypt has been active in forging security cooperation among Arab governments to prevent such an occurrence. The role of Egypt's Minister of Interior, General Hasan al-Alfi, at the January 1995 meeting of the Arab Ministers of Interior is a case in point.

Managing the Islamic challenge may become one area of contention in U.S.-Egyptian relations. In some instances, the United

States has advocated compromise and a dialogue with some (nonviolent) Islamic groups. Some American diplomatic contacts with Islamist groups have become a source of concern to Egyptian officials. Given its disastrous experience in Iran, where an Islamic revolutionary regime took U.S. diplomats hostage and overturned decades of established links with the country, the United States is probably trying to avoid a repetition of that experience by maintaining links with some of these groups. Incumbent regimes are likely to tolerate such links only as long as they are not perceived to be encouraging their growth.

Egypt and the United States in the New Geoeconomic Environment

It has been argued that the world is moving from geopolitics to geoeconomics. With the end of the Cold War, military strategic concerns are likely to lessen in importance. Instead, more policy emphasis will be given to economic considerations. Evidence demonstrates the accuracy of this assertion, and Egypt is already adjusting its regional role to accommodate these circumstances.

This regional change, however, is not entirely unfavorable to Egypt. Egypt is not without elements of geoeconomic influence: it possesses a large, potential market with a great deal of purchasing power; it has an elaborate infrastructure that has yet to be fully utilized; it has mobile and skilled manpower; and it has a definite competitive advantage in the culture industry. These can and will be used to strengthen Egypt's regional role in favor of stability and moderation. Both factors favor U.S. interests. Moreover, the U.S.-Egyptian relationship now has a strong economic component.

Despite strong cooperation, however, U.S.-Egyptian relations cannot be divorced from a regional context. It is not likely that the two countries will see eye to eye on all regional issues, especially those of geostrategic and political matters—e.g, the peace process, Libya, and the nuclear issue. As with other partners, it is only natural that their views will continue to converge and diverge based on differing perspectives. What is important, however, in the more fluid international environment, is that these differences be debated and resolved through diplomatic means and in the context of the ties that bind the two countries together.

Note

1. Robert Satloff and Daniel Pipes, "Amr M. Mousa: A Nationalist Vision for Egypt," *Middle East Quarterly* 3, no. 3 (September 1996): 61, 62.

U.S.-EGYPTIAN DEFENSE RELATIONS

Chas. W. Freeman, Jr.

The Egyptian-American partnership needs a new strategic underpinning and focus. That focus should be on Egyptian-American partnership in the maintenance of the regional order and stability beyond the Levant. . . . Such a partnership and focus could be the basis for long-sustained American domestic political support for appropriate military assistance to Egypt.

As the end of the century nears, the defense relationship between the United States and Egypt faces challenges and uncertain transitions. Some of these derive from changed international and regional circumstances, some from the contraction of spending by the United States on its Armed Forces and economic and military assistance to foreign allies and friends. Still others arise from changed missions for the Egyptian Armed Forces and the requirement for long-deferred adjustments in the military's force structure and role in Egyptian society.

Ambassador Chas. W. Freeman has been Chairman of the Board of Projects International, Inc., since 1995. Previously he had an extensive career in the U.S. Government, including the positions of ambassador to Saudi Arabia and Assistant Secretary of Defense for International Security Affairs, where he was responsible for managing U.S. defense relations with all regions of the world except the former Soviet Union.

Origins of the Relationship

The U.S. defense relationship with Egypt was born in the circumstances of U.S. global rivalry with the former Soviet Union and the historic but initially shaky Camp David Accords of 1978. The first U.S. military assistance to Egypt was part of a massively funded military-assistance effort that benefitted American allies and friends throughout the globe. The motivations for this assistance effort were more political than military; its political base of support in the United States came from Israel, its American partisans, and others concerned to sustain the Arab-Israeli peace process, not from the U.S. defense establishment.

All these conditions have changed or are in the process of changing in the closing years of the 1990s. The Soviet Union is no more. American foreign policy has a regional, rather than global focus, and the willingness of the American people to fund a global role is increasingly uncertain. U.S. military-assistance programs for all countries other than Israel and Egypt (plus a token contribution to Jordan) t have already been phased out. As Congress strives to cut the deficit while meeting long-neglected domestic requirements, its attention is targeted increasingly on foreign aid. As the peace process strains for a finish line, the pressure on the budget will increase. As Egypt loses its unique status as an Arab neighbor at peace with Israel, the emphasis of Israelis and their American supporters on assistance to Egypt can no longer be taken for granted. Finally, the focus of U.S.-Egyptian political cooperation has been the management of the Arab-Israeli peace process. When peace comes, the two countries must find equally compelling common purposes to replace this task as the basis for continuing close ties.

New Emphasis of American Policy

The focus of American military concern in the region has meanwhile shifted to peacekeeping operations and the security of the Gulf. This offers the promise of new directions for U.S.-Egyptian military cooperation. At present, however, this remains more promise than reality.

Peacekeeping

Egypt has already emerged as a significant participant in a number of peacekeeping operations of direct concern to the United States. Egypt's willingness to stay the course in Somalia reflects many factors, including its traditional interests in the Horn and in the security of Arab League members, as well as its leading role in the international community and the United Nations. The Egyptian role in peacekeeping in Africa has been much appreciated and directly supported by the United States. In Bosnia, Egypt's military participation in the U.N. Protection Force (the U.N. force engaged in enforcing the cease-fire in the former Yugoslavia) has been similarly valued by the United States, which has a position on the issues that is closer to Egypt's than to many of its European allies. Egypt's increasingly active role in the management of security issues in Africa and in Islamic councils adds to its military importance to the United States. That importance rests mainly, however, on Egypt's status as the only Arab partner of the United States able to contribute on a large scale to joint military operations beyond its borders.

The Arab Gulf

In the era of the Shah, U.S. policy had assigned Iran the role of primary manager of challenges to Gulf security from within the region itself. The collapse of imperial Iran and U.S. estrangement from Tehran has forced the United States to undertake a much more direct role in the Gulf than it had earlier contemplated. The Camp David Accords and the forging of new defense ties with Egypt, Oman, and Somalia followed closely on these events. It was not, however, until the Iran-Iraq war was succeeded by the war for Kuwait that the United States looked seriously to Egypt as a partner in Gulf security. Egyptian participation in the coalition effort to liberate Kuwait made a major political and significant military contribution to its success. This naturally focused American attention on partnership with Egypt for the defense of the Gulf.

At the same time, however, the Gulf War and its aftermath revealed numerous difficulties in the way of such a role for the Egyptian Armed Forces. Egypt's inability to deploy quickly or on its own to the Gulf region during Operation *Desert Shield* is a military case in point. So also are incompatibilities of military doctrine, planning processes, and operational concepts between American and Egyptian forces that hampered their cooperation in Operation *Desert Storm*.

Moreover, the appearance of wartime unity was quickly succeeded by postwar bickering among the Gulf Arabs and other members of the Gulf War coalition. The Gulf Cooperation Council (GCC) has failed to contrive a solid mechanism for military cooperation among its members. In the absence of such a mechanism, effective military cooperation by the GCC with Egypt or other non-Gulf Arab states is difficult to imagine. Although some Gulf armed forces now participate bilaterally in U.S.-sponsored regional exercises involving Egypt, little bilateral military cooperation has developed among Egypt, Saudi Arabia, and other Gulf states.

This failure is the result of many factors. Egypt lacks the resources to do much on its own even if the Gulf Arabs were more welcoming. Neither the GCC nor the United States has been willing to fund an Egyptian role in Gulf defense. The Gulf Arabs, for their part, are apparently content to assign the United States the primary role in their defense. The Americans combine great military capability with limited ambitions in the Gulf. Gulf Arabs recall the centuries-long history of Egyptian political intervention and military operations in the Arabian Peninsula, and they fear Egyptian ambitions and financial demands may prove greater than the military capabilities Egypt could place at their disposal. The Arabs of the Gulf seem to prefer that Egypt act as an American military auxiliary, rather than assume a larger and more direct part in Gulf defense, which might make them dependent on Cairo. The U.S. proclamation of its unilateral willingness to contain Iran as well as Iraq has deprived the Gulf Arabs of effective incentives to rethink this logic. Some GCC members continue in fact to see a post-Saddam Iraq, rather than Egypt, as their best regional counterweight to Iran.

Egypt's Changing Security Environment

Egypt's regional and domestic security environment has also changed. As the Camp David treaties have settled into place and the peace process has unfolded, Egypt has had less and less reason to be concerned about the possibility of hostilities with Israel, the only neighbor capable of mounting a massive and direct military threat to Egyptian territory or seriously challenging the Egyptian Armed Forces. Egypt's management of its relations with Libya has reduced the threat from that quarter, though not without generating some relatively minor friction with the United States. Sudan poses no threat at all in conventional military terms, though it has emerged as a center of Islamic militancy sympathetic to the terrorist activities of domestic Egyptian extremists. The United States, which shares Egyptian concerns about Sudanese complicity in terrorism, has drawn closer to Egypt as a result.

The Accomplishments of Cooperation

Over the past 15 years, the United States has granted a total of nearly $20 billion for Egyptian force modernization. The list of equipment provided under this program includes some of the most modern systems in the U.S. arsenal.[1] In addition, over $25 million has been expended to educate and train Egyptian officers in the United States. This, by any accounting, is an impressive program of cooperation, and Egypt has come to depend on it. Some sources reckon that support from the United States accounts for as much as half of Egyptian defense spending.

Over much of this period, dialogue between Egypt and the United States on defense matters centered on the Egyptian need, as Washington perceived it, to reconfigure Egypt's Armed Forces to correspond to changing roles and missions and to reduce defense manpower to manageable and affordable levels. This included the phasing out of most of the obsolete Soviet equipment in Egypt's military inventory. These objectives gained the agreement in principle of the Egyptian military, but they were not fully put into effect. The delay in the downsizing and reconfiguration of the Egyptian Armed Forces will exacerbate the challenges to that country as it adapts to the more demanding military missions and changed American funding levels that the future is likely to bring.

Problems of Force Structure and Manning

Egyptian Armed Forces remain large and heavy, fully capable of meeting any of the threats Egypt confronted in the past. They are, however, vastly larger and heavier than required to meet any currently conceivable external threat to Egyptian national security. (Heavy armored units are also less relevant than more mobile, lightly armed forces would be to the internal security problems that pose an increasing problem to the Egyptian Government.) The expense of maintaining these levels of manpower and obsolete equipment is a major drain on the Egyptian treasury, diverting funds from more productive investment. The Egyptian military is trying to rectify these deficiencies but lacks adequate funding. This funding will not come from abroad under current circumstances; it can come only from the savings to be realized by drastic downsizing of the armed forces and retirement or disposal of its surplus equipment.

Such downsizing, however, raises the specter of further additions to the already swollen ranks of the unemployed in Egypt. Largely for this reason, the Egyptian Government has hesitated to carry it out. Egypt needs urgently to examine the experiences of Taiwan in the 1950s and 1960s, the People's Republic of China in the 1980s and 1990s, and the United States in still more recent years. Each of these countries carried out a radical reduction in manpower and retirement of obsolete equipment in order to modernize smaller but more militarily effective forces. Each successfully fostered economic growth without adding significantly to unemployment. Taipei pioneered, and Beijing may have perfected, the commercialization of military industry and engineering services. Egypt needs to do the same, not only to solve the problem of employment for demobilized soldiers, but also to make its underutilized military industry efficient and profitable. Accomplishing such "defense conversion" should become a principal task of U.S.-Egyptian defense cooperation.

The Future of U.S.-Egyptian Military Cooperation

As noted, it is doubtful that the current pattern of U.S. assistance to the Egyptian Armed Forces can continue much longer. Nevertheless, it is in the interest of both countries to continue cooperation to meet the requirements of regional order and peacekeeping. The basis for this must be a new Egyptian-American formulation of strategic partnership that can serve the interests and help meet the defense requirements of both countries.

The United States military will increasingly need the cooperation of its Egyptian colleagues to meet the challenges of maintaining security and internationally acceptable levels of order in the Afro-Asian region centered on Egypt. The recent radical downsizing of the U.S. Armed Forces implies increasing reliance on coalitions with regional forces to meet the challenges of major regional crises. Egypt is the only Arab partner with the potential to make a significant contribution to such coalitions beyond its borders.

This necessary restructuring of the Egyptian Armed Forces would also serve purely Egyptian interests. It would create an Egyptian military capable of unassisted power projection within a radius of several thousand kilometers and rapid deployment to meet any conceivable threat on Egypt's borders or within them. If the Egyptian forces assigned to this mission were to adopt the NATO-compatible military operating concepts and standards used by the United States, this would open the prospect of effective Egyptian cooperation with European as well as American forces and considerably expand Egypt's options for both external military operations and national defense.

Equally important, such a partnership could provide a new focus for U.S. military assistance to Egypt that could garner political support in the United States. It could gain such support from those concerned about security in the Gulf and Africa as well as about the security of Israel and the consolidation of a comprehensive Arab-Israeli peace.

Conclusion

Bilateral defense cooperation between Egypt and the United States helped to consolidate the Egyptian-Israeli peace, significantly reducing the external threat to Egyptian security. It has produced a major modernization of the Egyptian Armed Forces, one that enabled them to play a very important role in the war to liberate Kuwait. It has also helped make possible Egyptian activism in international peacekeeping operations. This bilateral cooperation has continued for 15 years, however, on a basis that is now increasingly in question. Moreover, it has failed to produce an appropriate opening for Egypt in the Arab Gulf or to bring about the level of military restructuring needed to fit the Egyptian Armed Forces for the future, rather than the past. For all these reasons, the Egyptian-American partnership needs a new strategic underpinning and focus. That focus should be on Egyptian-American partnership in the maintenance of regional order and stability beyond the Levant. U.S. assistance should be redesigned to develop Egyptian forces capable of rapid deployment throughout the region in coalition with the United States. Such a new partnership and focus could be the basis for long-sustained American domestic political support for appropriate military assistance to Egypt.

Note

1. Aircraft provided include C-130s, E-2Cs, F-4Es, F-16A/Bs, and F-16C/Ds. Helicopters include UH-60 Blackhawks, SH-2G Seasprites, and AH-64A Apaches. Chaparral, Harpoon, Hawk, Hellfire, Maverick, Sidewinder, Sparrow and TOW missiles have been provided to the relevant branches of the Egyptian Armed Forces. The Egyptian Navy has received patrol boats, Knox Class frigates, and several types of small craft. Armored personnel carriers, armored cargo carriers, tanks, tank recovery vehicles, and self-propelled antitank artillery have gone to the army.

EGYPT'S SECURITY CONCERNS

Ahmed M. Abdul Halim

Egypt's regional and international role is undergoing a transition. . . . While economic considerations will greatly affect Egypt's regional and international role, national security policy will continue to focus on preserving the state and its interests from external aggression, on securing and maintaining its regional role, and on the economic and social welfare of its people.

The end of the Cold War and the collapse of the Soviet Union as a regional player have led to the emergence, at least temporarily, of the United States as the world's sole superpower and the most influential external actor in the Middle East. This dramatic change in the international system has imposed certain constraints on the ability of regional states to maneuver and, in particular, on their capability to diversify sources of foreign aid and support. The change has also generated international momentum toward emphasizing economic power and capability, although not to the point of ignoring the role of military power. Given these international trends, a state that is not economically strong and has not joined a viable economic bloc will not be able to play a prominent

---

Major General Ahmed M. Abdul Halim (Ret.) is head of the Military and Strategic Unit at the National Center for Middle East Studies in Cairo. He is the author of *Five War Zones* and has written many studies for the Al-Ahram Strategic Studies Center and the University of Cairo.

international role, even if it possesses extensive military power. In short, a country's status today is increasingly based on what it has to offer economically, rather than its military power. The end of the Cold War competition has also minimized the international role played by the Non-Aligned Movement (NAM). The NAM loss of status, especially among those countries that were its leaders, has been exacerbated by changes in the international economic environment, the decline of their economies relative to the West, and its growing debt problems.

Changes in the Middle East have been equally momentous. In Egypt, for example, the Arab-Israeli conflict has for half a century had a clear and substantial impact on the mobilization and allocation of Egyptian resources. The first phase of this conflict, marked by peace agreements and the increased difficulty of using military power, is coming to an end. It is now becoming necessary for regional states, including Egypt, to think about the reallocation of their resources in ways that will bring a full peace dividend, enhance regional cooperation, and strengthen peace. This does not mean, however, that a country's ability to defend itself and to preserve its national security can be ignored. The key task is to convert from mobilization for military and strategic goals to mobilization for economic and social aims, while balancing the requirements of external security with those of domestic peace and stability.

Another regional transformation has involved the liberalization of local economies, including the transfer of parts of the economy from the public to the private sector, as a method of reconciling the goals of economic development and social stability. But liberalization and privatization have also raised a number of issues, including the appropriate role of the government in the country's economic structure and the nature of the relationship between economic and political changes. The solution of such issues will influence the degree and direction of political liberalization, the diversification of skills available to society, and the replacement of structures needed to manage the institutions of state.

These are the changes that Egypt must take into account in planning and mobilizing its national resources. At the same time, these changes will influence Egypt's perceptions of the challenges, threats, and opportunities it faces.

Threat Perception

The Israeli Factor

It is a widely held view in the Middle East, including Egypt, that the United States is more favorably disposed toward Israel than the Arabs, and that in Arab-Israeli peace negotiations the U.S. generally adopts the views and ideas put forth by Israel. The interests of Israel and Egypt are not synonymous, so this American orientation has had a negative impact on Egypt, notwithstanding an Egyptian-Israeli peace treaty, Egypt's role in securing and maintaining peace in the region, and its role in stabilizing the Middle East and the Levant, two areas whose security is linked.

With respect to the threats facing Egypt and the size of the Egyptian Armed Forces required to meet these threats, the United States has adopted a point of view similar to that of Israel. In the course of discussions within the Multilateral Working Group on Arms Control and Regional Security (ACRS), Israel has called into question the size of Egypt's conventional forces and its future strategy and advocated the "necessity" of reducing these forces to a minimum. If accepted, the Israeli perspective would lead to an imbalance between Egypt's military capabilities and its need to secure its national interests. The Israeli emphasis on conventional forces ignores the fact that Israel is the sole Middle East possessor of a nuclear capability and the capacity to use space for military purposes. In addition, it has an enormous arsenal of conventional forces that surpasses in efficiency and capability all the Arab states put together. Such an imbalance automatically poses a threat to the weaker side and is thus a source of regional instability. Notwithstanding its apparent goal of regional peace and stability, the United States supports Israel in its endeavor to maintain this imbalance.

Underlying this policy is an American assumption that there is virtually a complete compatibility of interests between itself and Egypt in the region; this view disregards the reality that Egyptian security interests require an independent Egyptian capacity for action. American policy in the Gulf, which has resulted in excluding Egypt from a role in Gulf security, and U.S. attempts to reduce Egypt's conventional capabilities are points of difference between the two countries.

The Rationale for Military Power

Threat assessment is only one of the bases determining the size of a state's armed forces. Military requirements are determined by a number of political, economic, and strategic factors. In Egypt, these include:

- The continued existence within the region of states with nonconventional capabilities, as well as the possession of superior conventional capabilities. The use of such forces, intentionally or by mistake, or even threat of such use to achieve foreign policy objectives constitutes a direct threat to Egypt. Whatever the reason for possession of such capabilities, the effect is to pose a threat to Egypt.
- The need for a reasonable balance of power in the region. A situation in which one state has complete military superiority allows it the luxury of threatening its neighbors at a time of its choosing and for reasons real, imagined, or even mistaken.
- The ability to secure and defend Egypt's economic and social development goals. Among the most important of these are the establishment and expansion of production plants, the creation of various investment projects, and the construction of new cities. Such infrastructure requires a defensive umbrella. There is little point in pursuing economic and social development if the benefits are vulnerable to external threats.
- The potential need for regional or international use of force. Notwithstanding the movement toward peace, destabilizing threats persist. Egyptian use of force will be governed by the potential for political and military cooperation with other concerned states, chief among them the United States. Recent examples of Egyptian-American military cooperation and coordination include the international alliance established after

Iraq's invasion of Kuwait in 1990 and Egyptian participation in the international emergency forces sent to Somalia and Bosnia.
• The need for a dependable Egyptian force as a guarantor of regional security and stability. This role is crucial. It is true that Israel sees its superior military might as such a guarantor, but Israel's military forces cannot be used to stabilize the region, precisely because its forces are perceived by its neighbors as one of the causes of instability. Only Egypt's forces can provide this military ballast.

Constructing a Military Balance

The calculations that determine the size of a state's armed forces are thus intricate and complex. The most important factor, however, is the necessity of reaching a reasonable and acceptable regional balance of power, one that considers the threat perceptions of each country and does not create a situation in which one state's perceived security needs create a perception of threat among other states. Such a balance is crucial for stability. Once this principle is accepted, then the size of the armed forces can be determined, together with the quantity and quality of its equipment, its operational plans, and its strategic uses, taking into account the concerns of other countries in the region. It is also important to take into account how military and political alliances can affect state security. The ability of a state to draw on regional and extraregional sources of support play an important role in an analysis of defense needs. Historically, close ties between the United States and Israel have increased the latter's security, now enhanced by the fact that the United States is the most important, if not only, external influence in the region.

To achieve stability, all states in the region should adopt a defensive doctrine and act on it, by acquiring only the tools necessary for defense and rejecting an "excess" of power that could be perceived as a threat to other parties in the region. Peace should be maintained also by using the tools of peace, including economic cooperation and social exchanges.

Military Posture

Egypt's military force posture is based on the following considerations:

- The current development of Egypt's Armed Forces is directly related to Egypt's assessment of Israel's abilities, most notably in the nuclear and space fields. From the Egyptian perspective, Israel's regional military dominance creates the potential for instability, thus compensatory measures are important to ensure the security of all states in the region.

- In spite of the Egyptian-Israeli peace treaty, the Declaration of Principles between Israel and the Palestinian Liberation Organization, and the Jordanian-Israeli peace treaty, defense expenditures of all states in the region are likely to remain high, in comparison not only to Western countries but also to other developing states. At a time when the emphasis is on development, heavy allocations for defense will continue to drag on the region's economies at the expense of social needs like education and health.

- Egypt's military, like others in the region, is undergoing a transition from quantity to quality, most apparent in the type of weapon systems employed. The transition has required extensive resources, creating an additional burden on the Egyptian economy.

- The United States is the primary source of weapons and approximately $1.3 billion in annual military aid; hence, the development of Egypt's military force is directly related to cooperation with the United States. Egyptian efforts to diversify its sources of weapons has not been entirely successful. The U.S. and Egypt hold joint military maneuvers, indicating joint interests and obligations between the two countries.

- Egypt has the potential to develop a military industry. However, the withdrawal of the Arab Gulf states from the Arab Authority for Industrialization has had a negative impact on this industry. A military industry requires extensive capital investments that, for a small state, like Israel, must be mainly drawn from external sources. The United States has been a large contributor to Israel's military industry. The existence of a sophisticated and varied military industry is another factor working to Israel's advantage, enabling it to have greater freedom of action than is the case for Egypt, which has to rely on external sources of weapons, often with political conditions attached. The imbalance in capabilities and independence creates regional insecurity.

• Egypt's military planning is conditioned by Israel's refusal to join the Nuclear Non-Proliferation Treaty (NPT) or its renewal in 1995. Its nuclear capabilities face no international restrictions, and the argument that Israel's nuclear weapons cannot be used for strategic or military purposes is not tenable. Similarly, the argument that Arabs should not be concerned about Israel's nuclear capability now that there is peace, or that these weapons constitute a guarantee of continued peace, ignores the fact that a peace based on pressure from the United States and a threat of Israel's nuclear weapons is neither real nor secure. Regional states cannot permanently accept such an Israeli challenge and will seek to eliminate or balance the threat by finding a suitable equivalency. The only basis of lasting peace is the Egyptian initiative for the creation of a region free of nuclear weapons and other weapons of mass destruction. The adoption of such a program is a crucial step in arms control.

• Finally, Egypt's force posture is affected by threats of terrorism, threats to its water resources, and threats to its economic development caused by continued tensions in the region.

The U.S.-Egyptian Equation

In their evaluation of these threats and the response required, the United States and Egypt agree on some points and differ on others. Quite clearly, both are concerned about the Iranian nuclear program and the general direction of Iran's foreign policy, but they differ on U.S. full support of the Israeli nuclear program, which constitutes a threat to the whole region. While the United States and Egypt have a close relationship, strains are created by Washington's support for the policies and positions of Israel. In the absence of any competition, the United States now has an opportunity to pursue independent policies in the Middle East that recognize the complexity of American interests. Given the extended period of peace that has existed between Israel and Egypt, it is difficult to understand why Israel continues to position most of its land and air-forces on the border with Egypt, sustains such complete military superiority over combined Arab military capabilities, and maintains its nuclear and space programs.

The Foundation of Security Strategy

In a period of movement toward regional peace and cooperation, most importantly in the economic realm, Egypt must nevertheless maintain the vitality and capability of its armed forces. To do so, it must emphasize improving their quality. The structure and disposition of Egypt's Armed Forces must correspond to the strategic balance in the region. Egypt's defensive strategy is thus based on possessing:

- Ground forces capable of defending and protecting all Egypt's borders and its national interests
- An air force and air defense system capable of protecting Egypt's air space
- A navy and coastal defense force capable of protecting Egypt's coastlines, vital navigation routes in the Mediterranean and Red Seas, and the security of its ports.

The basis of Egypt's military strategy is "defensive deterrence," that is, maintaining the capability to protect Egypt's national goals, most importantly the defense and security of Egypt. The aim is to attain an acceptable regional balance in the land, air, and sea. The adoption of a defensive strategy requires changes in doctrine, force structure and disposition, and readiness, not only for Egypt but for all other regional states.

Such a change of strategy and military disposition will require regional arms control. For Egypt, arms control will require certain principles. The first is regional transparency and a regional register of the capabilities of all states, including nonconventional fields.

The second is mutual confidence-building measures, beginning with agreements on arms limitation, moving toward arms reduction, and eventually reaching the elimination of conventional and nonconventional weapons that are most destabilizing, especially nuclear weapons. The third is agreements on the means and methods of inspection and verification to ensure that arms control agreements are implemented. Finally, there should be balanced and fair guarantees provided by an external party (particularly the United States) to ensure that all the regional parties, without exception, adhere to the agreements.

Arms control agreements must also take into account the economic impact of military spending. However, while the negative impact of defense spending is well known, it should also be recognized that armies play an important role in the region's societies. In Egypt, the Armed Forces are a means of alleviating unemployment and of providing vocational training to youths, whose new skills can then benefit society. The Army also plays an important role in addressing internal crises, such as those caused by natural disasters—the Egyptian Armed Forces played a key role in dealing effectively with the earthquake of 1992 and the floods and fires in 1994. The capacity to assist in civilian projects also has international application, as with Egypt's assistance in Somalia in December 1992.

Conclusion

A strong Egypt that is able to help maintain and extend peace in the Middle East is in a good position to strengthen regional ties with the United States. As President Husni Mubarak once noted, Egypt's strength still depends on its ability to focus on economic production and reform. Economic development, in turn, will depend on regional peace and stability. Regional peace and stability are also influenced by the policies of external powers, especially the United States. Egypt recognizes that there may be a reduction, and even elimination, of American aid to Egypt, due to domestic political and economic circumstances. While such a change would be detrimental, Egypt is prepared to bear the consequences. The pursuit of economic reform and development is an Egyptian national interest and should not be dependent solely on external aid.

As the external environment changes, so, too, must the foreign and domestic policies of states. Egypt's regional and international role is undergoing a transition, with some factors gaining prominence and others reduced in importance. While economic considerations will greatly affect Egypt's regional and international role, national security policy will continue to focus on preserving the state and its interests from external aggression, on securing and maintaining its regional role, and on the economic and social welfare of its people. Development, social cohesion, and the ability to compete in the world economy are key goals of the state, for they are the basis of Egypt's stability and its ability to play a positive role in the region.

The defense of a state's security is the primary responsibility of its armed forces, but security is not simply a military matter. It also includes political and economic considerations, and there is a great need for additional study on the peaceful resolution of conflicts and ways of strengthening peace. Peace cannot be based on the dominance of one side, as this will lead to resentment and instability. In the final analysis, peace, if it is to be stable, just, and comprehensive, must be based on equal rights and obligations for all regional states. Such a peace can be strengthened by regional integration and cooperation and by the development of an environment in which security is preserved through political, rather than military, means. The development of such a peace is in the interest not only of the regional states but also the United States.

III. U.S.-Egyptian Relations

THE FUTURE OF THE
U.S.-EGYPTIAN PARTNERSHIP

Ahmed Ismail Fakhr

Both Egypt and the United States have assets and capabilities, but they will need to establish a common dream. Both must view the instability in their common world as a common threat—a threat to both countries, both peoples, both ways of life.

Since 1979, the average Egyptian has seen and felt the deepening and strengthening of the relationship between Egypt and the United States. This putative Egyptian "man-in-the-street" has also come to the conclusion that Americans know more about Egyptian foreign policy, economic reform, democratization, security and human rights than Egyptians themselves. Egyptians believe not only that Americans know these things, but also that the U.S. bilateral relationship with Egypt allows the United States, when it is deemed appropriate, to influence external and domestic decisions in Cairo.

Major General Ahmed Ismail Fakhr (Ret.) is Director of the National Center for Middle East Studies, Cairo, and Chairman of the Popular Local Council of the Cairo Governorate. He has had fellowships at the Royal College of Defense Studies, London, the National Defense College, Cairo, and the National Defense University, Washington.

Is there a reason, then to question the nature of this relationship on the eve of the 21st century? The importance of the answer to this question became relevant only after sampling major segments of Egyptian society on their attitudes toward and understanding of this critical relationship. This informal poll—an Egyptian "focus group" if you like—revealed great variations in perception and many apprehensions over the relationship. These views spanned a number of generations, including the Nasser generation, which participated in the 1956, 1967, and 1973 wars; the Madrid peace process and multilateral negotiations with the Israelis, when Egyptians moved from a perception of Israel as threat to Israel as adversary and then neighbor and regional partner; the Sadat generation and the new business class, which has progressed from operating in a planned, totalitarian economy to dealing with privatization and a market economy; and a new, young post-Sadat generation, the recipient of religious dogmas as the only solution to their problems.

Differing U.S.-Egyptian Perceptions

These interviews have led to the following observations and conclusions on the Egyptian-U.S. relationship. First, there is a flaw in the relationship. The structure of relations looks firm from the outside, but the foundations on both sides are not completely sound. The reason is that the relationship has been built on two sets of inaccurate, different, but not necessarily conflicting, assumptions. What are they?

In the 1960s, the United States assumed that Nasser was a new Hitler, that Egypt was going "Red," and that "Arabism" was a threat to American interests. The Egyptians, on the other hand, viewed the United States as the enemy, the new colonizer, even a "devil." Each party constructed its relationship on the basis of these assumptions. Both were mistaken.

In the late 1970s, when Egypt concluded a peace with Israel and then abandoned the Soviets, Egyptians assumed that Americans would put an end to Egyptian sufferings, create parity with Israel, and raise their living standards. The United States, on the other hand, assumed that Egyptians would concentrate on

Egypt and forsake their "Arab" dimension, and could therefore be taken for granted. The United States began to talk about establishing military bases and facilities in Egypt and creating an organic interdependence between Egypt's basic needs and annual U.S. economic aid. Both were wrong.

In the 1980s, the loudest voices in Washington projected the collapse of the Egyptian economy; Egypt, they claimed, was a bottomless economic pit, a basket case with a bleak future. On their side, the Egyptians perceived the United States not as a friendly advisor but as a power encouraging International Monetary Fund (IMF) interference in Egypt's economic planning, with no sensitivity to potential social costs. As was the case previously, both assumptions were incorrect.

What is the situation today? Egyptians perceive that American assumptions are focused on the following issues:

- Americans fear there is no guarantee for the future of the existing regime; in this U.S. view, domestic control is at stake, and civil disorder has crossed previously inviolable limits.
- Corruption is rampant and is destroying Egypt's social structure.
- Egypt does not appear able to cope with the necessary fiscal and economic reforms, and as a result, radical Islamic groups are likely to seize power.
- The bottom line, in this reasoning, is that Americans believe their interests are threatened.

On the other hand, Egyptians have a different reading of American regional intentions:

- America's desire to restore its economic stability will mean seeing Egypt as a market for American goods and services, not as an exporting country.
- In the Gulf, U.S. security has meant the elimination of any Egyptian role there.

- America will organize its economic assistance regionwide, not state to state, to assure that Israel will be the dominant economic power in the region.
- One of the outstanding outcomes of this inquiry was that the Egyptians felt that American criticisms of human rights practices were directed against Egypt but neglected continual Israeli violations.
- Arms control will mean constraints on everybody except Israel.
- In funding economic assistance, America will give preference to those who meet the criteria of a "pro-democracy doctrine" that reflects Western patterns; nevertheless, the United States violates its own policies and proclaims values of democratization and human rights when it serves America's perceived interests.

Both sets of current assumptions need to be reviewed if Egypt and the United States are to have a healthier relationship.

A second observation is that both Egyptians and Americans now have different focuses. Egyptians are focusing on U.S. strength, while Americans are focusing on Egyptian weaknesses. Egyptians believe that the United States is capable of solving most international problems and managing most world crises. When contradictions appear between perceived U.S. abilities and resulting actions, Egyptians assume that the United State is able, but not willing, to act. This is a major cause of the accusation that the United States has "double standards."

A third observation is that strategies, policies, and programs rarely provide the inspiration for people to support a relationship. What provides inspiration is a national dream. Egyptians feel that there is not now, nor has there ever been, a common American-Egyptian dream. They see an American-Israeli dream, an American-Turkish dream based on NATO membership, and even an American-Gulf dream. Dreams, once realized, work as examples to be followed by other regional parties. They help to transform the relationship from the realm of tactics to that of strategy.

Egypt and the United States share vital interests in protecting access routes and waterways—the Mediterranean, the Suez Canal, the Red Sea, the Bab al-Mandab Straits, the Indian Ocean, the Gulf, and even the Nile River, but remarkably, the two partners do not have a well-defined common strategic threat. With the end of the Cold War, all they have today is a common preoccupation with security.

When the former Soviet Union was America's major threat, it was Egypt's main friend. When Israel was Egypt's major threat, the Jewish state was America's main regional ally. The only time that Egypt and the United States had a common threat was during the Gulf War. Egyptians believed in the so-called "new international order" led by the United States and fought alongside the United States to push back the Iraqi invasion of Kuwait. Today, the world is witnessing a new international disorder led, again, by the United States.

When Egyptians perceived Islamic extremism as a threat to their domestic stability, they thought Egyptians and Americans had a mutual understanding of the challenge. Yet both parties appear to have drawn different conclusions from the phenomenon. When Egyptians undertook to confront Islamic extremists, Egyptians heard reports, to their bewilderment, that the United States was secretly contacting them. One conclusion, drawn by some Egyptians, is that the United States assumes the present Egyptian regime is in decline and it is therefore trying to strengthen and, if possible, shape the growing political-religious movements that could eventually dominate Egypt's social, political, and economic institutions.

Egyptians, however, do not believe that extremist movements will be able to seize power in Egypt. They perceive the region as under control, despite current headaches. Although Egypt's political leadership and government are not enjoying the same public support they have in years past, Egyptians admire the skills of their statesmen. They are, however, accorded the highest honor and support only when they contribute in some meaningful way to the unity of the Egyptian people and to their material welfare and security.

Commonalities: The Ties that Bind

It is important to note that, although Egyptians and Americans may have different assumptions and perceptions, these differing perspectives need not lead to conflicts. Rather, they point toward a need to bridge shared misperceptions and to understand respective points of view better. Only then will the health of the future relationship be guaranteed.

Both Egypt and the United States have the assets, capabilities, and will need to establish a common dream. Both must view the instability in their common world as a common threat—a threat to both countries, both peoples, and both ways of life. Egyptians appreciate American aid, both economic and military, but both they and the Americans need to look to the future, not dwell on the past.

The most important conclusion to be drawn from these sample interviews is that the majority of Egyptians, including even some segments of the Islamic movement, do not want to lose American friendship. There may be complaints about the relationship, but not serious criticism. The relationship is valued by most Egyptians.

Egyptians feel no necessity to apologize for the relationship with the United States. When mutual interests coincide, Egypt will protect them, even by blood, as the second Gulf War showed. Extremism may spread in Iran, Algeria, Sudan, and other states, but it cannot dominate the region unless it succeeds in Egypt. For this reason, Egypt is the regional bulwark against the spread of Islamic radicalism. Containing these movements in Egypt is the way to diminish the threat to American regional interests.

Without Egyptian efforts, there would have been no hope for the Palestinian-Israeli implementation of the Declaration of Principles (DOP) or the implementation of the common Jordanian-Israeli agenda. Because of Egypt, Israel can fly its flag today in Muscat. Egypt's impact is of such importance that its maintenance is one of the major declared national interests of the United States.

Egypt is of major value to the United States, but it must not be seen as simply an extension of the U.S-Israeli relationship, nor should Egypt be viewed simply as a mediator in the peace process. Egypt is, rather, a pivotal partner in reaching peace. In the future, Egypt will still serve as a mediator in solving regional conflicts, because peaceful relations are not automatically expected to solve all political, economic, social, and security disputes in the region. Peace provides only a friendly atmosphere in which to solve contradictions through negotiations, dialogue, and conflict prevention. The future belongs to the United States and Egypt, if they work together and recognize each other's interests. Both will lose the present and the future, if they do not succeed in formulating a new foundation for U.S.-Egyptian relations.

Program for Action

What sorts of steps could the United States and Egypt take to move toward a better understanding and common objectives in the future? First, both sides need to devote more time to forecasting issues of importance to the two countries. If such a forecast is accurate, it could help to define probable differences between Egypt and the United States. Some of these differences are already surfacing in the U.S. media and they need to be addressed.

U.S.-Egyptian relations may be entering a new phase that could be called the "unprogrammed approach." That is, every action, every incident, every decision by either party are likely to be assessed and measured against previous perceptions and assumptions, some of which, as indicated, may well be inaccurate. If allowed to proceed in that direction, the Egyptian-U.S. relationship could enter a "crisis situation," resulting in increased uncertainty. This, in its turn, would only increase the possibilities of mis-understanding, misconception, and misinterpretation.

Such a phenomenon could lead to a divergence of assessments, not only between the two countries but also within the same administration. It would become extremely grave if one or another of the parties arrived, as a result of its own assessment made on the basis of its own perception, at a conclusion that the other party is damaging its national interest. This would negatively affect the mutual flow of resources between the two countries and could also be damaging in the security field where cooperation must be preceded by a common vision and a clear agreement.

A second conclusion is that the United States and Egypt need to establish a new method for the management of mutual relations to avoid a "crisis situation." The Mubarak-Gore initiative to establish a joint economic committee is an excellent one, but it is not sufficient by itself to chart a new path for future Egyptian-U.S. relations in all their diversity. To accomplish this, a High Coordinating Committee, comprising officials, business people, and intellectuals from both sides, should be established and meet biannually. As a spinoff, there might be standing committees with a mandate to improve cooperation in specific fields, such as joint marketing strategies for export-oriented businesses, tourism, or medical cooperation.

The main need right now is for a mechanism for improved consultation and better understanding between the two societies. By definition, such a mechanism should not and cannot be confined simply to government representatives. It must include intellectuals, entrepreneurs, legislators, the media, local government officials, and security and defense specialists. In short, it must be truly representative of both societies, if it is to help avoid a coming crisis.

Conclusion

U.S. and Egyptian interests coincide far more than they collide. That fact, along with all the new variables on the international scene and the new emerging powers in the new world order, makes it incumbent on the United States, the super power, and on Egypt, the regional power, to arrive at a new partnership, one that will emphasize common interests while providing a means for solving inevitable differences.

EGYPT AT THE CROSSROADS

Phebe Marr

The United States and Egypt need to build a new foundation for their relationship as they head into the 21st century. They have already taken some steps in a new direction, but in a rapidly changing regional environment, the outcome cannot yet be predicted. In the broadest terms, this foundation must be based on peace and prosperity.

Egypt is at a crossroads, in its domestic policy, its regional role, and its relations with the United States. On the domestic front, Egypt faces the choice between fundamental economic and social reform, or clinging to substantial vestiges of its former statist policies. Since 1974, Egypt has made considerable progress in movement toward a market economy, but more needs to be done before it can meet the economic criteria for self-sustained growth. On the political front, Egypt has greatly reduced the threat of violence from Islamic militants, although moderate, "mainstream" Islamic movements still present a political challenge to the Government. But Egypt must rise to the challenge of creating political space for new leaders, new ideas, and a new direction that look to the future rather than to the past.

On the regional front, Egypt is playing a more assertive role after a decade of isolation following its peace treaty with Israel. It has helped broaden the peace process to include other Arab states and plays an active part in mediating between the Palestinians and

Israel. In 1990-91, it was at the forefront of the Arab military effort to contain and roll back Iraq's aggression against Kuwait, and it is strengthening economic and security ties with the Maghreb. Recently, Egypt shows every sign of reviving its traditional role as the leader of an Arab bloc committed to wresting a better deal in negotiations with Israel. The nature and direction of Egypt's region role raise questions for the future. If the peace process moves to fruition, is Egypt prepared to move beyond a cold peace to normal relations with Israel? Will Egypt's aspirations exceed its grasp, overextending its capacity and resources and derailing its promising economic development? Is Egypt still too enmeshed in the Arab-Israeli dilemma for its own good? Above all, can Egypt reconcile its regional Arab role with the demands of the global market?

With respect to U.S.-Egyptian relations, the trends outlined in this volume have had mixed results. Egypt's economic progress on the domestic front has received a positive response from the United States as well as from the business and financial communities. There is also some U.S. relief that Egypt does not appear threatened by destabilization from radical Islamic elements. Egypt's regional policies, however, are stirring some unease in the United States. This discontent has focused on Egypt's moves to freeze normalization with Israel as a means of leveraging Israeli concessions in the peace process; Egypt's attempt to compel more transparency in Israel's nuclear program than can be accomplished in the near term; and its willingness to have relations with regional neighbors (Libya and Iraq) ostracized by the United States. On its side, Egypt is increasingly disillusioned with stagnation of the peace process and wants a more activist U.S. policy in moving it forward, as well as a reshaping of the security environment with respect to Israel's nuclear advantage. As the partnership matures, Egypt is increasingly sensitive about its bilateral relationship being held hostage to relations with Israel, rather than standing on its own foundation. It seems clear that in changing times, the relationship needs a new vision that takes account of new regional realities and Egypt's changing situation.

Egypt's Domestic Stability

The Political Dimension

Nowhere is Egypt's choice between past and present clearer than in the political sphere, where Egypt seems poised somewhere between lethargy and change. One of the major questions emerging from this volume is whether Egypt's leadership will be able to summon the "will" to undertake the political changes necessary for Egypt's growth in the 21st century. Indeed, rather than potential turmoil, Egypt may be suffering from too much political stability. According to Tahseen Basheer, the root of the problem lies in a tacit social contract between the government and the populace, ushered in by the 1952 revolution. The population acquiesces in large measure to government control in return for an array of social services. Successive Egyptian presidents have altered the contract slightly, allowing for a degree of pluralism, a more open press, and greater adherence to the rule of law, but have stopped short of tolerating real dissent or allowing genuine opposition in the assembly, thus stifling creativity and the potential for change. As a result, the contract that once gave the government legitimacy has now led to inertia, which must be overcome if Egypt is to make the choice for change—political, economic, and ideological. The question for Egyptian leadership is whether it will be willing to open up a political system that has thus far provided it with security and continuity.

Indeed, to produce the required political and economic change, new leadership may be needed. As John Waterbury indicates, in this area Egypt is more likely to get continuity than transformation. For decades, Egypt has been governed by men recruited from the administrative hierarchy of the state. These have generally been technocrats, selected for their expertise, rather than politicians, capable of mobilizing public support for change. Only Islamic leaders today could play this role, and they are unlikely to lead Egypt in the direction it needs to take. Entrepreneurs are likely to play an increasing role in any future scenario because of Egypt's need for foreign investment, but it is not clear that they can break the mold. Hence, the most likely political future is a continuation of the current alliance between moderately authoritarian rulers and technicos, which could trap Egypt in a vicious cycle. The only way the current government can perpetuate itself is by economic growth, and yet such economic growth can come about only by abandoning the status quo.

The Islamic Challenge

If a dramatic change in leadership is not likely, neither is an overthrow of the regime by Islamic radicals, a threat greatly exaggerated in the West. Indeed, Egypt may well have turned the corner in its efforts to gain control over militant Islamic groups and their terrorist activities, although the threat has by no means been entirely eliminated. As Saad Eddin Ibrahim points out, the recent wave of Islamic militancy is only the latest in a long historical progression of such movements. However, it has been by far the most violent and widespread. Current members of such movements are younger, more rural in origin, less educated, and more skilled in their violent craft than their predecessors. The retreat of Nasser's social contract and a reduction in government subsidies and benefits have alienated the lower middle class, a disaffected group that forms the main source of Islamic activism. However, since 1995, violence perpetrated by these movements has subsided under heavy-handed measures taken by the government. Although militancy has not disappeared (it survives mainly in the neglected rural provinces of upper Egypt), its impact on Egypt's stability has been marginalized.

If Islamic violence has been tamed, mainstream Islamic movements still have appeal and continue to be the medium of expression for opposition to the regime. As John Esposito points out, the Muslim Brotherhood (MB) is the real alternative to the government and, as such, represents its main challenge. It is one that is likely to persist and can be dealt with only by opening the system to vigorous political competition and by dynamic economic growth.

In confronting the Islamic challenge, the Egyptian Government has gone in the other direction, moving from a position in the 1980s in which mainstream Islamic movements were given some political space in which to operate (in contrast to militants who were jailed), to one in which the lines between the two have been blurred and in which Muslim Brotherhood activities have been persecuted along with violent movements. This has brought a period of calm to Egypt, but it may be driving moderate movements underground and in a more radical direction.

Economic Progress: Slow but How Sure?

Ultimately, the key to Egypt's future lies in its economic decisions, and here Egypt may be closer to a real threshold of change, after years of slow steps, than is generally recognized. In this arena, Alan Richards makes a forceful case that Egypt needs to make a "break for the market" rather than continuing a policy of "dilatory reform." Egypt faces a real economic choice between the statist policies of the past and the free-market policies of the future, to which it claims to be committed. Egypt is in the process of structural reform, but its progress has been slow, especially in reducing government regulations, which hamper investment, and in privatization. Above all, the economy needs to provide more jobs for a growing, youthful population. The World Bank estimates Egypt must create 500,000 jobs a year for the next decade just to keep up with its rapidly growing labor force.[1] That will require an annual growth rate of around 7 percent.[2] While gradually increasing, the rate in 1997 was about 5 percent. Reaching 7 percent will not be possible unless national savings, now 18 percent of the GDP, rise to at least 25 to 28 percent.[3]

Egypt has made considerable progress in this direction at the macroeconomic level. It has been able to reduce its debt (in part as a result of its participation in the Gulf War) from 20 percent of the GDP in 1990 to less than 1 percent in 1997; its reserves have risen from $4 billion in 1991 to over $20 billion in 1996;[4] and its currency has stabilized. Some privatization has taken place, and private sector firms are doing relatively well. In 1996, over 90 companies were sold, giving the government over $2.8 billion.[5] This recent progress has generated a new climate of optimism, not only among foreign investors of high caliber, but also among Egyptians. Sensing a new market, some young Egyptians are returning from abroad, along with some Egyptian capital.[6] But Egypt must continue this direction and increase the pace if it is to break the cycle of stagnation. Key problem areas lie in privatization of less profitable industries; complex deregulation; tariff reduction; and drastic reform of an educational system that results in a literacy rate of about 50 percent.[7]

Moreover, as Hanna Kheir el-Din reminds us, the costs of reform must be considered as well. In the past, structural adjustment has led to maldistribution of wealth and an increase in poverty among some sectors of the population. As the Asian crisis has reminded everyone, the short-term political risks of structural adjustment must be well managed to achieve success, although Egypt may be over the worst of the short-term pain and on its way to a higher growth rate and an ability to attract foreign capital. The reform program is also vulnerable in the medium term. Egypt needs substantial investment and, above all, access to external markets, especially in the European Union and the United States. If these are not forthcoming, the reform could be threatened.

The Military: Egypt's Stabilizer

One factor that must be considered in Egypt's domestic dynamics is the military, which has been playing an expanded role in the economy. As Gotowicki points out, while the military's political role has been greatly reduced since Nasser's day, the defense establishment has been compensated in the economic sphere. Involvement of the Army in civilian industries and agriculture has had a mixed impact on Egypt's economic growth and structural reform.

On the positive side, the military has acted as an engine of growth in some high-tech sectors, such as communication systems, as well as provided employment. But some see the military, with low-cost labor and other advantages, as competing unfairly with the private sector, thus impeding structural change. In this view, a diversion of some of the resources devoted to the military (about a quarter of all government expenditure) into productive enterprises and into educational services could help to jump start the economy. These changes do not appear imminent, or even on the horizon, because the military is now seen as the stabilizing political force behind the regime.Thus, on the domestic front, we have come full circle. Almost all analysts agree that political, economic, and military factors have come together to produce a high degree of stability in Egypt on the eve of the millennium. But this stability has been achieved at a level of economic and political development as yet inadequate to solve Egypt's most pressing problems: population increase, lack of jobs, and maldistribution of wealth and privilege. Egypt has made progress on the economic front, with higher growth rates and some structural reform, and in the political arena, with more personal freedoms. Unless progress is continued in both areas, however, the long-term prospects for stability could be undermined.

Egypt's Regional Role

If the domestic scene shows signs of both change and stability, so, too, does Egypt's regional posture. The partnership with the United States remains a cornerstone of Egypt's policy, as does its importance to the United States, but since the Gulf War Egypt has been asserting its traditional role as regional Arab leader ever more aggressively, sometimes in directions that have put it at odds with the United States. This gradual transformation owes much to Egypt's enhanced domestic stability but even more to its greatly improved geostrategic position since the mid-1980s.

Egypt's failure to bring the rest of the Arab world along with it in 1979, when it signed a peace treaty with Israel, left Egypt isolated regionally and overwhelmingly dependent on the United States for support. For the next decade, the main thrust of its regional policy was directed toward its own reintegration into the Arab world. This was largely achieved in 1990, with the return of the Arab League headquarters to Cairo. In the aftermath of the Gulf War, Egypt worked to bring other Arab countries into the peace process in large part in an effort to vindicate its own earlier position. Paradoxically, the more success Egypt had in this endeavor, the more its regional role as a mediator appeared to diminish.

But movement in the peace process was set back by the assassination of Prime Minister Yitzhak Rabin in 1995 and the election of a Likud-led government under Binyamin Netanyahu. Even before this election, Egypt had begun shifting to a new regional role, that of mobilizing Arab support for improved peace terms on the Arab-Israeli front. How far Egypt can go in this direction remains to be seen, but this is a role more compatible with Egypt's traditional leadership niche and tends to sit more comfortably with members of its political establishment, many still influenced by the Nasserite heritage.

Indeed, as Rosemary Hollis indicates, a jolt in the peace process could be fortuitous for Egypt, so long as that process does not collapse. It may even give Egypt some additional time to make headway in its economic restructuring. While Hollis does not see Egypt transforming itself into an economic powerhouse, it should make some progress on this front, despite regional political vicissitudes. Politically, Egypt cannot be ignored because of its size, its influence, and its ability to reshape the region.

Meanwhile, Egypt is pursuing initiatives in other quarters as well. In the Maghreb, it is participating in the multifaceted Barcelona initiative with the EU, seeking incorporation into European markets, and establishing security links with its North African neighbors. It is also acting as a lifeline for Libya, where an estimated 500,000 to 1 million Egyptians remain employed. In the Horn of Africa, Egypt's role is more cautious than that of the United States in confronting Sudan's provocative Islamic policies, despite accusations that Sudan harbored some of those responsible for the June 1995 assassination attempt against Mubarak in Ethiopia. In the Gulf, its role, though cooperative, is likely to remain circumscribed, especially in the security field.

In assessing Egypt's new regional role, Abdul Monem Sa'id Ali strongly urges Egypt to grasp the nettle and boldly adopt the new geoeconomic agenda. Egypt cannot lead while it lags in economic development. Unless Egypt rectifies the economic imbalance between goals and resources, its hand will continue to be weakened. However, Sa'id Ali sketches a relatively ambitious agenda for Egypt: completing the peace process, building a regional geoeconomic structure of cooperation, and upgrading Egypt's regional capabilities through rapid economic reform. Others are skeptical as to whether Egypt, or any Middle Eastern country, can exercise such a role in the new geostrategic environment.

The New Geostrategic Environment

Whether any of these aims will be realized depends, in large measure, on the regional environment Egypt will face as it moves into the 21st century. Here, as Joffe points out, there have been major changes. First, as an area, the post-Cold War Middle East has been enlarged and now encompasses new regions formerly part of the Soviet Union. As a result, the Arab world, which previously dominated the Middle East, is now balanced by a component that is mainly Turkic and Iranian. Second, the Arab world has lost what cohesion it once had, particularly since the Gulf War, and is increasingly divided into blocs. In this new strategic environment, it will be more difficult for Egypt to exercise a "regional role." Nonetheless, Joffe sees Egypt pursuing a renewed initiative to recapture its old Arab position, although it is too early to say whether it will be successful.

Ali Dessouki also sees Egypt's new security environment as characterized by change and fluidity. Not withstanding this flux, Egypt will be a status quo power, with a deep interest in regional stability, which it needs in order to concentrate on domestic economic development and to attract investment. In his view, Egypt's role in the peace process is likely to be mixed; foreign policy elites are uneasy over the "rush to normalization" before Israel has withdrawn from occupied territory. Egypt will work for "substance" in the peace process and for regional cooperation and development, but only after settlement of territorial issues and a military balance that does not threaten Arab states, especially with respect to Israel's nuclear power. Meanwhile, Egypt will continue to coordinate an "Arab" position, a factor likely to raise strains in relations with Israel and the United States.

The regional Islamic factor is an uncertainty with which Egypt must deal. Should the balance in the area shift to an "Islamic bloc," because of the emergence of another Islamic state in the region, this would impose constraints on Egypt's cooperation with the United States. The United States and Egypt are not likely to agree on all aspects of this agenda; they will have to work out differences within a context of mutual interests.

Military and Security Policy

Significantly, on military policy, the heart of the U.S.-Egyptian security relationship, two authors in this volume point to sharply differing visions of the future. Chas. Freeman sees the U.S.-Egyptian defense relationship facing serious challenges in the future, because of changing regional circumstances and potential U.S. budget cuts. In the wake of the Cold War, the United States is searching for ways to reduce budgetary expenditures. Meanwhile, the Egyptian-Israeli peace treaty has reduced Egypt's threat from that quarter. These changed circumstances argue for a reduction in military manpower and a change in mission. The resources devoted to maintaining such a military could be better spent on confronting Egypt's economic challenges. Egypt's new regional mission should shift, in his view, to helping maintain acceptable levels of order in the Afro-Asian region, beyond the Levant. If Egypt moved even further to adopt NATO compatible military equipment and operating concepts, this would open more possibilities for Egypt to cooperate with Europe and the United States, and provide a new basis for continued U.S. funding.

As Abdul Halim's chapter makes clear, Egypt does recognize the need to reallocate resources and engage in regional cooperation, but he takes a very different view of Egypt's external security. He sees the regional imbalance between Egypt's forces and those of Israel, especially in the areas of nuclear and space capacity, as a continuing source of regional instability and a potential threat to Egypt, regardless of its peace treaty. This military asymmetry deprives Egypt of the capacity for independent action and allows Israel the luxury of threatening its neighbors if it chooses. Egypt also sees Israel's call on outside sources of technology and its refusal to sign the NPT as sources of threat, requiring some equivalency. Hence Egypt, while modernizing and streamlining its military, is not likely to downsize its forces to the extent suggested by many in the United States. While Egypt shares U.S. concern over proliferation and the spread of Islamic radicalism, its interests are not synonymous with those of the United States. Nor does it favor integration into the Western NATO framework. Rather, Egypt will seek an independent but cooperative role in the region and will maintain a military posture consonant with such a mission.

The U.S.-Egyptian Relationship

What do these trends portend for the U.S.-Egyptian relationship on the eve of the 21st century? After 17 years of collaboration, what adjustments must be made by both partners to accommodate the changing strategic environment of the Middle East? How can a positive relationship be maintained as some interests diverge?

The Egyptian View

In an insightful and thought-provoking essay, Ahmed Fakhr points out that the U.S.-Egyptian relationship, though seemingly solid, may not have such firm foundations. Over the last two decades, both sides have proceeded on the basis of differing perceptions and assumptions. Despite mutual misperceptions, however, both sides have common interests, to include security of communications routes and a desire for regional stability. Despite some domestic criticisms, Egypt values U.S. friendship and wants to keep it. What is needed is a new strategic vision to fit the changing regional environment, and a practical program to put it into effect. Above all, the United States and Egypt need better mechanisms to identify and forecast issues of importance to both and to bridge the communications gap.

One of the best ways to build a bridge, in Fakhr's view, would be to expand the current economic commission, which deals with the privatization and reform effort, into a general commission that meets periodically to iron out grievances, address differences, and keep communications open.

The U.S. View

These conclusions, drawn from previous chapters, show that numerous forces, inside and outside the Arab-Israeli arena, have combined to create a new situation for both countries that is gradually modifying their relationship. The United States, now the only superpower, has global interests and concerns it must balance against regional interests and bilateral relations. At the same time, it has diminishing resources (including public interest) to spend on international affairs. Egypt, no longer isolated regionally, is emerging as a more independent force, with its own national interests, some of which do not replicate those of the United States. This new situation, in which both powers have multiple, overlapping, but sometimes contradictory interests and concerns, is likely to become the norm for the future.

The U.S. Transformation

If Egypt is undergoing a transformation, so, too, is the United States. First, in the absence of the Soviet threat, the United States has downsized its military and the budgetary outlays devoted to defense. Since the end of the Cold War, the U.S. military has shrunk from more than 2.1 million to about 1.4 million; expenditures have gone from about $400 billion to about $250 billion annually (from about 6 percent to about 3 percent of the GDP).[8] This has included much of the U.S. defense posture in Europe for out-of-area contingencies, such as those in the Gulf. U.S. troops in Germany, once numbering 350,000, were fewer than 100,000 in 1997 and scheduled to be reduced even further.[9]

Second, and even more important, the Gulf War shaped a new U.S. threat perception and a new security architecture to go with it. In U.S. strategic planning, regional threats, such as those posed by Iraq and Iran in the Persian Gulf, have superceded the global Soviet threat and have provided the likely contingencies for force planning. While these plans are periodically reviewed, the regional threat contingencies are likely to remain as the cornerstone of U.S. military planning.[10] In the Middle East, this strategy has been articulated as "dual containment" of Iran and Iraq. While this policy has been subject to criticism and is eroding in practice as changes in regional dynamics occur, the policy itself is likely to change only slowly as threats appear to subside. While the United States has assumed the lion's share of the burden of this containment[11]—with substantial financial help and host-nation support from GCC partners—it is a strategy requiring support from regional allies outside the Gulf, such as Egypt, if it is to be sustained. Egypt provides not only a broader Arab framework for the policy but also important logistic support when necessary by allowing Western forces to use its airfields and its airspace to supply the Gulf. Further, its maintenance of the Suez Canal as a neutral waterway open to commerce and military transport is indispensable. Should this support disappear, U.S. protection of Gulf oil flows would be difficult indeed.

For the United States, several new global challenges with regional implications have also emerged. Chief among them is the proliferation of WMD, particularly among states currently hostile to the West. With the exception of North Korea, the chief adversarial proliferators are in the Middle East; one, Libya, is a neighbor of Egypt. Others include Iran, Iraq, and Syria. Slowing the spread of these weapons and reducing current arsenals are chief aims of the new U.S. strategy. While Egypt shares these goals, it is also profoundly concerned over the largest Middle Eastern proliferator, Israel, which has an undeclared nuclear arsenal that Egypt wants reduced or eliminated. On this issue, it finds itself at odds with the United States.

The United States is also concerned with an array of transnational threats, less potent than the former Soviet menace but nonetheless disruptive to regional stability and the security of U.S. regional allies. These include civil wars that spill across borders and create refugee crises, drug trafficking, and above all, the threat from terrorism, particularly that sponsored by radical Islamic elements like those that undertook the bombing of U.S. embassies in Kenya and Tanzania. On this issue, Egypt and the United States are in basic agreement, but Egypt may be unwilling to take the sharp-edged measures often advocated by the United States when it comes to dealing with neighbors such as Sudan and Libya and important Middle Eastern players such as Syria and Iran.

Domestic Political Dynamics

The United States faces a different global security environment and a different domestic political situation as well. In Washington, as in other capitals, the absence of the Cold War has focused attention on domestic concerns. One result has been that both the administration and Congress have put issues, such as a balanced budget, health care, and economic growth well ahead of international affairs. Elections to Congress in 1994 and 1996 reinforced this trend, with a strong surge of new freshman from the heartland committed to less government at home as well as abroad.[12] This decline in public interest in foreign affairs is also reflected in opinion polls and in the amount of time devoted to foreign subjects on major news networks, which provide the basis for informing most U.S. citizens.[13] In political discourse, there is an increasing and disturbing "unwillingness to do the hard work of exercising international leadership and an urge, not merely to share, but to shed its burdens."[14]

Some have seen this syndrome as a new U.S. penchant for unilateralism. Rather than taking the time and effort to work on coalition politics, the United States, according to these critics, recognizes its indispensable power in the new world order and avoids spending political capital and resources on diplomacy. But when it is necessary to act, it does so on its own, or with a handful of allies who share its views, often with a minimum of consultation. At the same time, the absence of an overarching and dominant threat has weakened the transatlantic coalition that was the mainstay of global politics for decades. The very diversity of the "new world order," the competition for international trade, and the multiple but overlapping threats to security have made it much more difficult to keep coalitions together. The erosion of NATO cohesion in Bosnia and the fraying of the Gulf War coalition on policy toward Iran and Iraq provide examples. In the latter case, it is less important that U.S. and European goals have diverged—all remain interested in preserving a secure flow of oil from the Gulf—than that roles have changed. Europe's main relationship to the Mediterranean and the Gulf is a commercial one (hence its interest in trade), but it is the United States that provides the security umbrella and absorbs most of its expenses (hence its emphasis on sanctions and military deterrence). Similar differences exist between the United States and its regional partners. While the United States is more prepared to use punitive measures to enforce peace, regional allies, who must live with the targeted neighbors on a daily basis, prefer diplomacy or political tradeoffs.

This new set of circumstances is likely to complicate relations between the U.S. and Egypt. Egypt's new assertiveness, its attempts at a regional leadership role, and its variegated interests in the Middle East and beyond may lead to some sharp differences with the United States on regional policy. A relationship that was once characterized by a high degree of interdependence may become, on occasion, contentious. The differing assumptions and perceptions raised by Ahmed Fakhr may well come to the fore, if relations are not nurtured. Indeed, they are already in evidence. On several issues, U.S. and Egyptian policies increasingly diverge. This is particularly true in the peace process, where Egypt has taken stands at variance with the United States on the pace of normalization with Israel, in nonproliferation issues, and in dealing with Libya.

Additional new irritants could lie ahead as well. A Congress increasingly concerned with budget cutting and possibly irked by Egypt's differing positions on key issues could reduce its aid package. While Egyptians claim they would "understand" cuts made on economic grounds, provided they also extended to Israel, unilateral cuts could have a devastating impact on the relationship.[15] Even benign cuts will have some negative effect. Egypt is likely to compensate by shifting funds from the civilian sector to the military, a process that reverses the order of priorities needed, and such cuts would sever a multitude of links with the United States, especially among the military, that have proved mutually beneficial. Even without aid cuts, if Egyptian positions continue to diverge from those of the United States, especially on peace process issues, voices are likely to be heard from Congress, from the vocal and influential pro-Israeli lobby and others for "pressure" to be exercised against Egypt to bring it into line. These, too, are likely to make the relationship contentious.

Notwithstanding these difficulties, strong mutual interests between the two countries should mitigate these contradictions. As Ali Dessouki points out, Egypt is a status quo power and, one might add, a moderate one with a good record of responsible international behavior. Its favorable relationship with the United States is now entering its 18th year. The United States and Egypt have faced stresses in the peace process before, and relations have survived. While they may differ on tactical measures to survive gathering storms, both would suffer greatly from its collapse. A moderate Egypt, cooperating on expanding the zone of peace in the area, is essential to the U.S. position in the region. Should Egypt become more openly hostile (as in Nasser's day) or even coolly neutral, Israeli security would be much more difficult to maintain at much greater expense, while the U.S. position in the Gulf, especially the fraying Dual Containment policy, would be badly undercut. Moreover, a shift in Egypt's position could herald a change in the regional balance, which would be detrimental to U.S. interests throughout the region.

For this reason, among others, both the United States and Egypt have a vested interest in holding the line on any deterioration in relations. In a situation where a faltering peace process puts stress on relations, the United States and Egypt must work to mitigate the damage and strengthen those areas where there are agreements. One such area is limiting the spread of radical Islam. For this reason, the United States and Egypt will probably continue to cooperate, within certain parameters, on antiterrorist policy, although both parties may disagree on the tactics to be employed.

Last, and perhaps most important, the United States and Egypt can be expected to cooperate on the new geoeconomic agenda. The agenda itself owes much to high-level U.S. efforts to shift the focus of the U.S.-Egyptian relationship from traditional strategic (and defense) issues to trade and economic growth. As the chapters in this volume attest, the effort has strong support from Egypt's educated elite, especially its economists. Even entrenched elements of the bureaucracy are slowly giving ground on the market economy. Above all, the efforts are beginning to show very visible benefits, in GDP growth, in investment, and in privatization. As promising gains are translated into increased employment, the process should generate continued momentum. Egypt itself is now making increased investment in education in an effort to address serious gaps in its skill levels. While these efforts could be sidetracked by a fractious peace process, it is also possible that the new geoeconomic agenda will take on a life of its own. The fact that Egypt held the Cairo Economic Summit in 1996, despite peace process problems, is a good indication that the new agenda is taking root—an agenda strongly supported by the United States. Egypt's continued economic development and its further integration into the global economy, especially through the EU sponsored Barcelona initiative and others like it, are the best underpinnings for Egyptian and regional stability and continued mutual cooperation with the United States.

Toward the Future

The United States and Egypt need to build a new foundation for their relationship as they head into the 21st century. They have already taken some steps in a new direction, but in a rapidly changing regional environment, the outcome cannot yet be predicted. In the broadest terms, this foundation must be based on peace and prosperity, both of which will involve costs and efforts on both sides if they are to be realized. It remains to be seen whether the United States is willing to make the requisite political investment required for peace and Egypt the investment for prosperity.

Peace with Israel must mean more than the mere absence of war; it must be built on a gradual reduction and elimination of the causes of conflict that drive the arms race in Egypt, on gradually establishing trust and confidence, and on habits of constructive discourse and personal interaction. In short, Egypt must be prepared for more normalization with Israel, and Israel for more progress on Palestinian issues. These will take years to build, but a better beginning needs to be made. Meanwhile, the old agenda of moving toward final status issues needs to be pushed ahead. Egypt has a role to play in nurturing bilateral relations between Israel and the Palestinians and multilateral relations within the region. Greater prosperity for Egypt can occur only in the absence of war, but it will also depend on a regional environment that does not sap its resources and misdirect the energies of its younger generation in prolonging a fruitless conflict. Egypt may now have time to play catch-up economically, but this will demand effort, sacrifice, and above all, a new set of values and aspirations for its younger generations. The United States must play a constructive role in fostering the environment that makes this possible.

To strengthen the relationship, two general directions could be pursued. First, U.S.-Egyptian ties need to be broadened. Interaction among critical political and security personnel at high levels is fairly constant, but this interaction needs to include larger numbers of people. Business interests, symbolized by the vigorous activities of the American Chamber of Commerce in Egypt, is one example, but this effort needs to be expanded. Intellectual contacts and activities are other promising areas. While the American University in Cairo and the American Research Center in Cairo form a nucleus, wider intellectual exchange would help generate sensitivity in the United States to Egyptian concerns and nurture a new spirit among a younger generation in Egypt. The same is true in a host of other fields—journalism and the media, information-age technology, environmental studies, arms control, and women and the family. In an era of greatly expanded nongovernment diplomacy, nongovernmental organizations and private institutions can be used to build a robust network of activities and contacts that will strengthen the relationship and enable it to better withstand the wear and tear of political vicissitudes.

Second, the United States and Egypt also need to deepen their relations. Ties already established need to be nurtured, not neglected. In this respect, Ahmed Fakhr's suggestion for a high-level commission that meets regularly to consider issues of concern to both countries across the board is worth serious consideration. There is a danger that a new spirit in Washington, far more interested in domestic issues than foreign policy, may neglect, or even take for granted, relations with steady friends like Egypt. A Congress interested in budget cuts, especially in foreign affairs, and deeply involved in partisan politics could foster that neglect. Worse yet, Egypt's increased independence on Arab-Israeli issues, its unwillingness to move ahead on normalization with Israel, and its stance on Libya and the NPT could cool relations with Congress. There is already some resentment in Egypt that relations are filtered through an "Arab-Israeli" prism, rather than standing on their own. In April 1997, congressional hearings were held to probe Egypt's domestic politics on human rights and its foreign agenda.[16] While a sturdy relationship should be able to survive public examination, these are warning signs of a fraying relationship. Egyptians, no less than Americans, need to engage in more consultation and exhibit a better willingness to meet mutual concerns.

In the end, the United States and Egypt may have to decide to agree to disagree on some areas, but more attention needs to be paid to the boundaries between the two and the reasons for disagreement. Above all, a new vision for the future must shift Egypt's horizon beyond the Arab-Israeli conflict and the regional military balance, to the new geoeconomic agenda of the 21st century. Egypt and the United States must concentrate on encouraging the promising steps taken by Egypt to restructure its economy and to move it to a take-off position. And it must encourage Egypt to move toward developing a more dynamic civil society and opening political institutions and positions to members of the new generation. In this endeavor, the United States will want to keep its eye on five issues:

- Is the younger generation in Egypt as committed to economic growth and a market economy as its predecessors were to the Nasserite vision of Arab nationalism or the current one to political Islam? Can a new vision of prosperity—even personal affluence—provide the kind of energy necessary to move Egypt forward? And how can the United States help encourage the shift?
- Will Egypt react to competition from other regional and global economies, especially those of Israel, at home, and of Asia, as a challenge to be met or with resentment and a negative response? Here, too, the United States can play a role in nurturing a positive attitude.

- Will the EU open its markets to Egypt and help foster the private sector, or concentrate on the North African countries where its domestic interests are more involved? The United States, too, needs to examine its trade posture toward Egypt and to encourage a shift from aid transfers to trade. The EU should be encouraged to make sure that the Barcelona initiative fully includes Egypt.
- Will the Egyptian state apparatus recede further from the political sector and allow new leadership to emerge? While this process entails some risk, its initiation and its astute management may be key to ending its inertia and underpinning its economic reform.
- Can the peace process be kept on track? Without at least some progress on this front, Egypt's regional role could diverge even further from the goals originally envisioned at the start of the process. Nothing would be more destructive to Egypt's new geoeconomic direction than a full collapse of that process.

It is clearly in the U.S. interest to keep Egypt moderate in its foreign policy and pro-Western in its political orientation. Egypt's domestic stability is essential to the maintenance of that position. After long, slow steps, Egypt is making real progress on the economic front. It would be a real disservice if flagging U.S. efforts on the peace process undermined or distracted from this effort.

Finally, the United States may have to learn to live with a gradually more assertive Egypt that follows national interests not always in sync with the United States. Egypt is unlikely to achieve a regional leadership role similar to that it held under Nasser, nor does it want to pay the costs of such a role. Instead, it is likely to be increasingly touchy about regional rivalry with Israel and Turkey, its exclusion from the Gulf, and differences with the United States over Libya, Iraq, and Sudan. These are not signs of weakness but of a more stable and self-confident Egypt that has dealt rather successfully with its Islamic opposition; that is undertaking economic reform and has a growing GDP and is increasing foreign investment; and that has been fully reintegrated into the Arab world after 18 years of isolation. While these may cause some problems for the new global superpower, the United States should recognize the fruits of its success. It is precisely these attributes for which it has worked for many years and that provide the basis for a new, more mature relationship with Egypt in the 21st century.

Notes

1. Amy Dockser Marcus, "Rising Sphinx," *Wall Street Journal*, April 10, 1997, 1.
2. David Gardner, "Egypt," *Financial Times Survey*, May 13, 1997.
3. Ibid.
4. Marcus; Sean Evers, "Egypt set for 'Home-Grown' IMF deal," *Financial Times*, October 11, 1996, 8; "Sovereign Report: Egypt," Fitch International Bank Credit Analysis (New York: August 1997); and "Special Report: Egypt," *Middle East Economic Digest,* October 3, 1995, 23.
5. Atef Obeid, Minister of Public Enterprise, lecture at the Washington Institute for Near East Policy, September 30, 1996, cited in *Policy Watch*, October 9, 1996, 2.
6. Gardner.
7. Ibid.
8. Fred Hiatt, "Defense: If Only They'd Debate," *Washington Post*, May 13, 1997, A17; *Department of Defense Annual Report to the President and the Congress* (Washington, DC: Government Printing Office), April, 1997, 16.
9. William Drozdiak, "US-German Partnership in Disarray," *Washington Post*, May 10, 1997.
10. The DOD Annual Report maintains that "The United States' strategy of engagement and enlargement requires forces that are able, in concert with regional allies, to fight and win two major regional conflicts that occur nearly simultaneously." This requirement "has been the most significant factor in determining the overall size and structure of US conventional forces." DOD Annual Report, 13. See also William S. Cohen, *Report on the Quadrennial Defense Review* (Washington: Department of Defense, May 1997), V.
11. Both Great Britain and France have participated with the United States in military operations in the Gulf.
12. Both the 1994 and 1996 congressional elections brought freshman classes with low levels of experience in any public office, much less international affairs. In both years, 40 percent of the newcomers had 2 years or fewer of any experience in government. This lack of experience

is compounded at the national level by a rapid turnover in office. By 1996, more than half of the House of Representatives (53 percent) had arrived since 1992 without prior service, while 40 senators were new to the chamber since 1992. Drawn from profiles of the congressional freshman class, *Congressional Quarterly* 53, no. 1 (January 7, 1995); 54 no. 45 (November 9, 1996); and 55, no. 1 (January 4, 1997).

13. A survey by the Chicago Council on Foreign Relations reveals that the American electorate favors "pragmatic internationalism" but shows a 33 percent decline in public support for protecting weaker nations; a 24 percent decline for human rights; and a 19 percent decline for foreign aid over the previous 3 years. Chicago Council on Foreign Relations, *American Public Opinion, and U.S. Foreign Policy 1995* (Chicago: Council on Foreign Relations, 1995).

14. Brent Scowcroft and Arnold Kanter, "The Perils of Going It Alone," *Washington Post*, February 3, 1995.

15. For an excellent analysis of the politics behind foreign aid to Egypt and Israel, see Duncan Clarke, "US Security Assistance to Egypt and Israel: Politically Untouchable?" *Middle East Journal* 51, no. 2 (Spring 1997).

16. Congress, House, Committee on International Relations, *Hearings on Egypt*, 105th Cong., 1st sess., April 10, 1997.

About the Editor

Phebe Marr is a Fellow at the Woodrow Wilson International Center for Scholars, where she is working on a book about Iraq. Previously, Dr. Marr was a Senior Fellow at the Institute for National Strategic Studies, National Defense University.

During the 1990-91 Persian Gulf crisis, Dr. Marr advised the U.S. Government and testified before Congress on Iraq. She has made frequent appearances on television as a commentator and is the author of several books and scholarly publications.